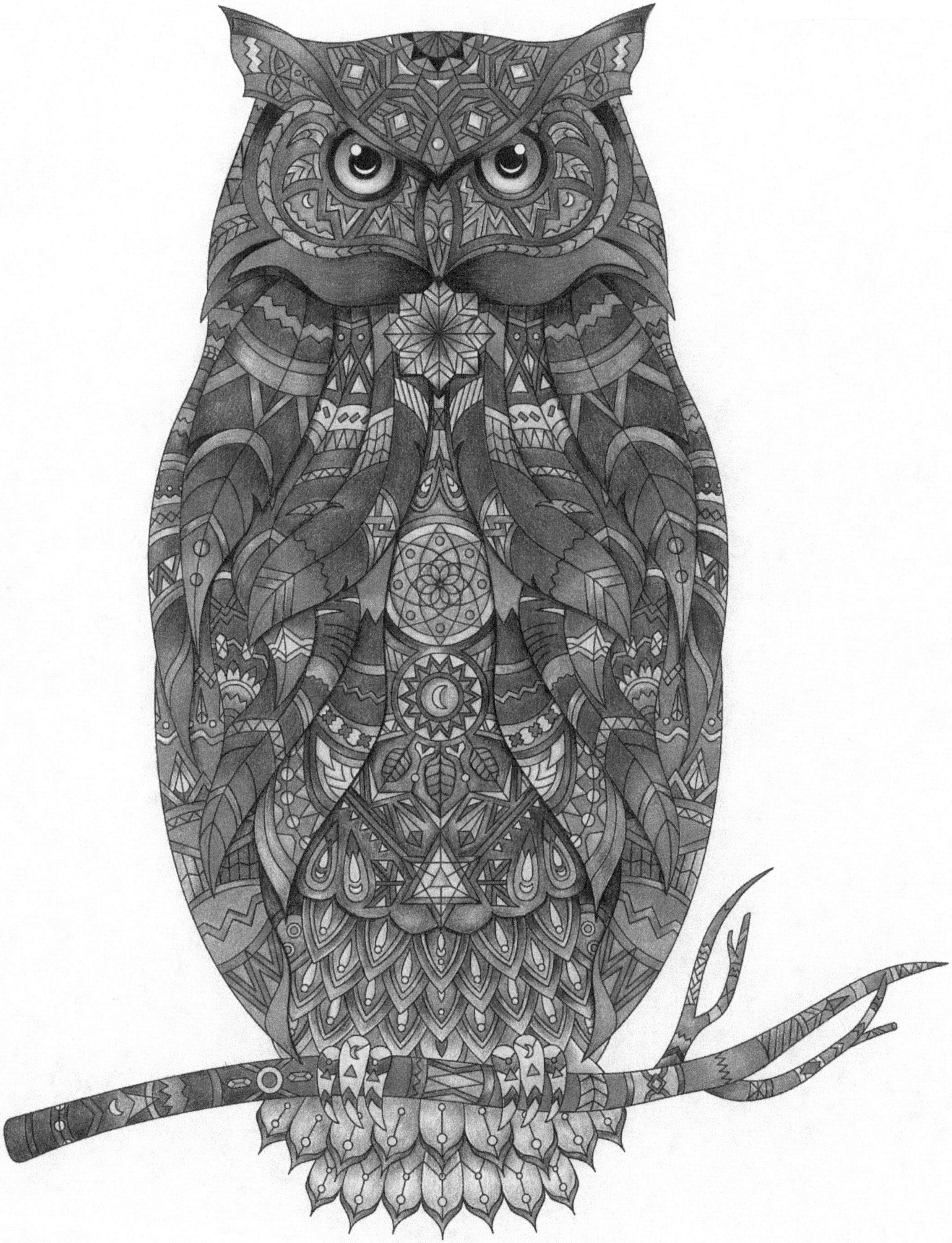

FANTASTIC OWLS
ADULT COLORING BOOK
COPYRIGHT © 2022
DR. ROBERT K. WHEELER JR.
ALL RIGHTS RESERVED
REPRODUCTION IN ANY FORMAT IS ONLY ALLOWE BY WRITTEN PERMISSION FROM THE AUTHR.
ISBN 9798366952378

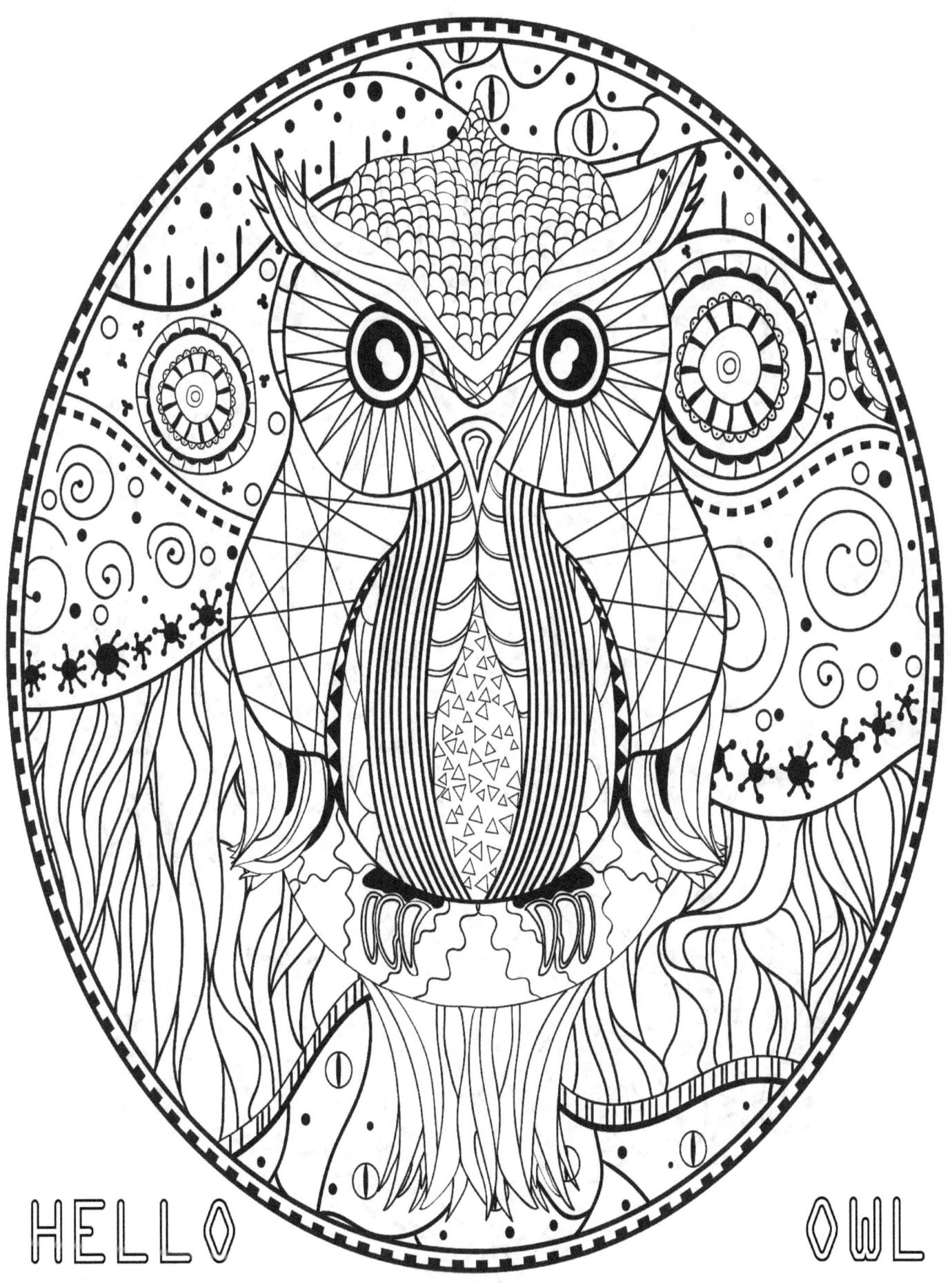

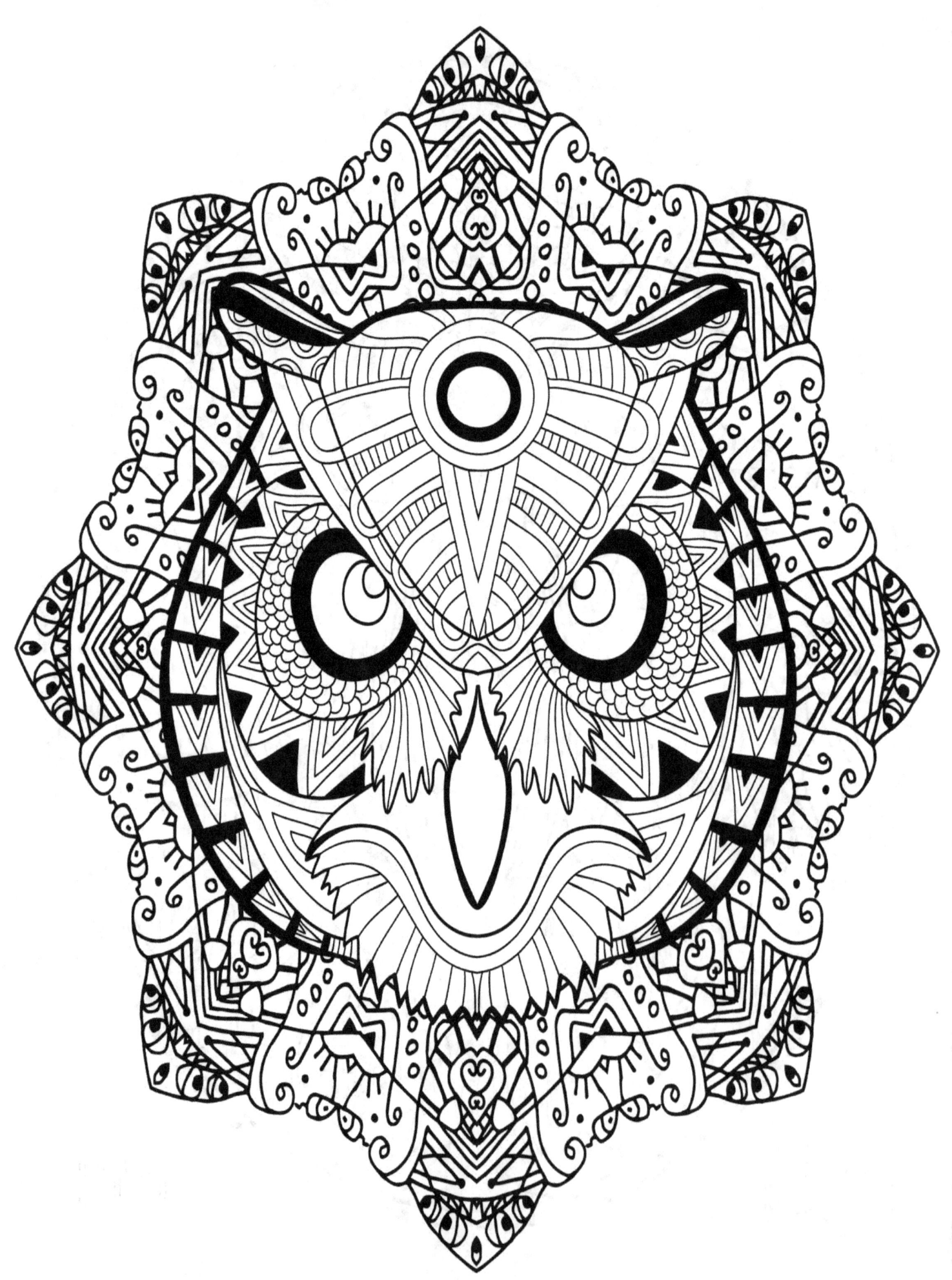

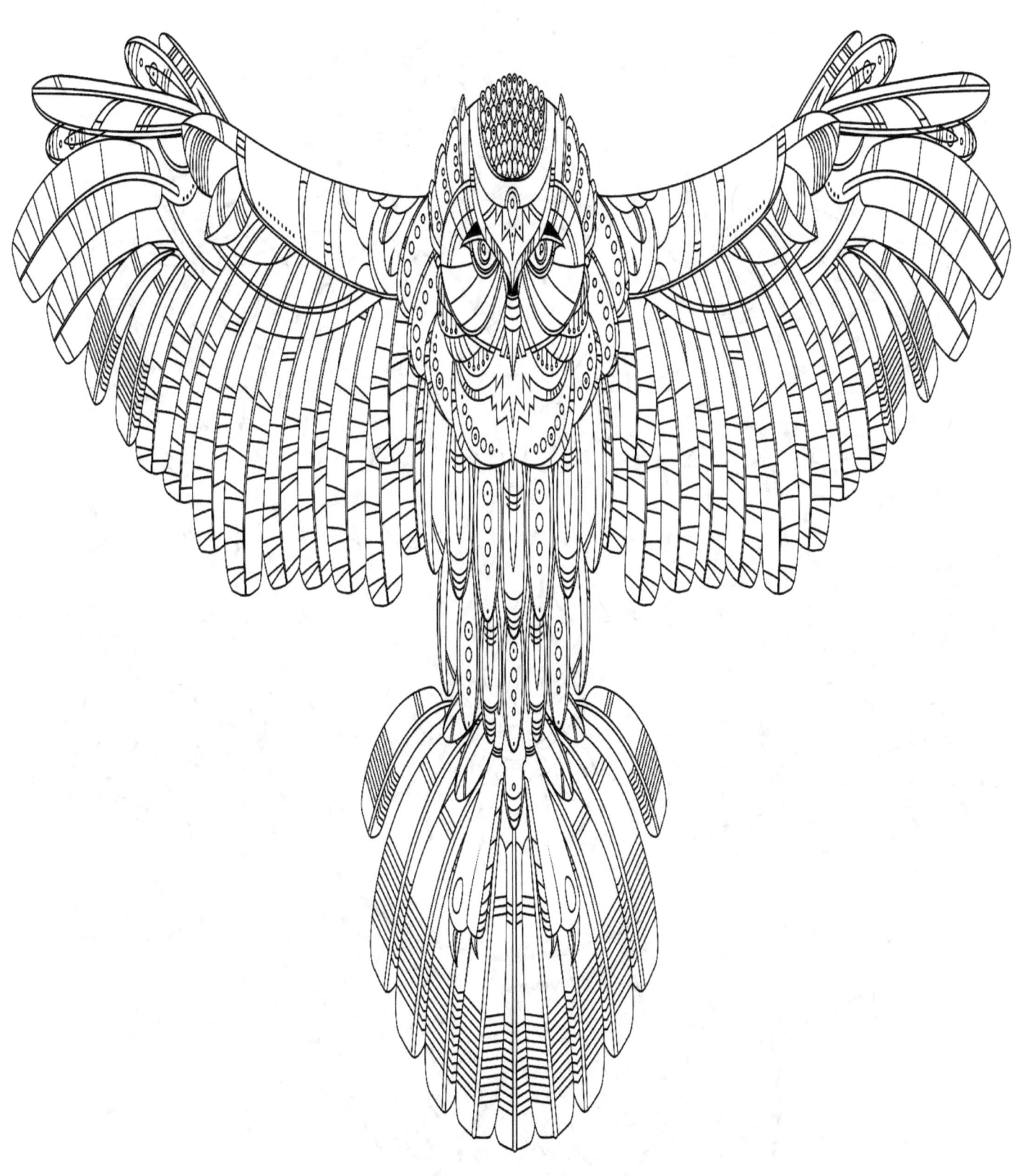

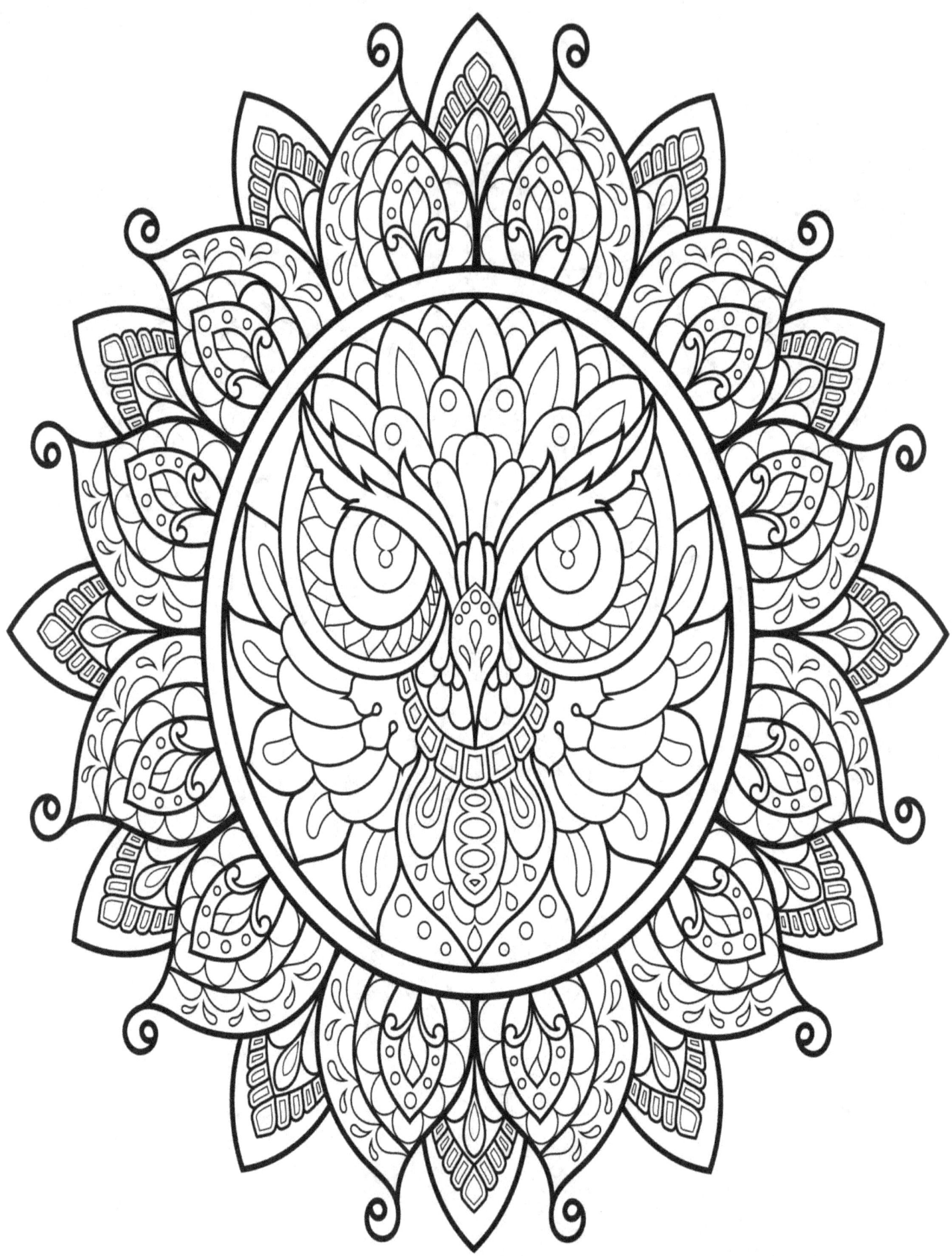

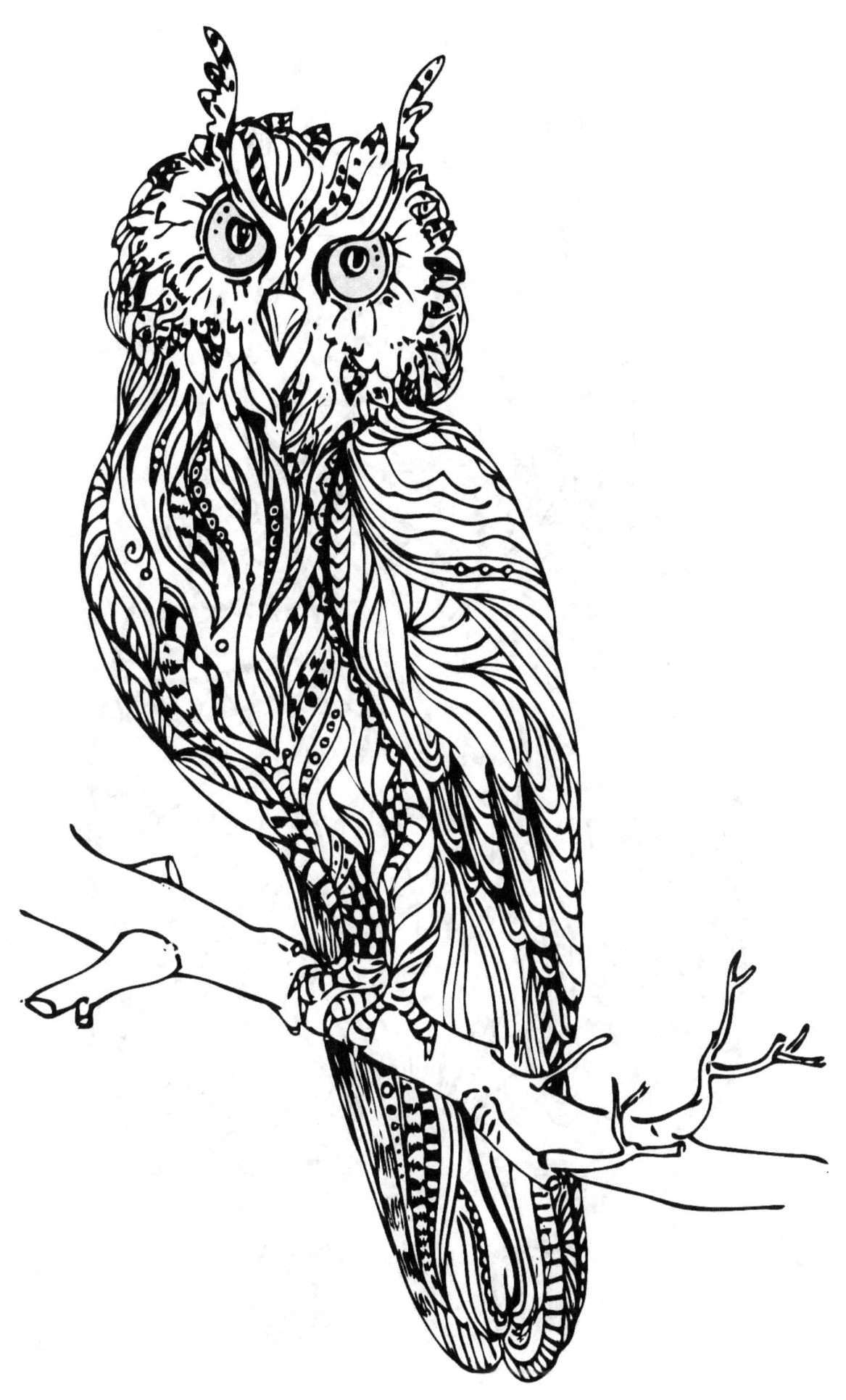

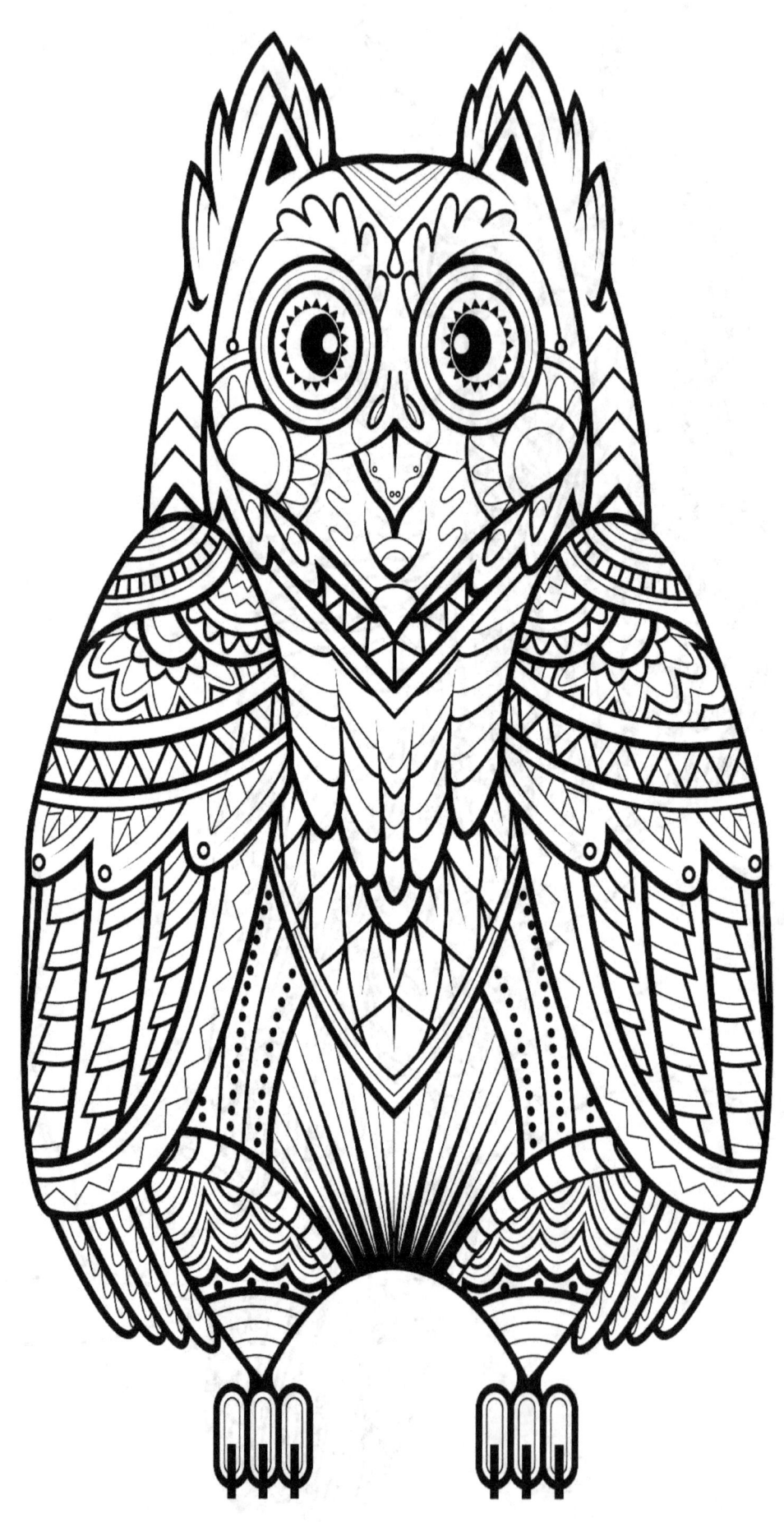

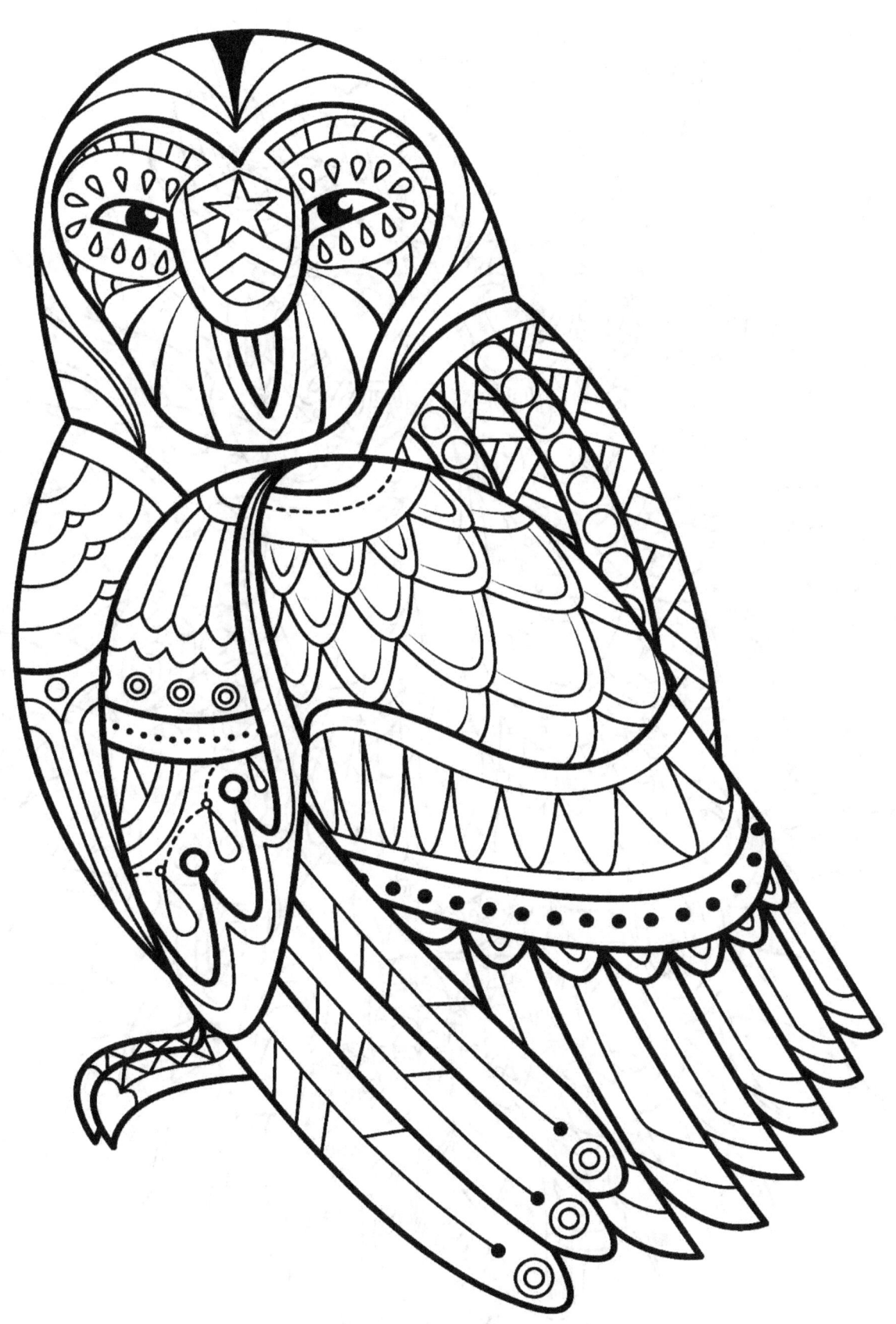

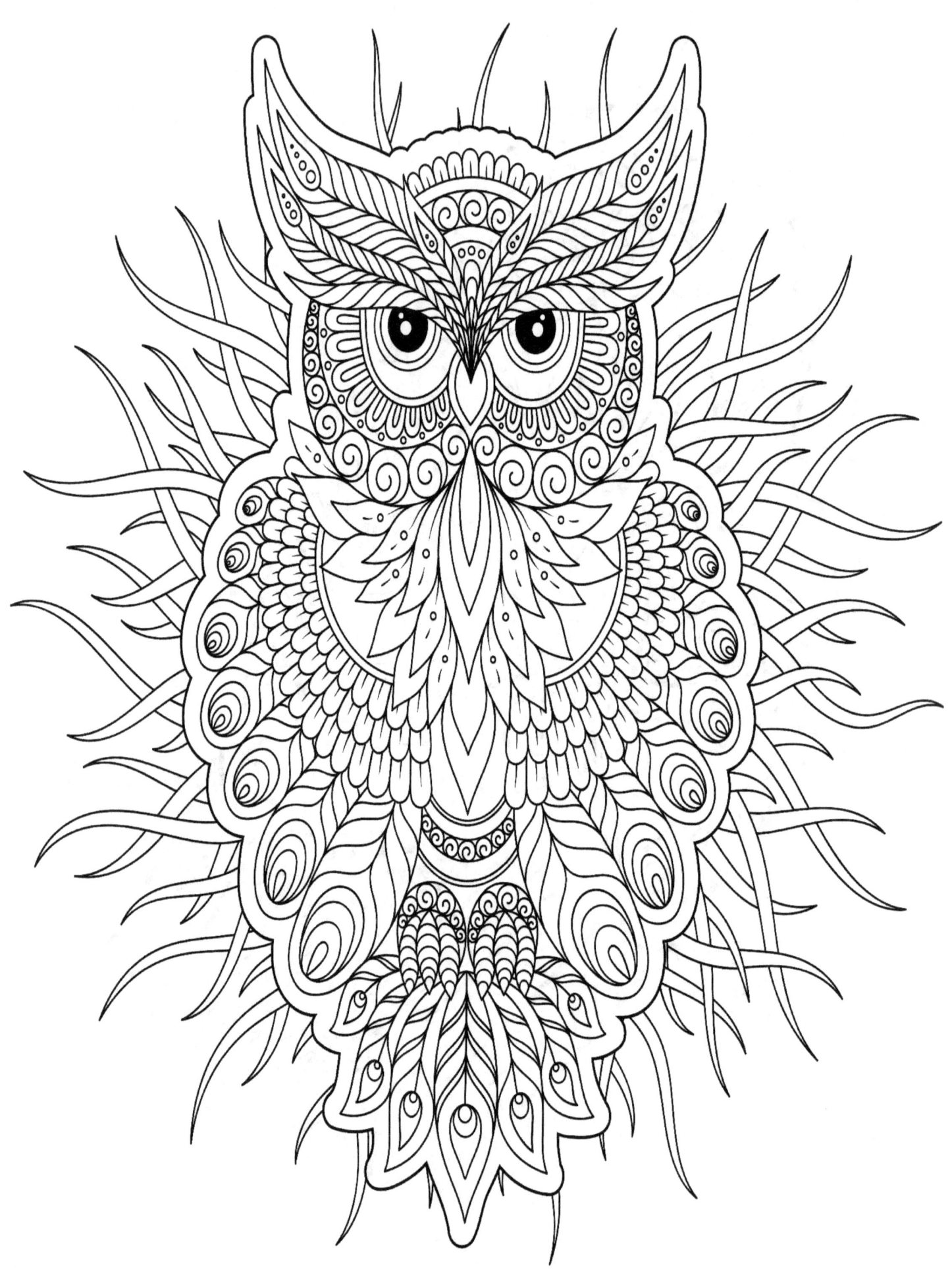

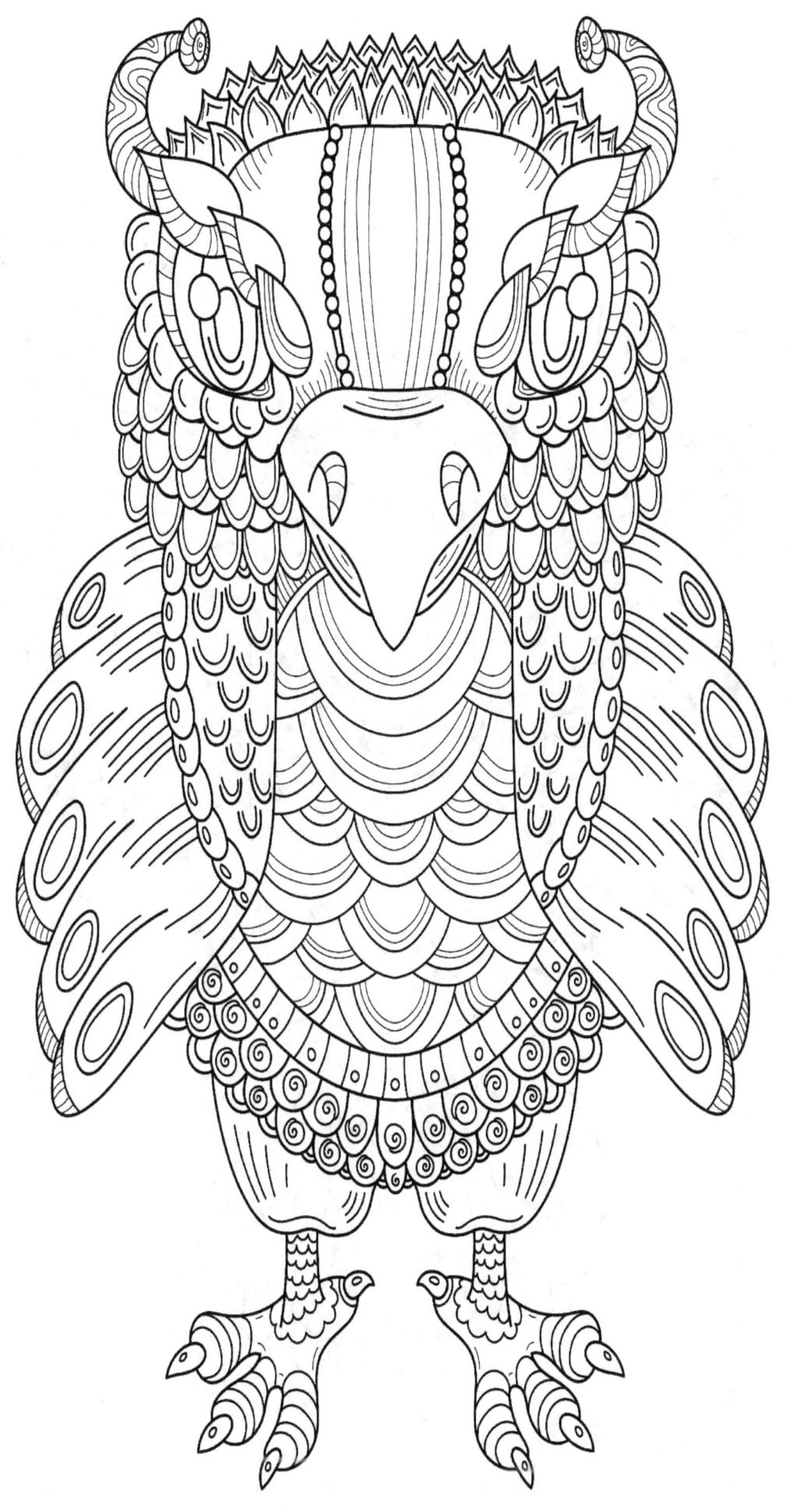

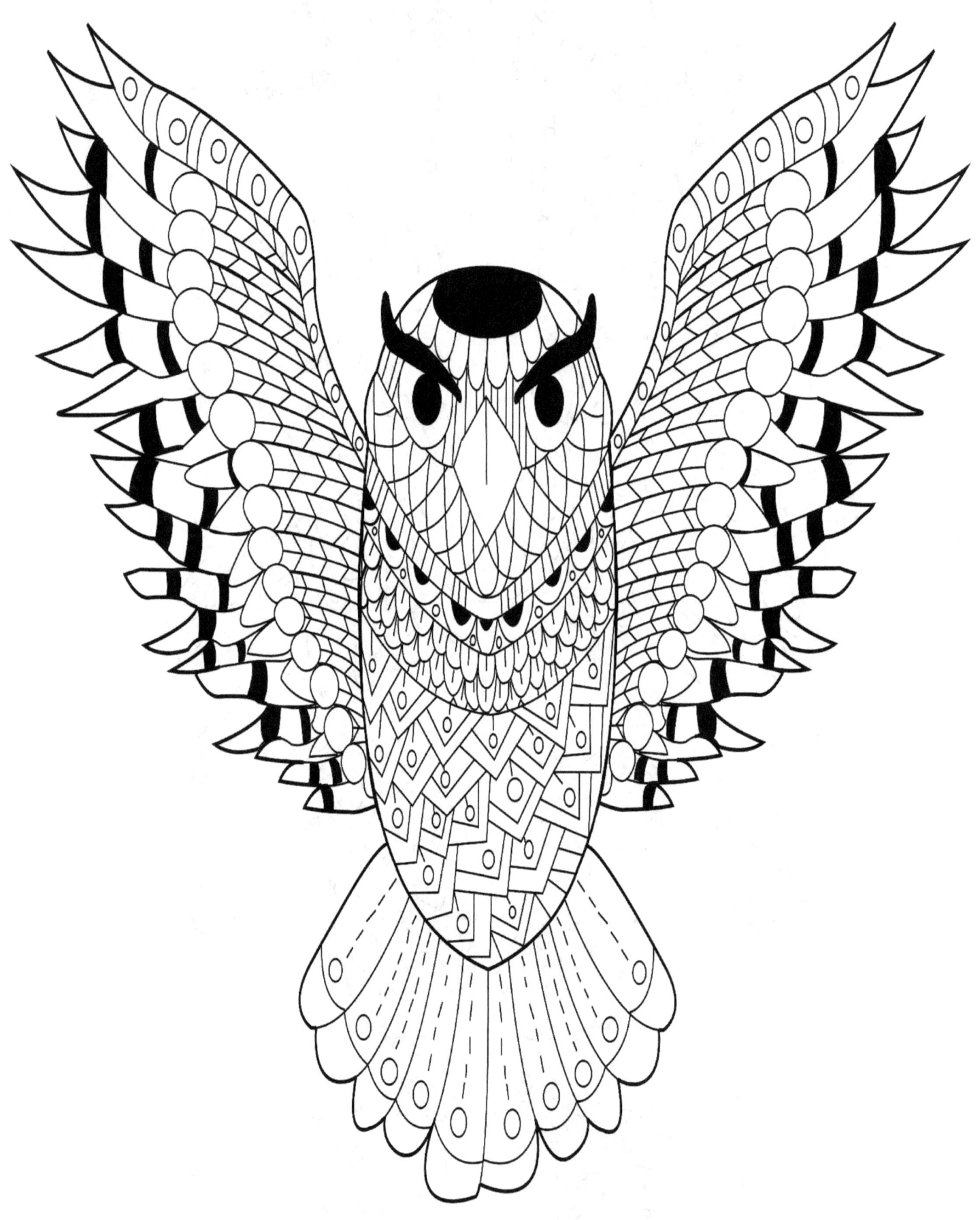

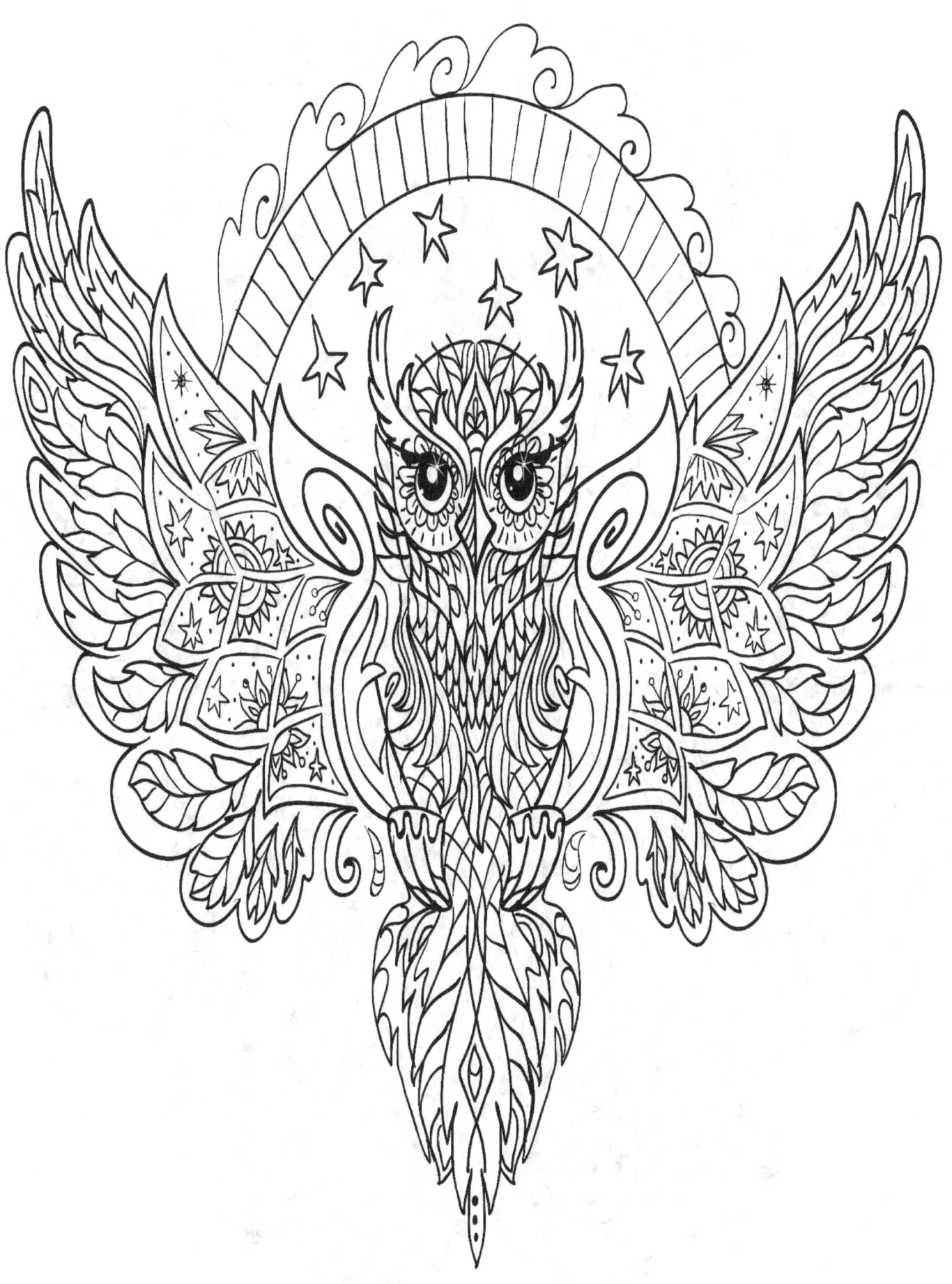

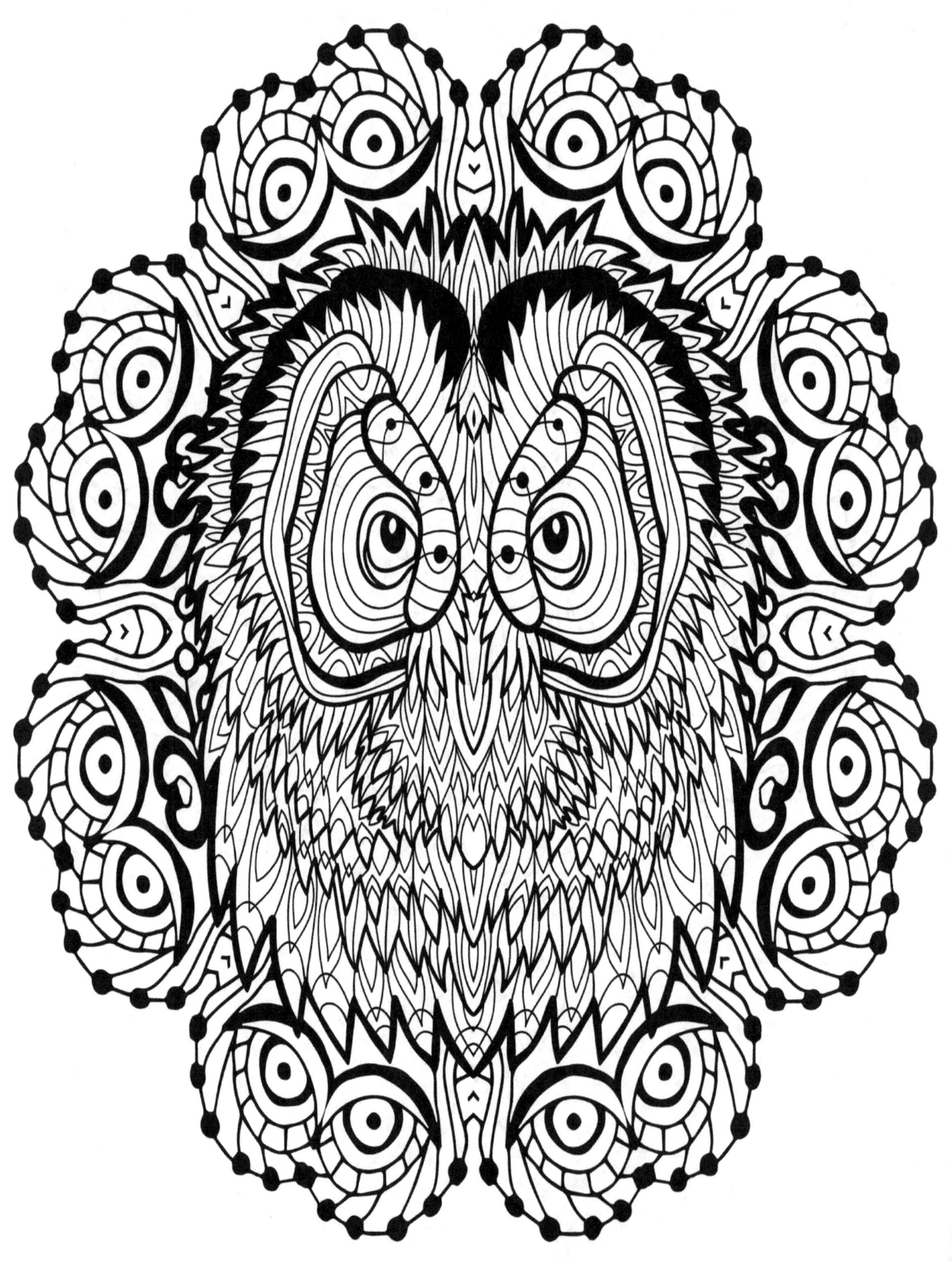

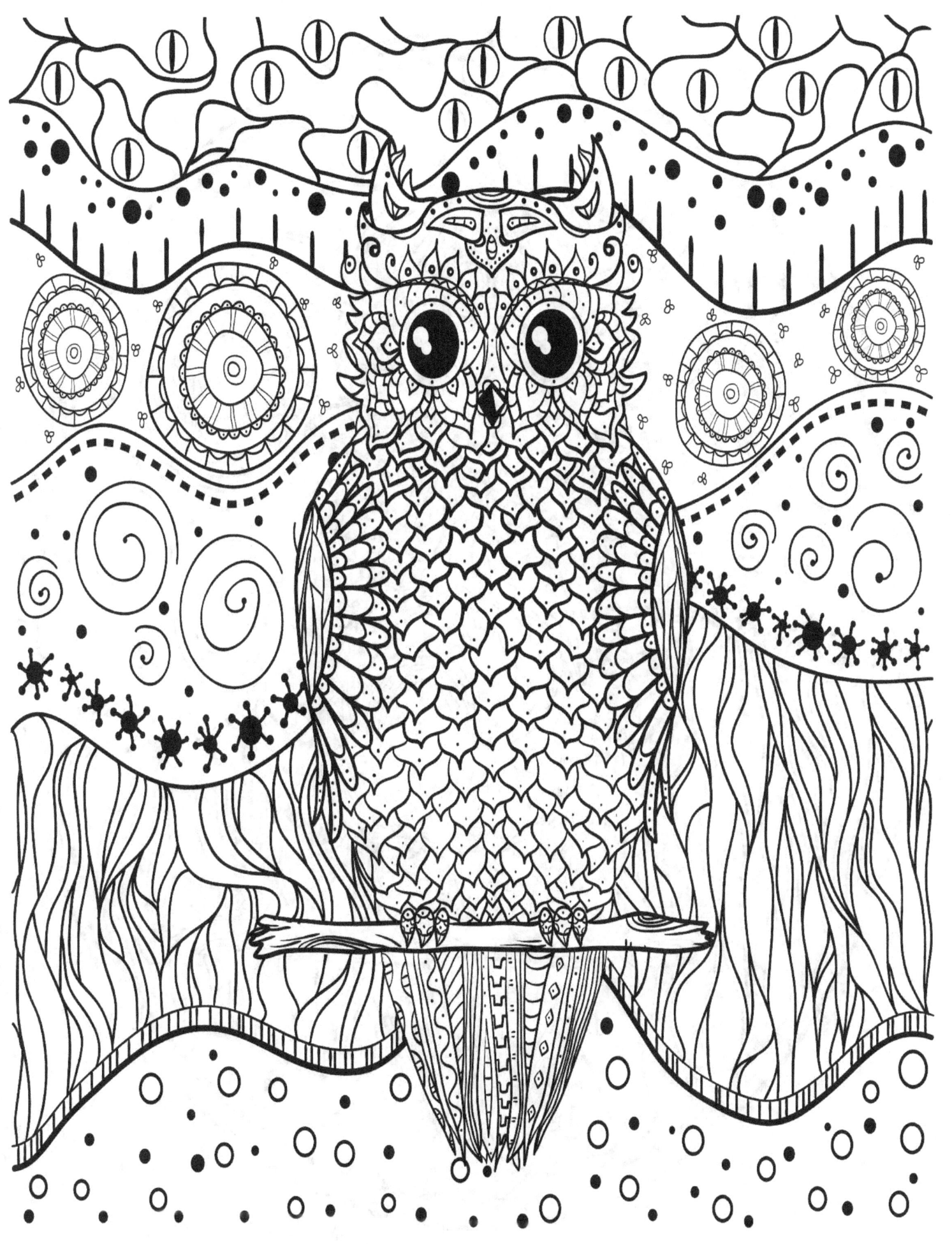

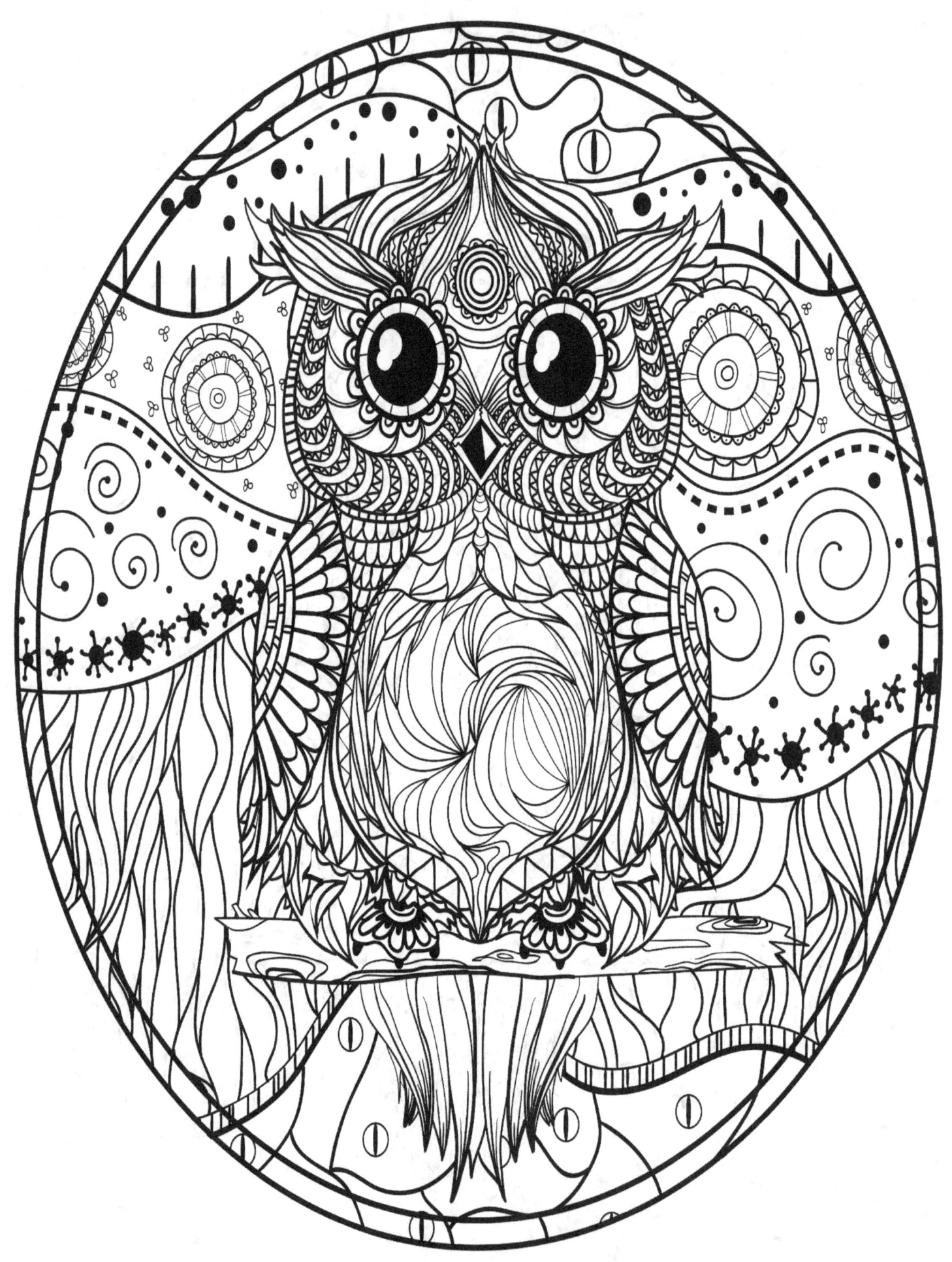

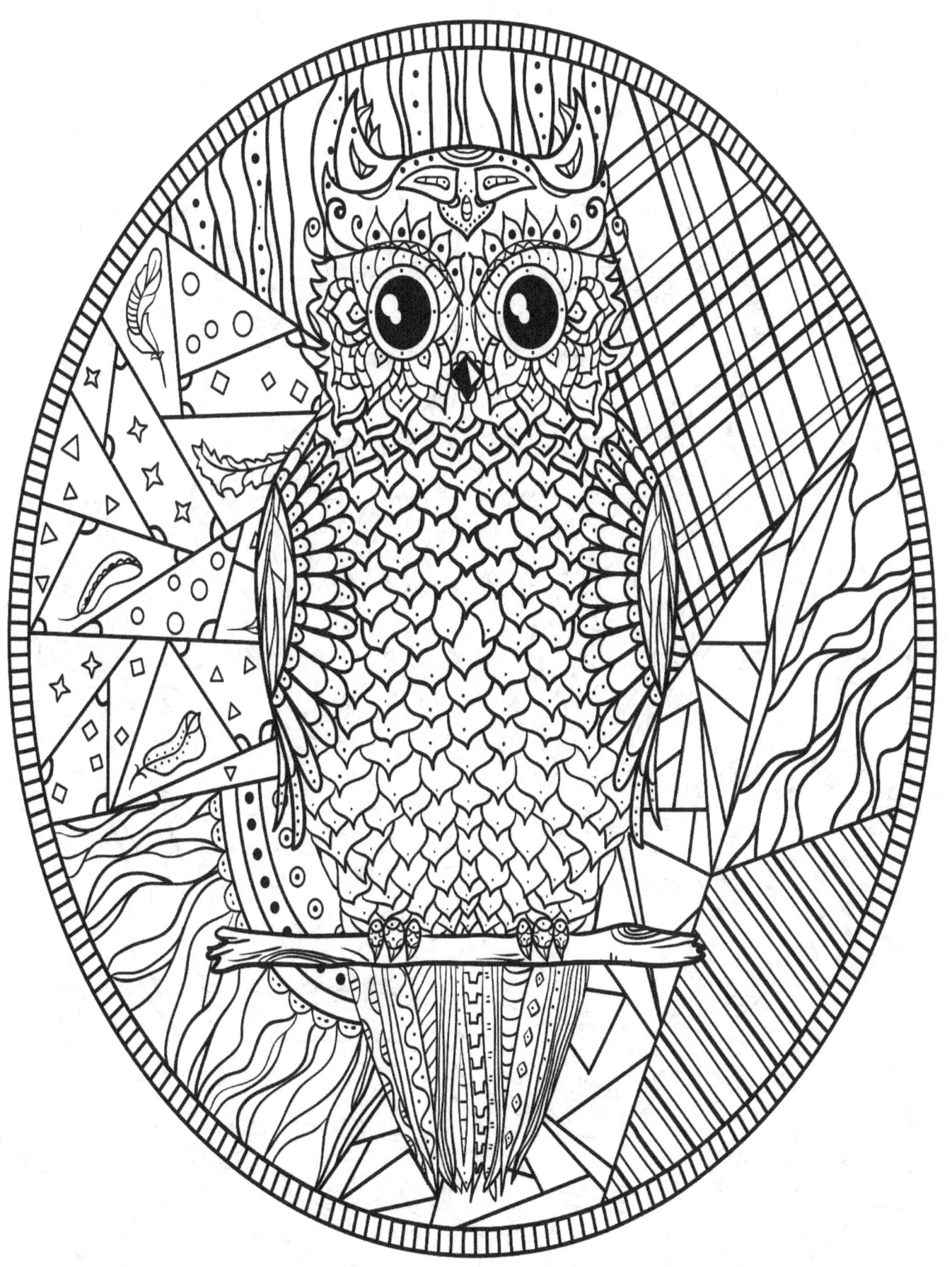

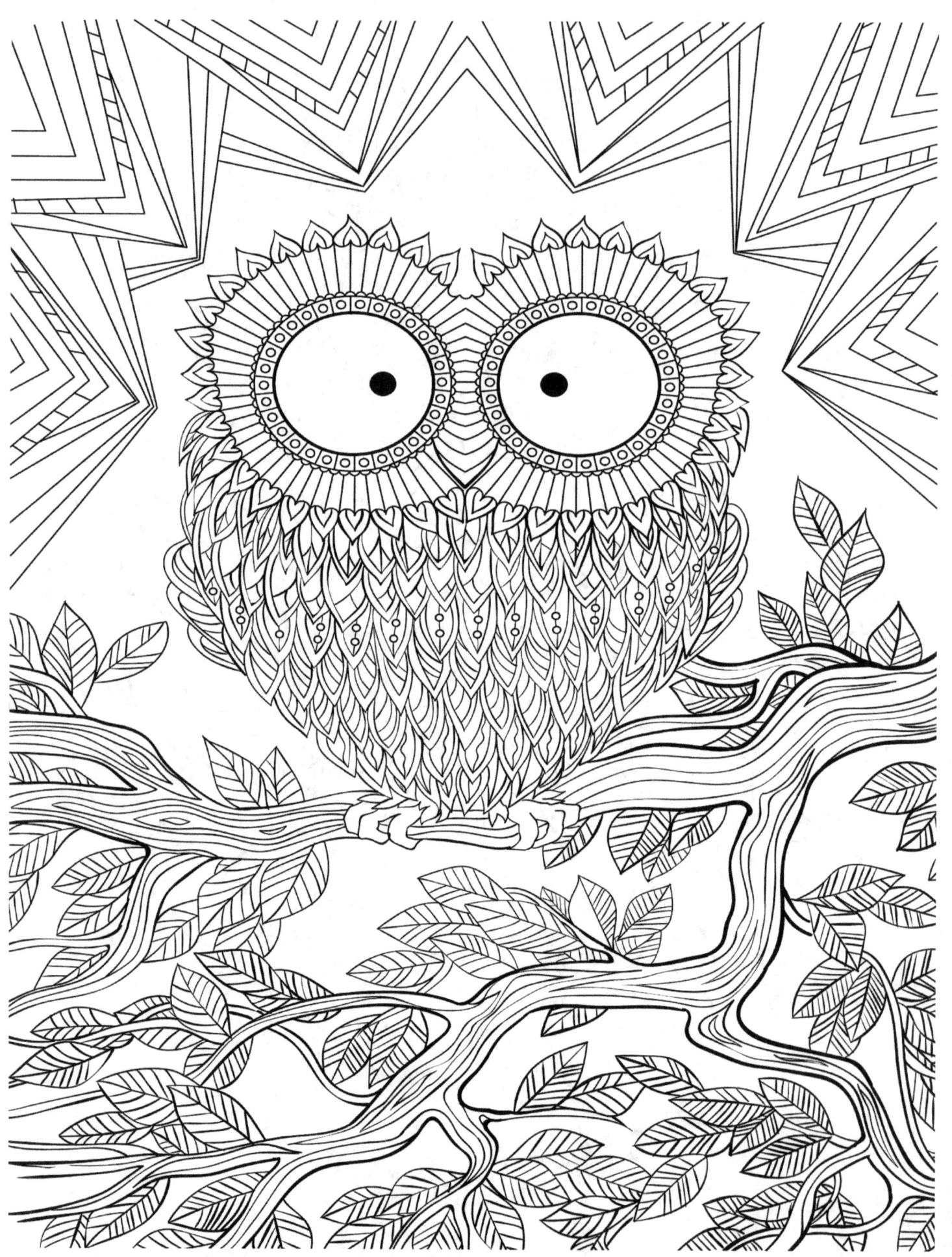

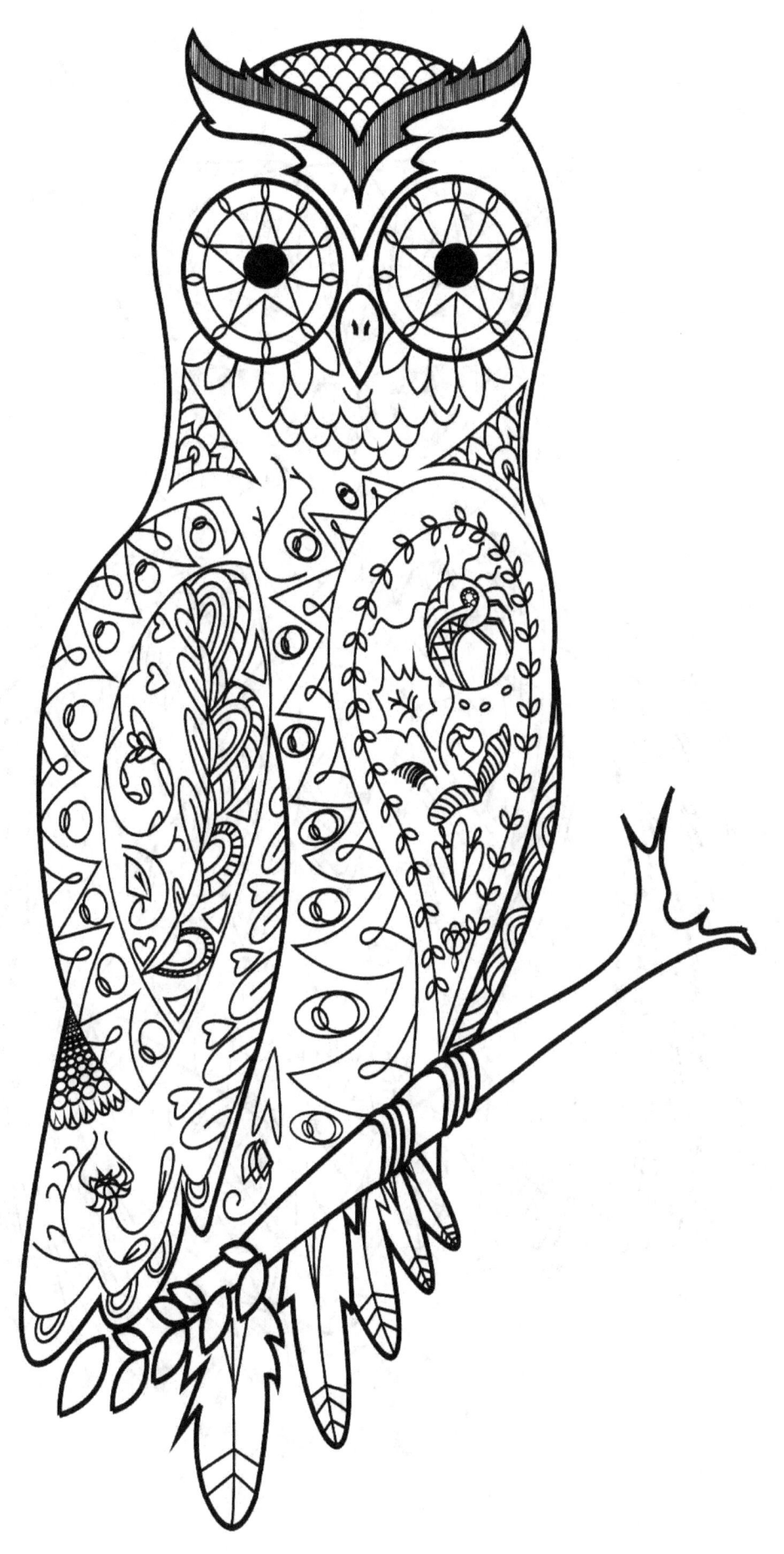

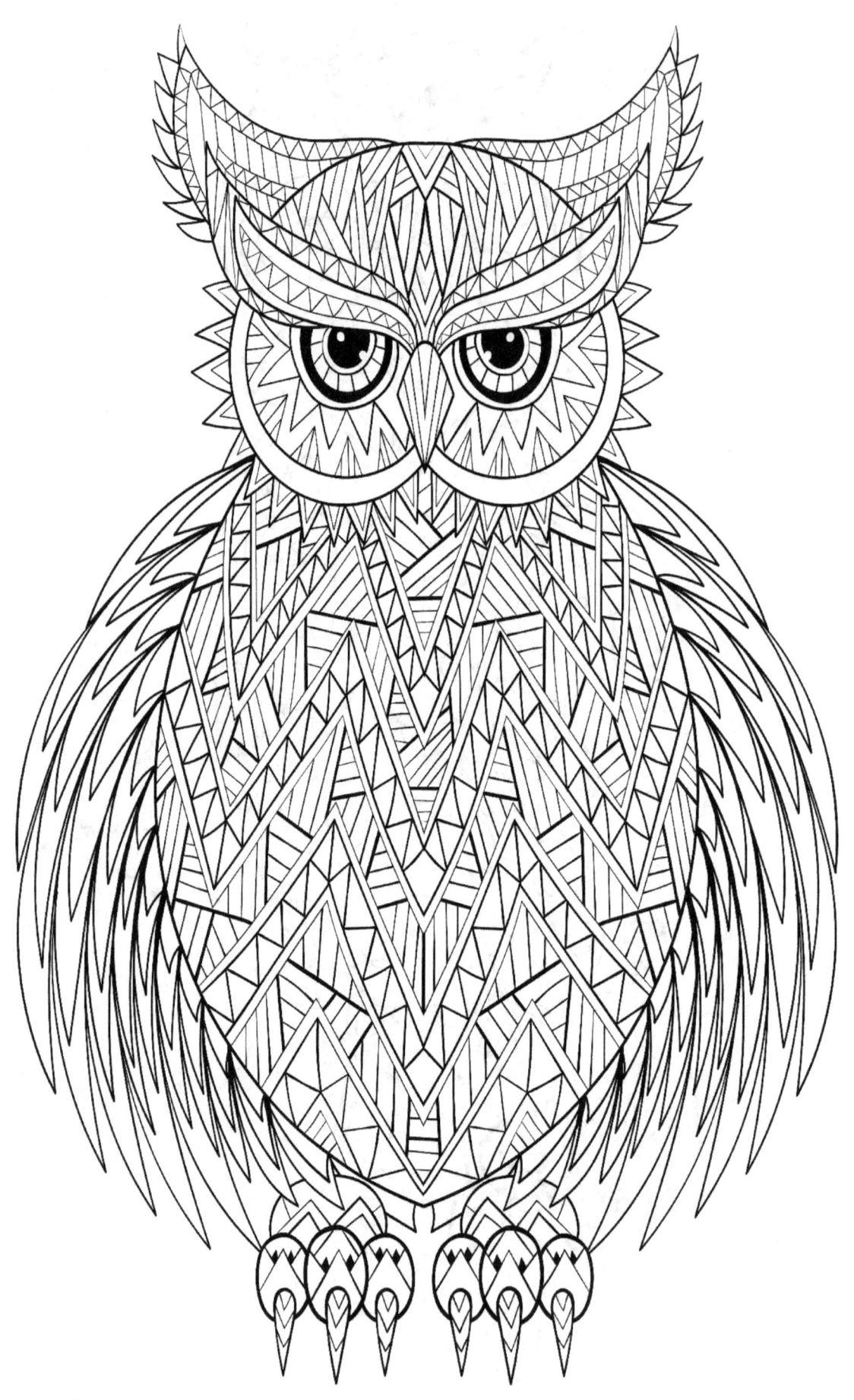

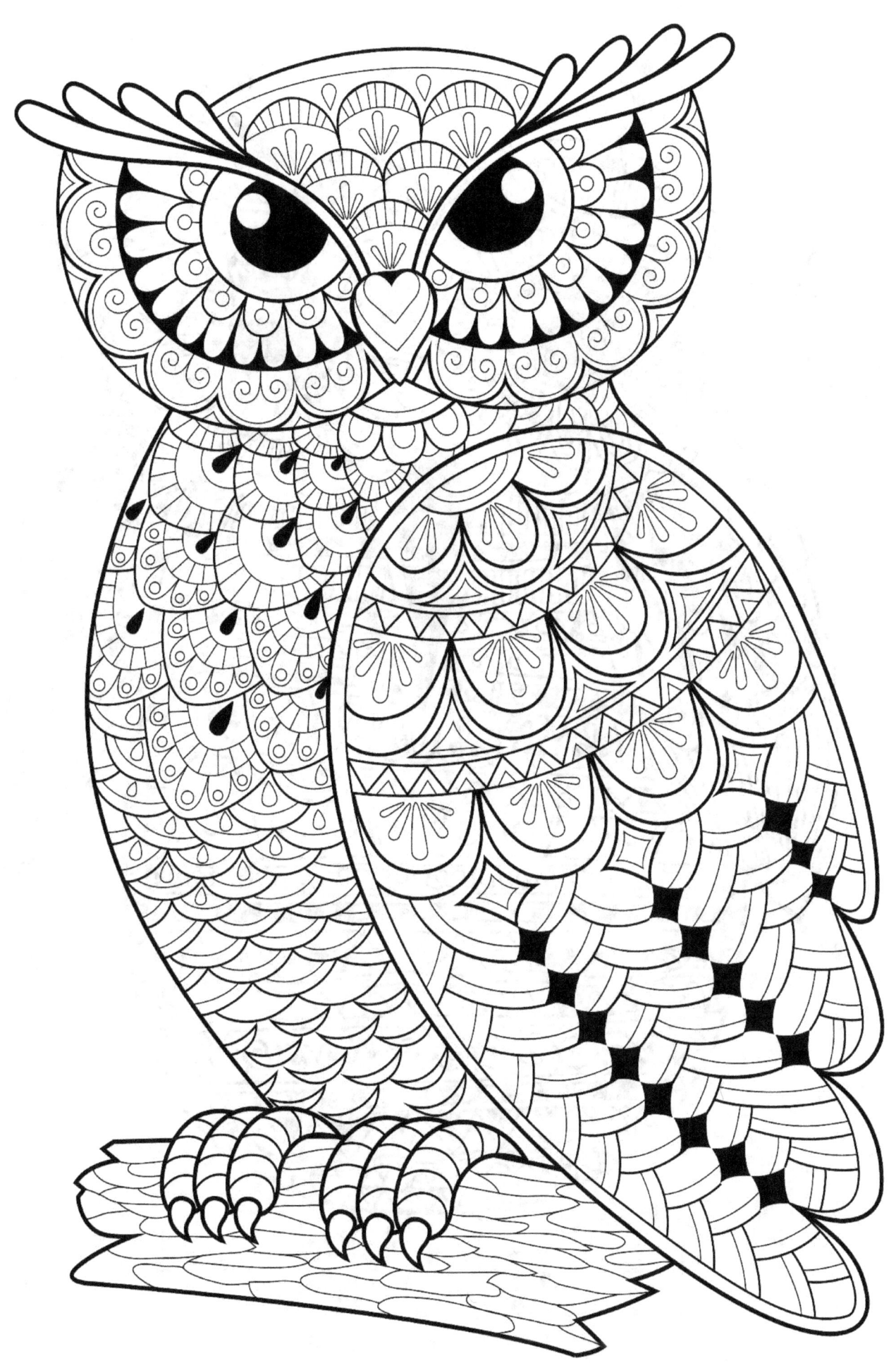

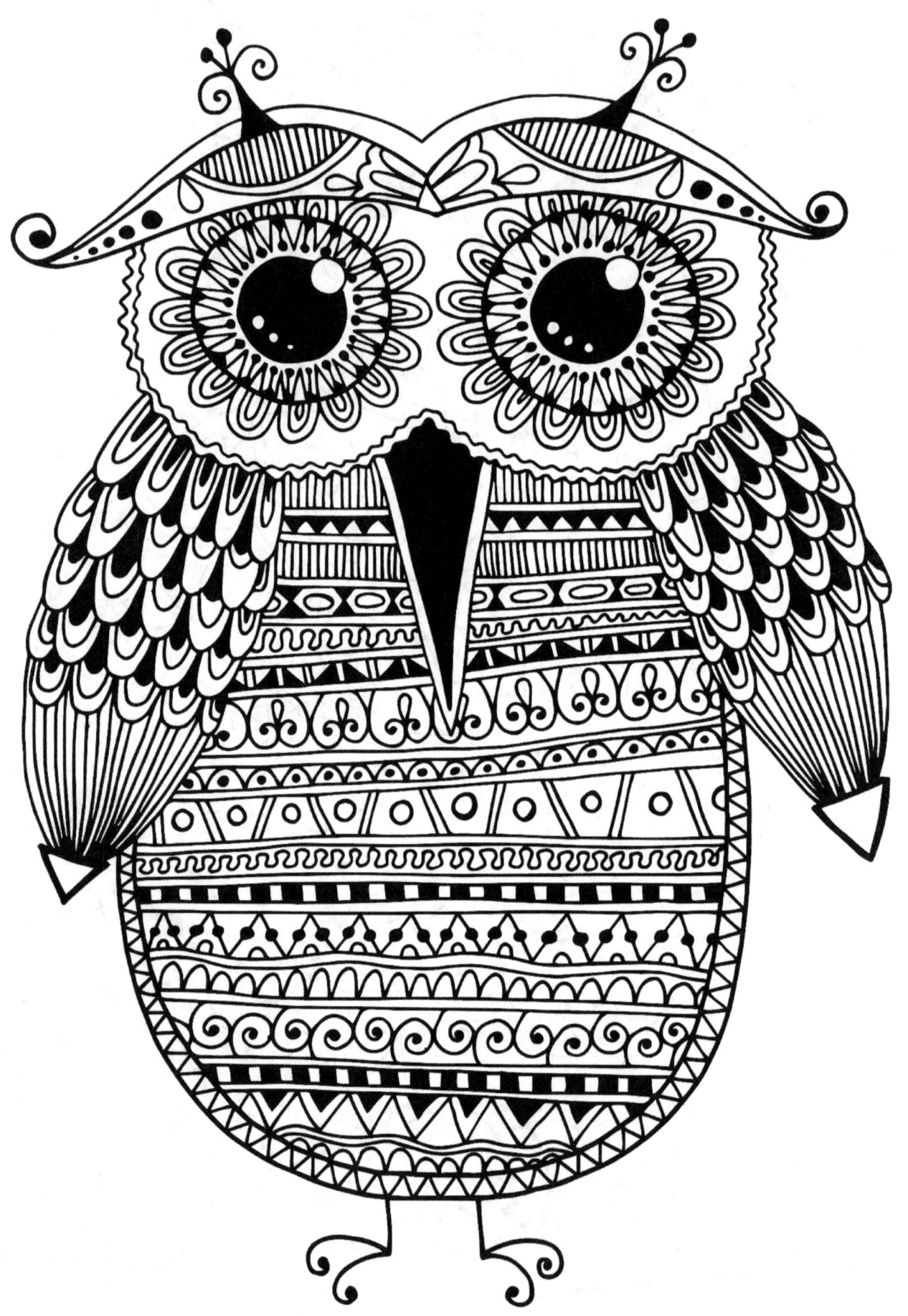

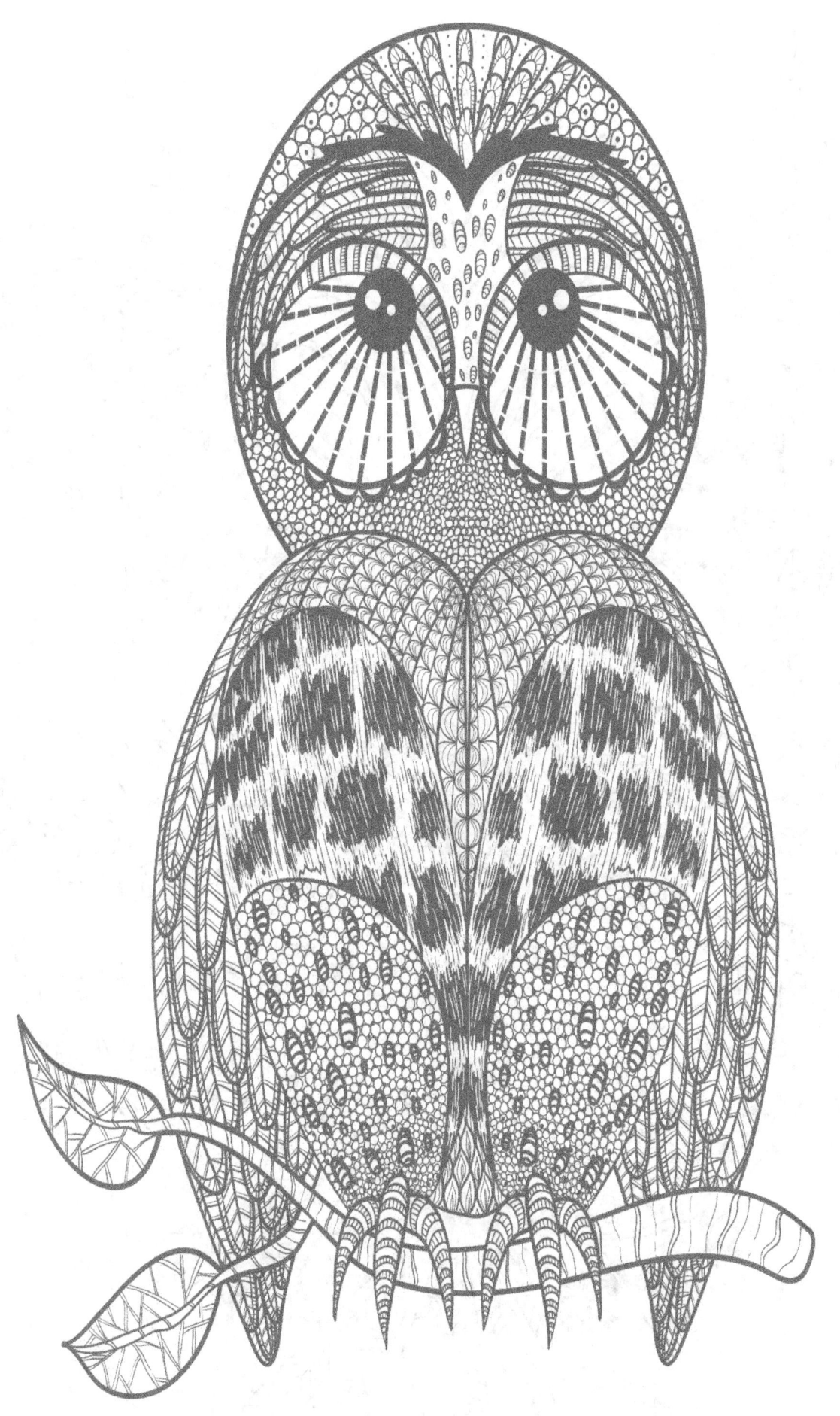

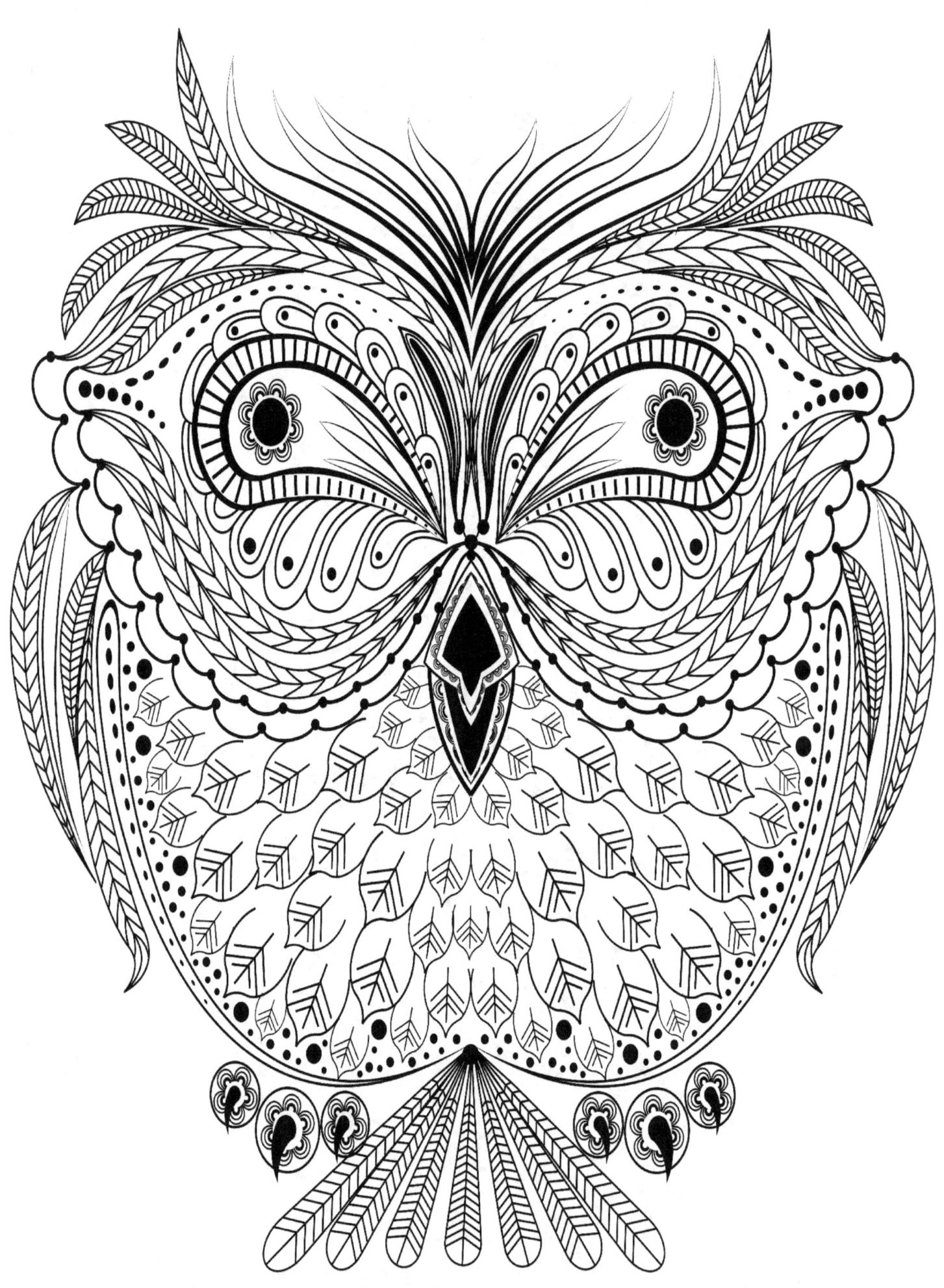

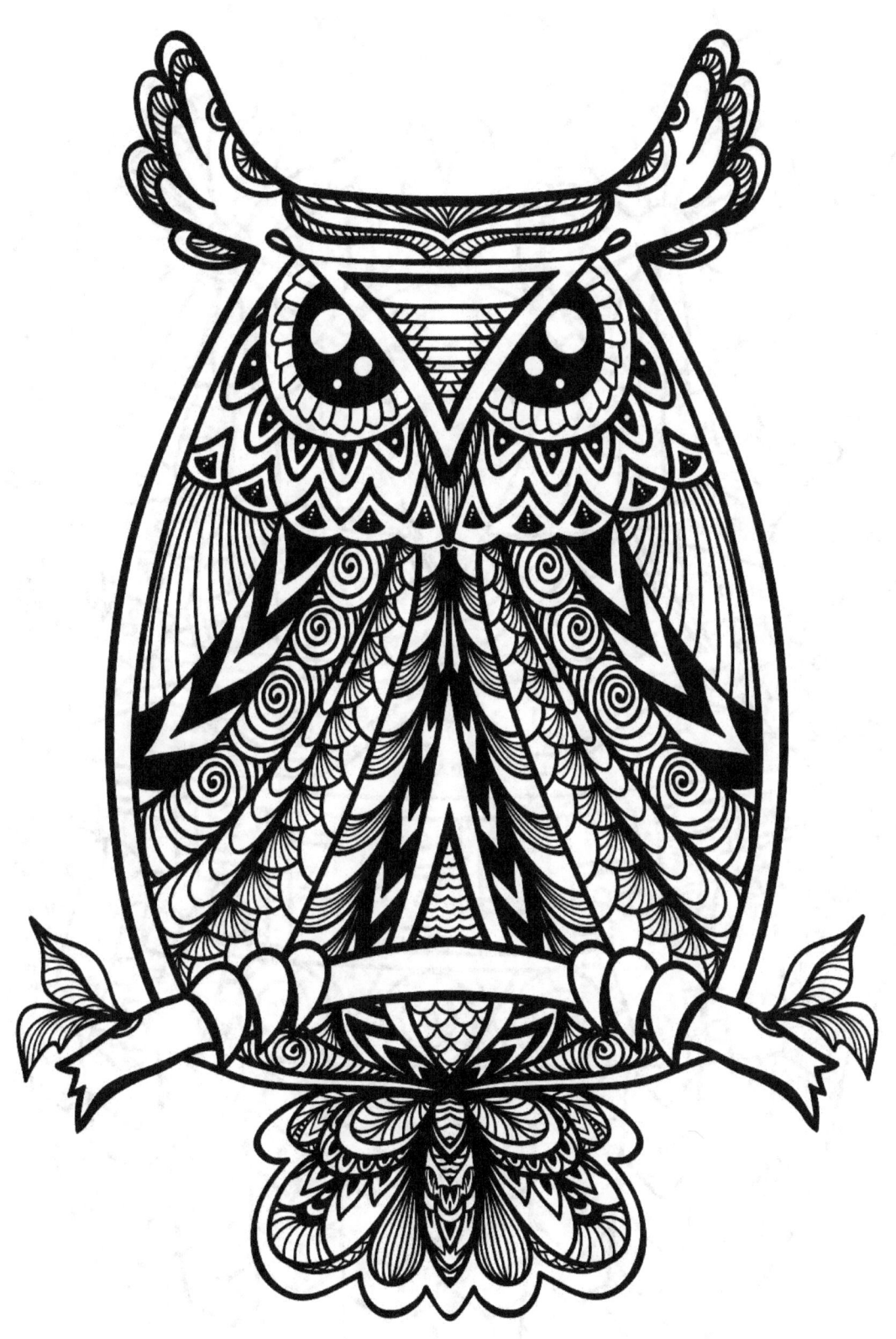

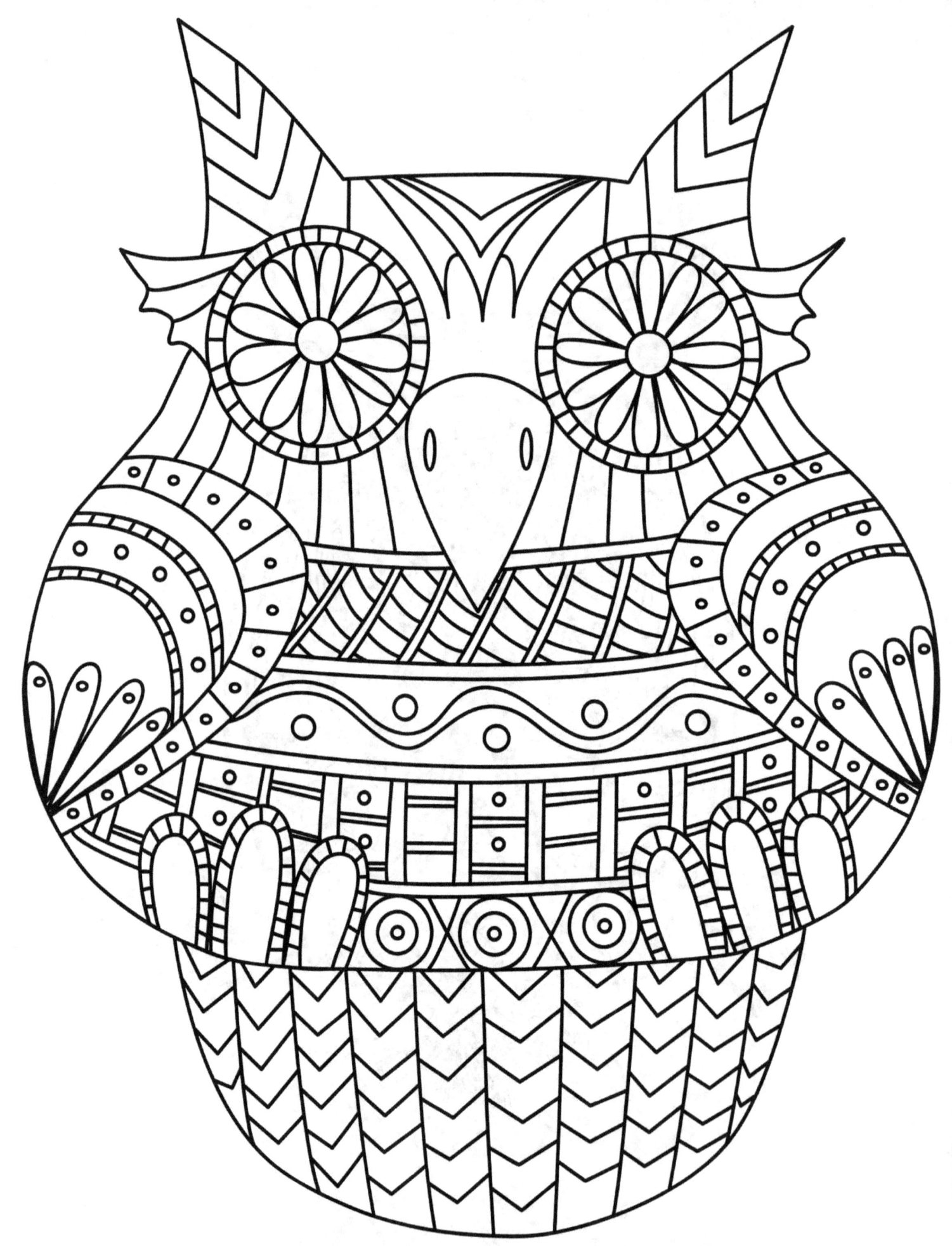

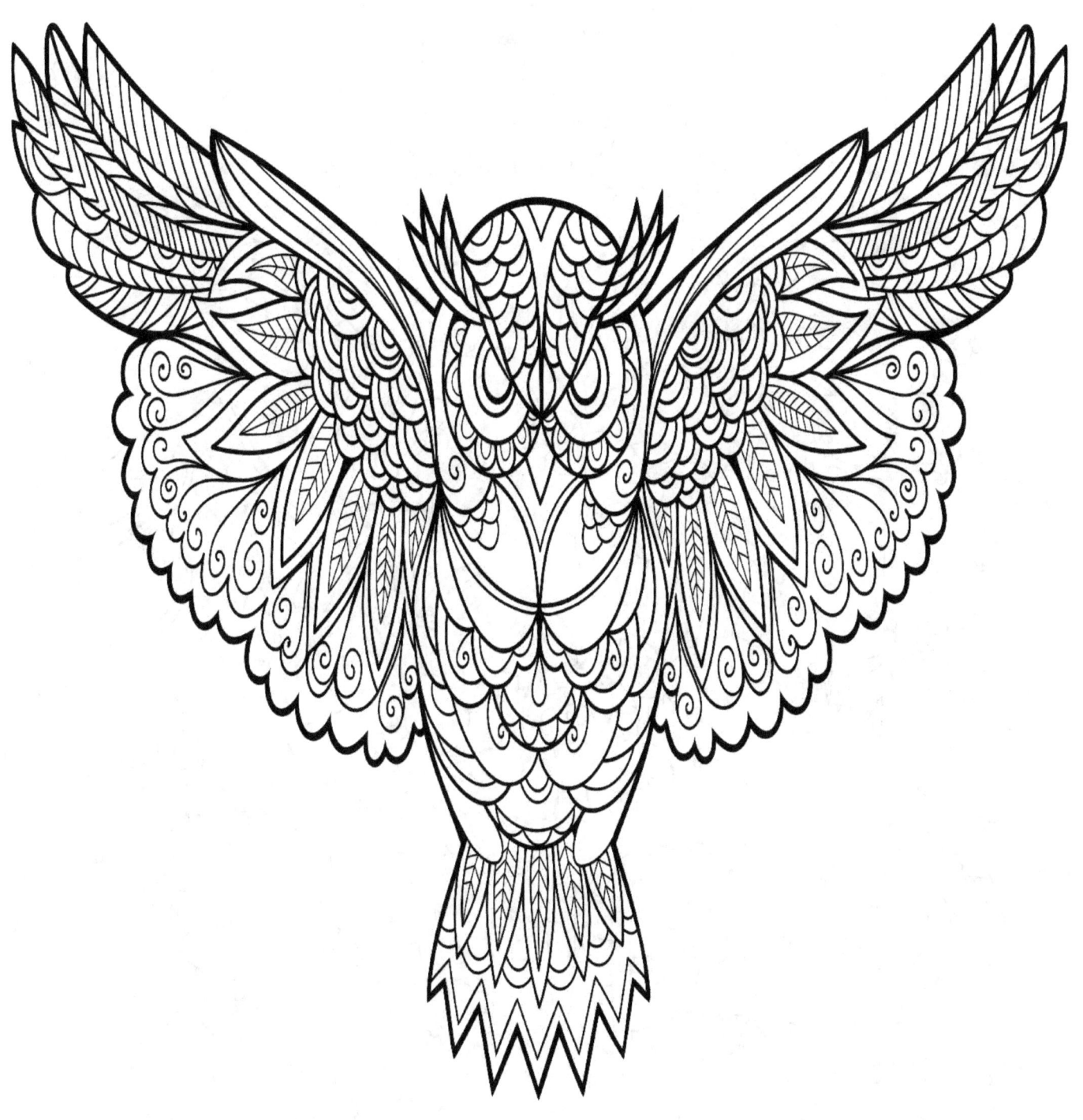

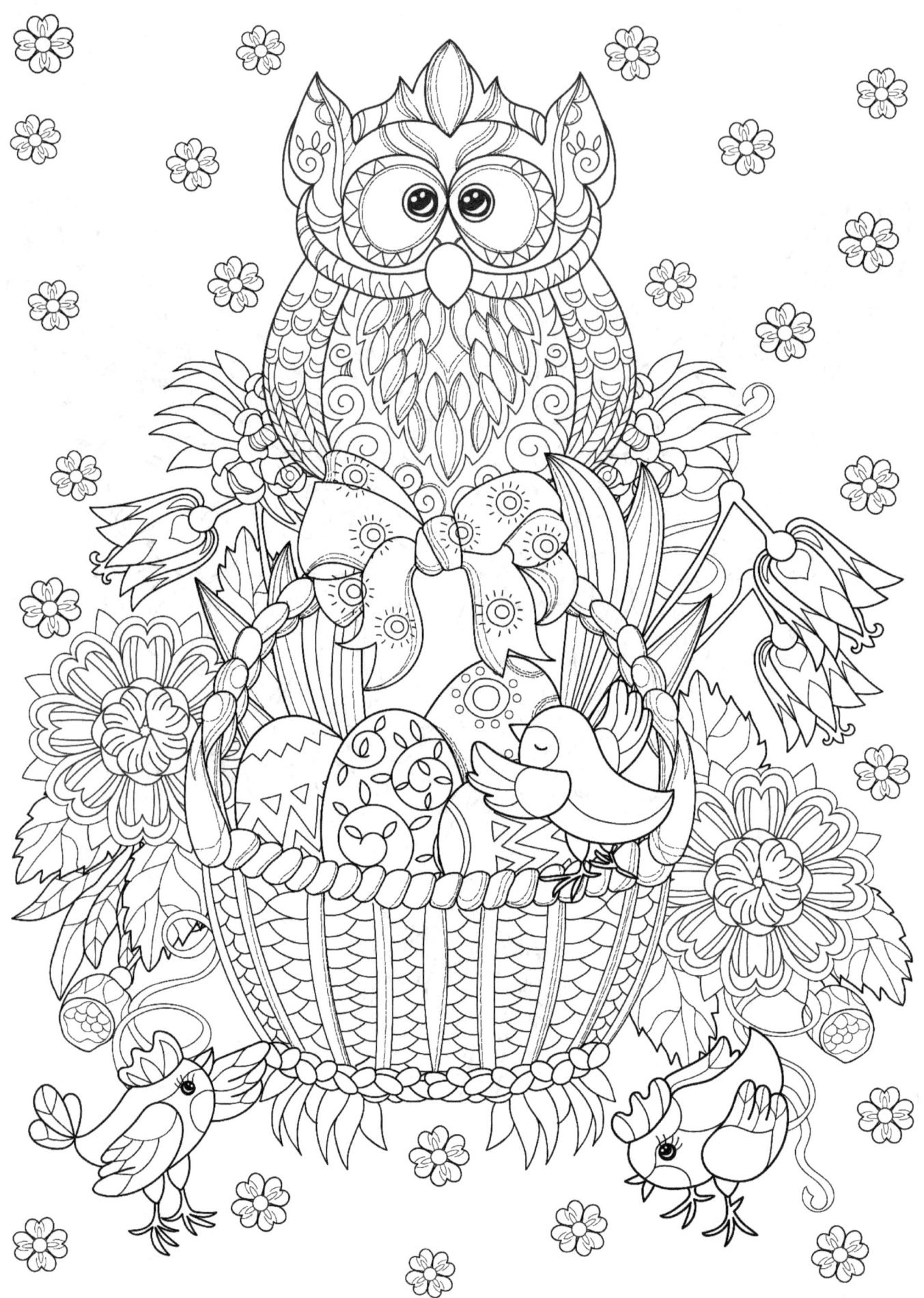

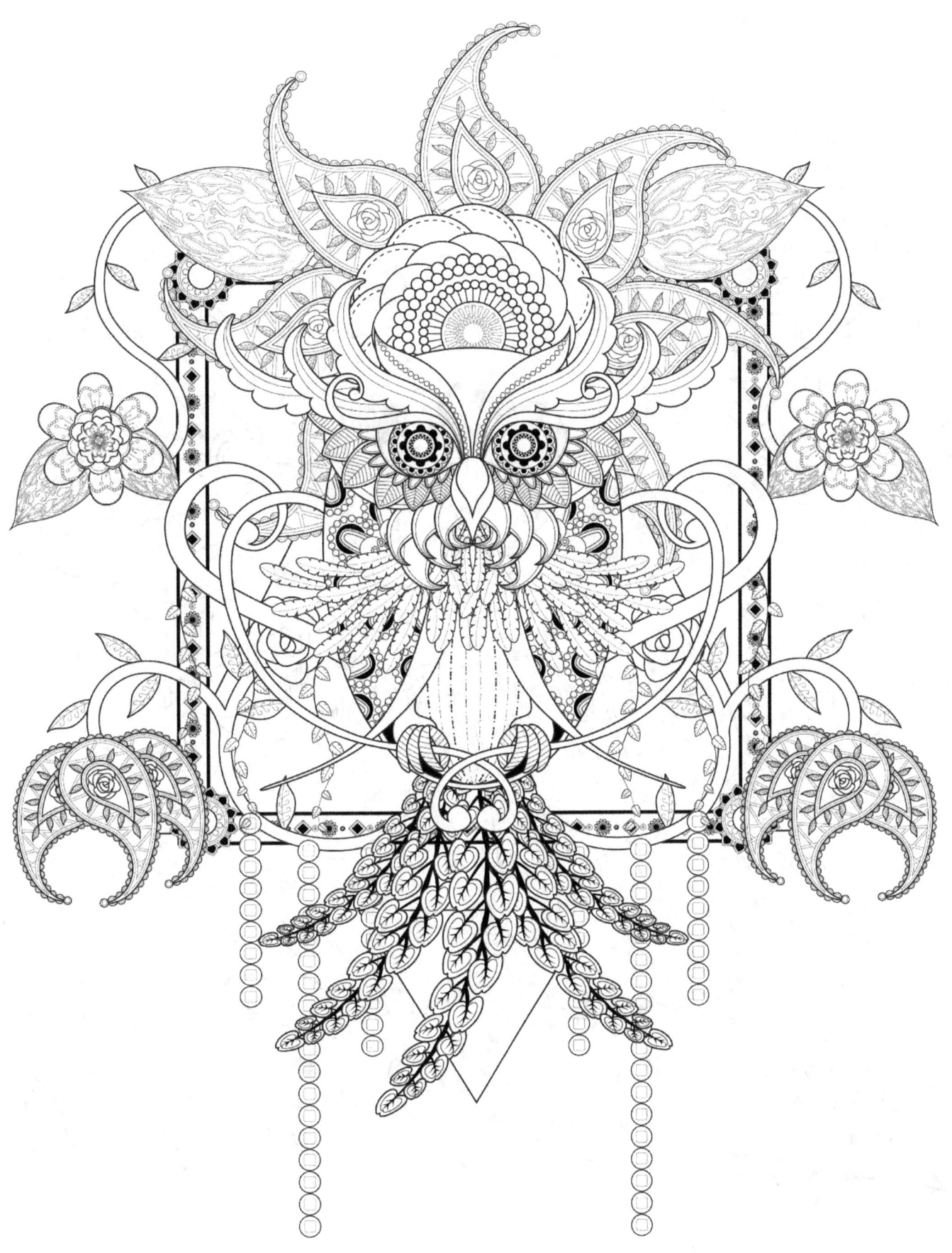

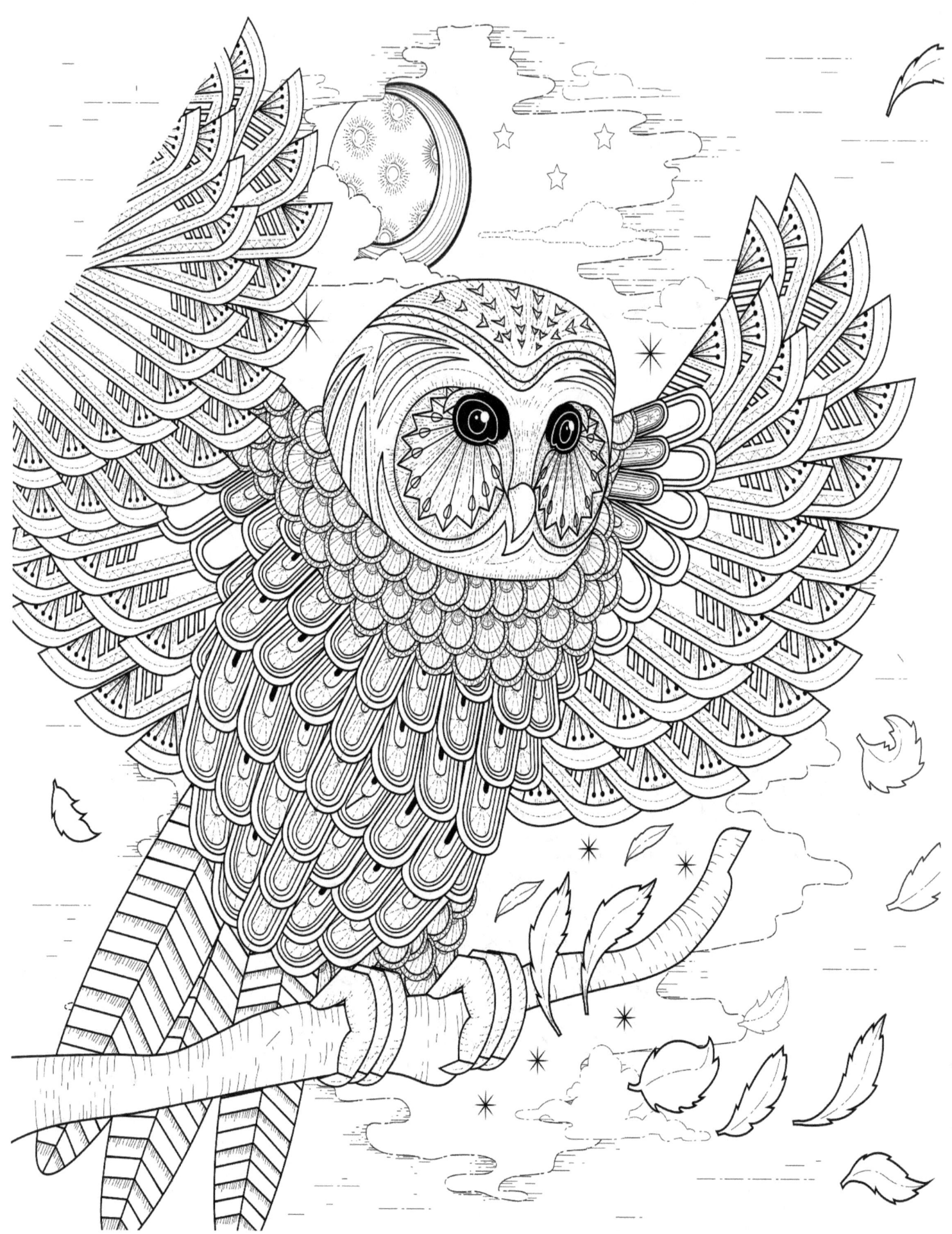

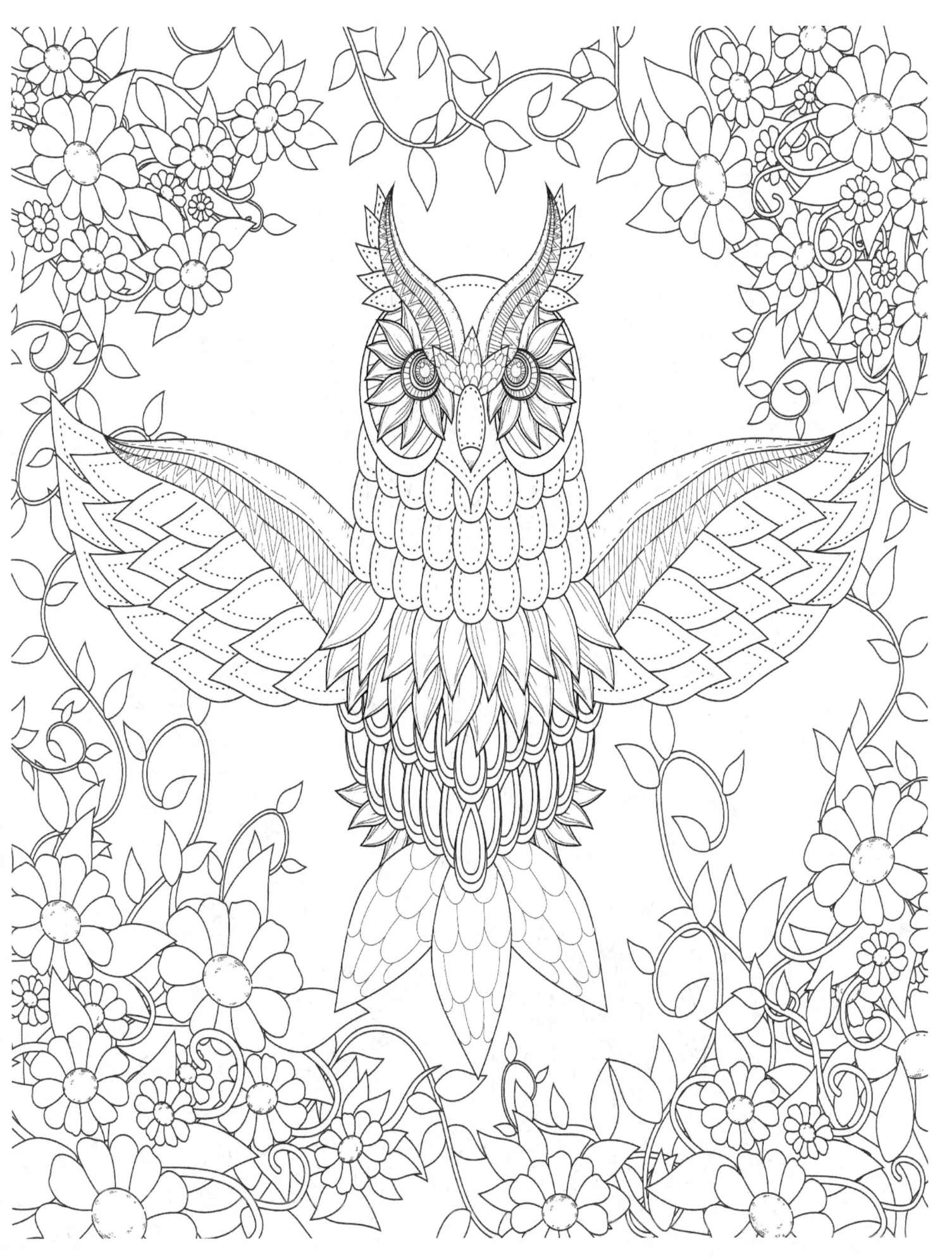

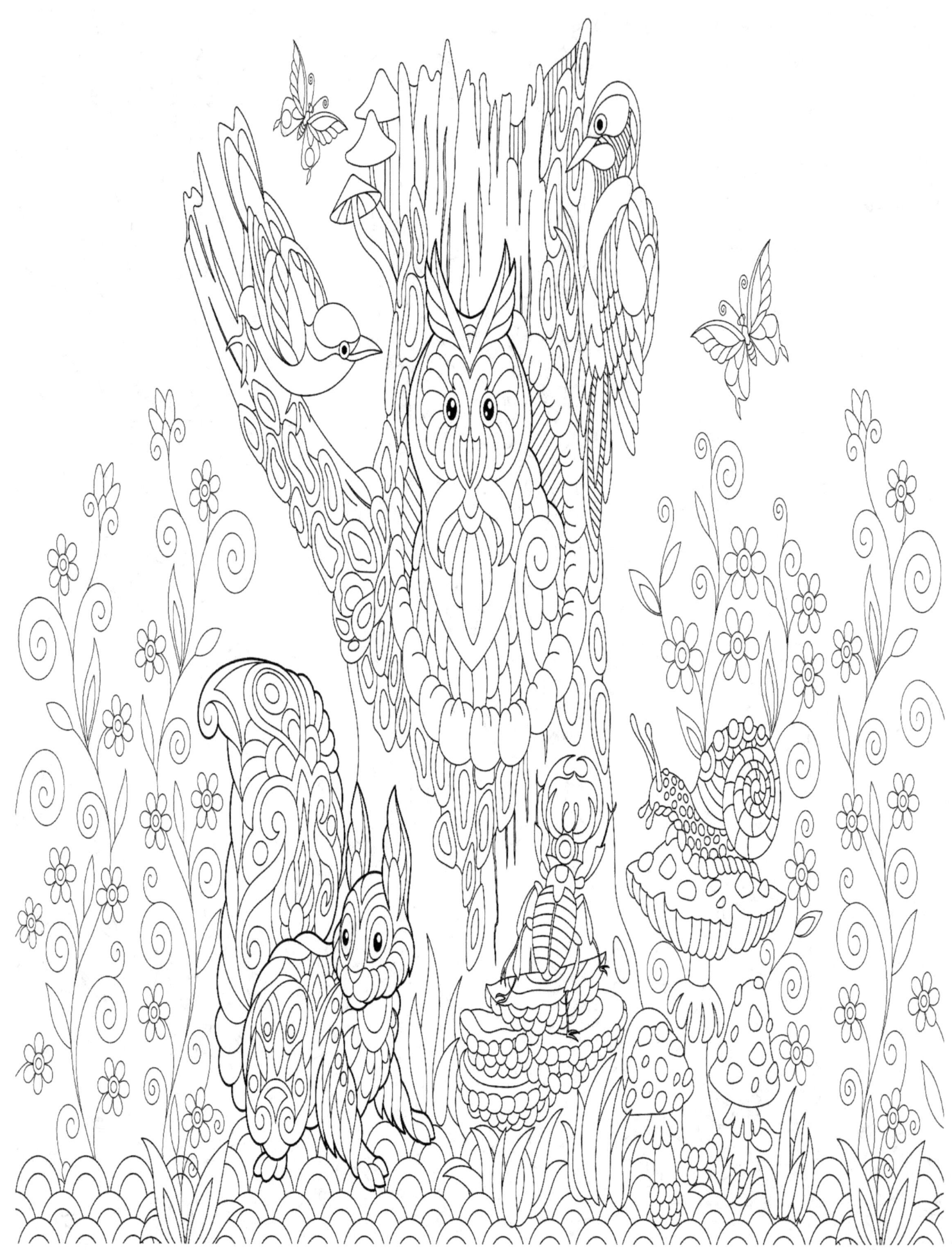

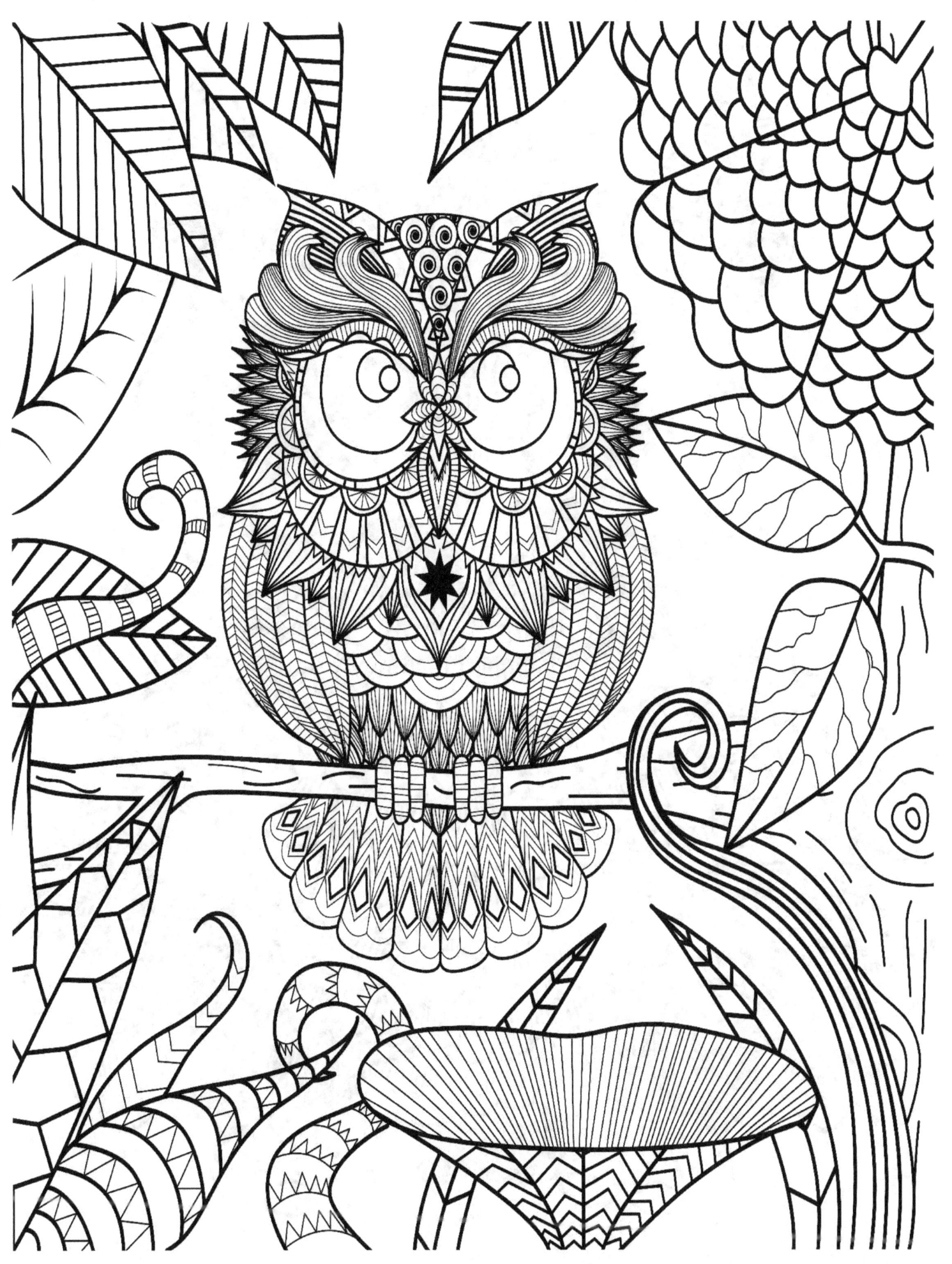

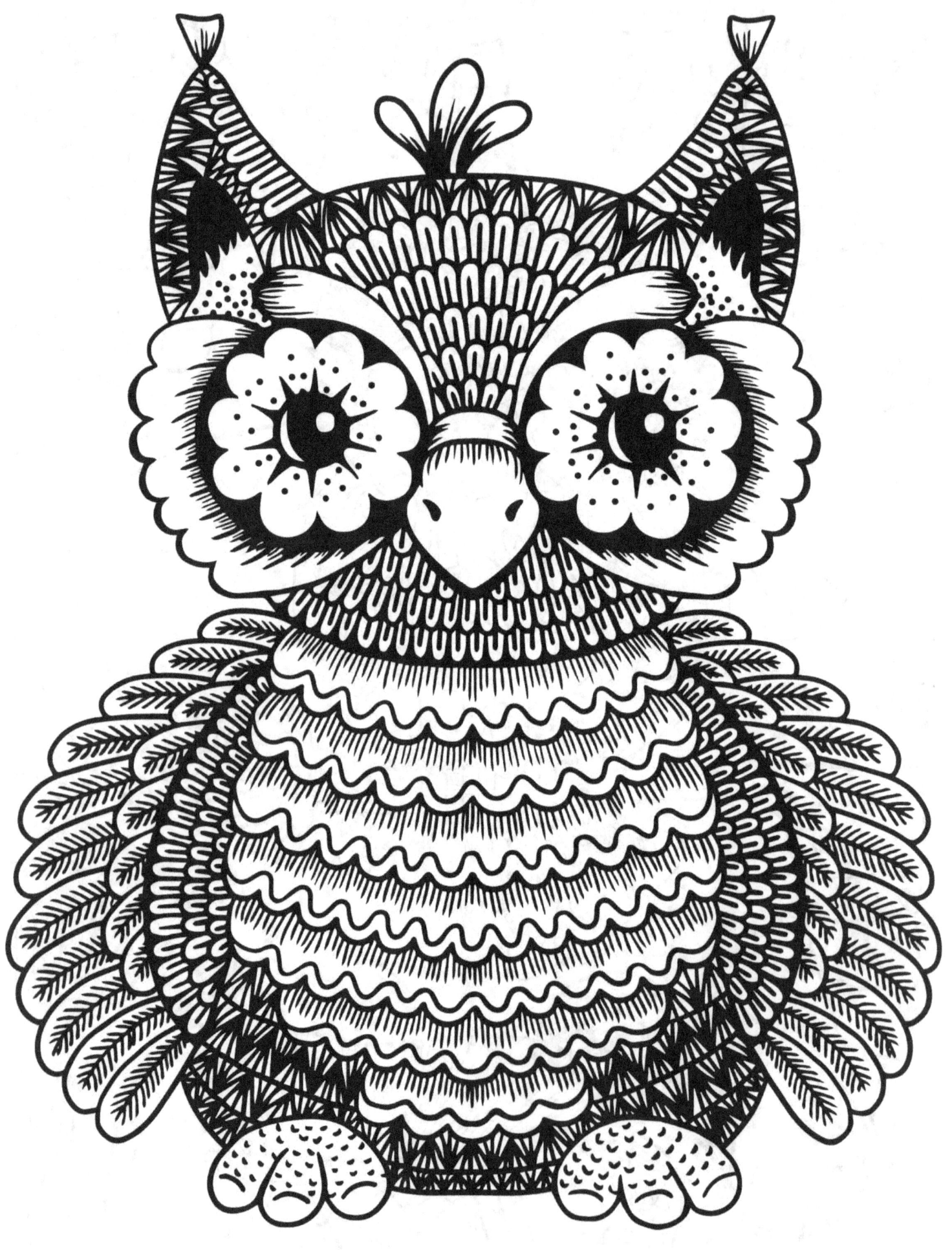

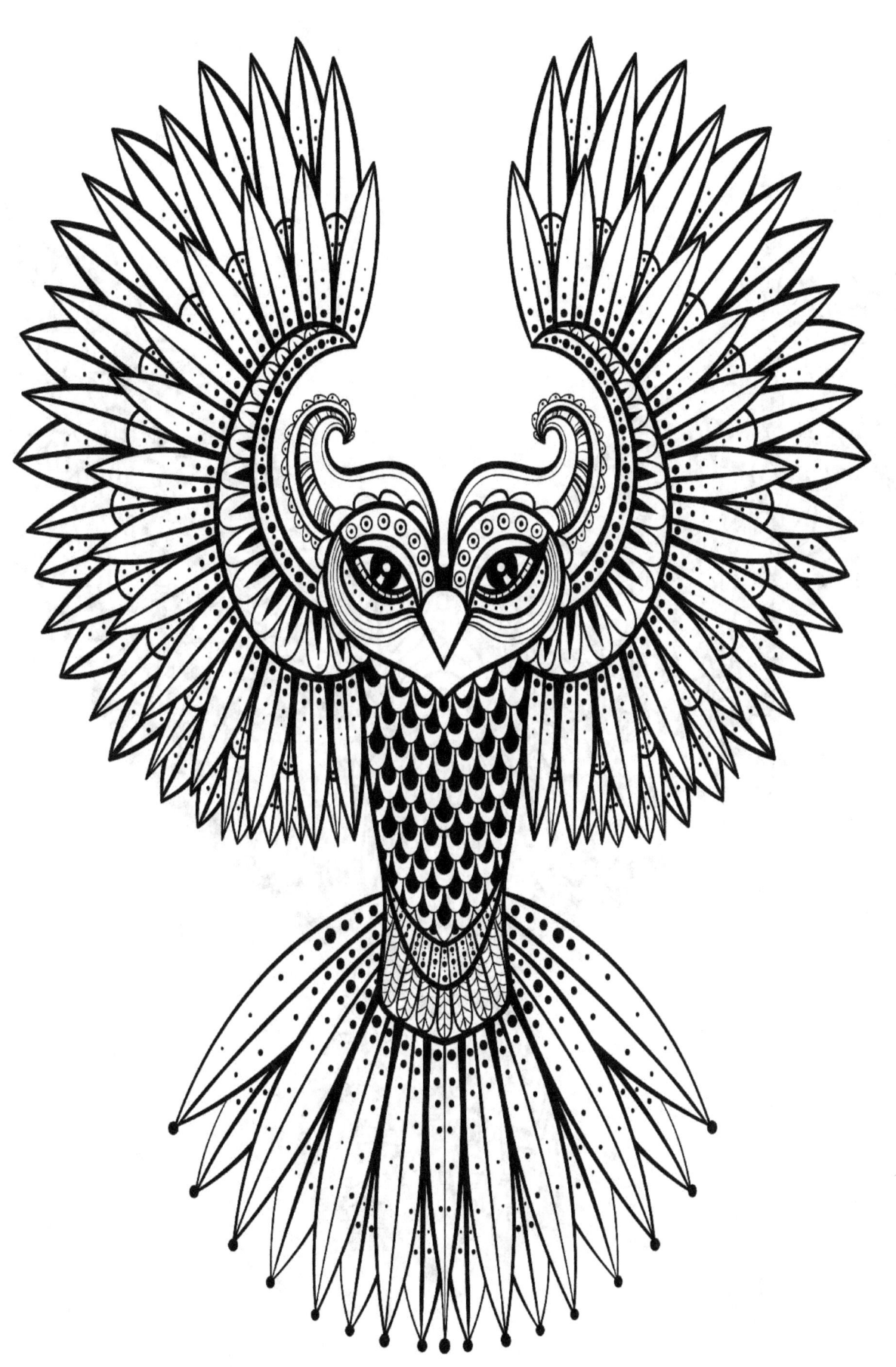

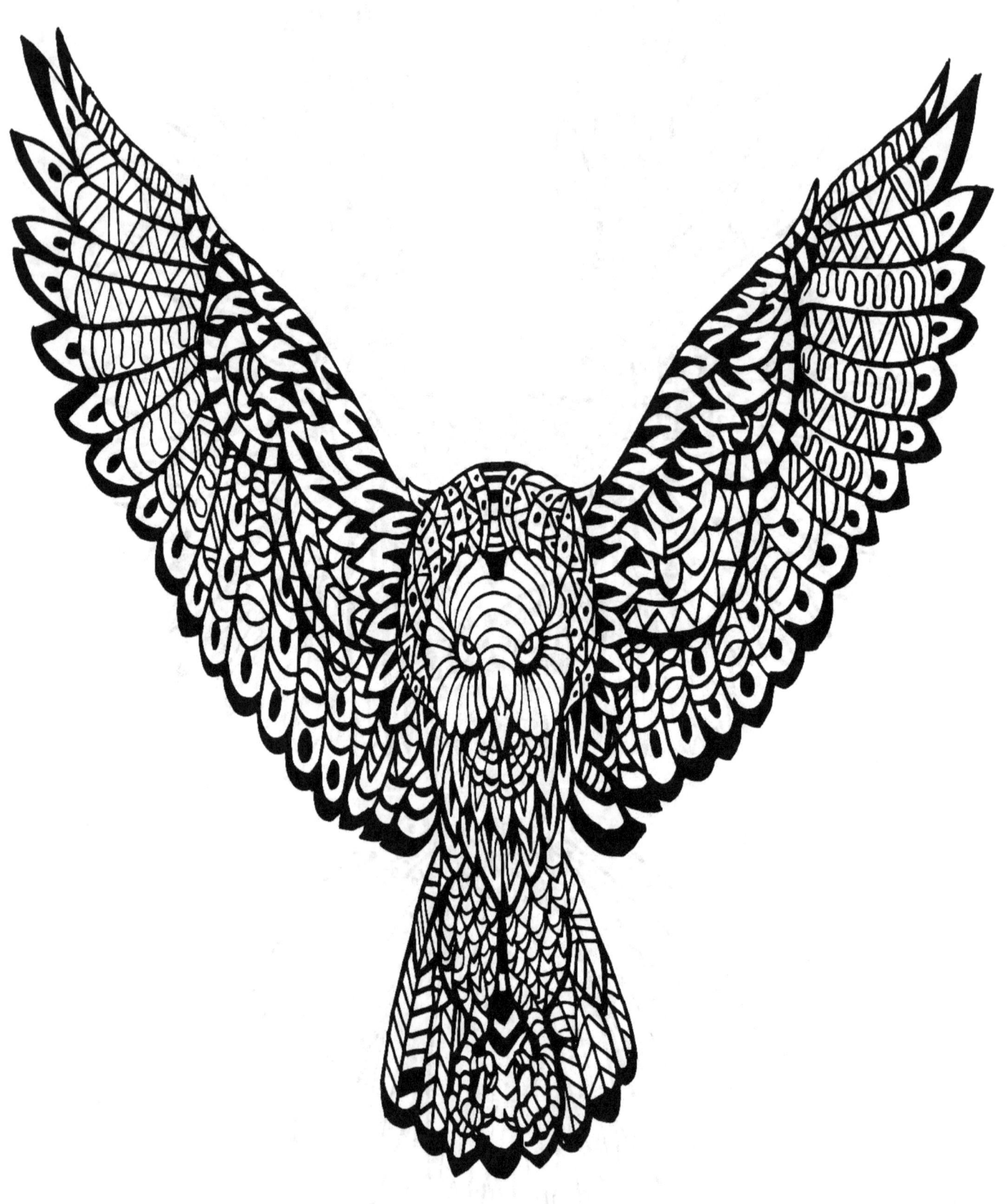

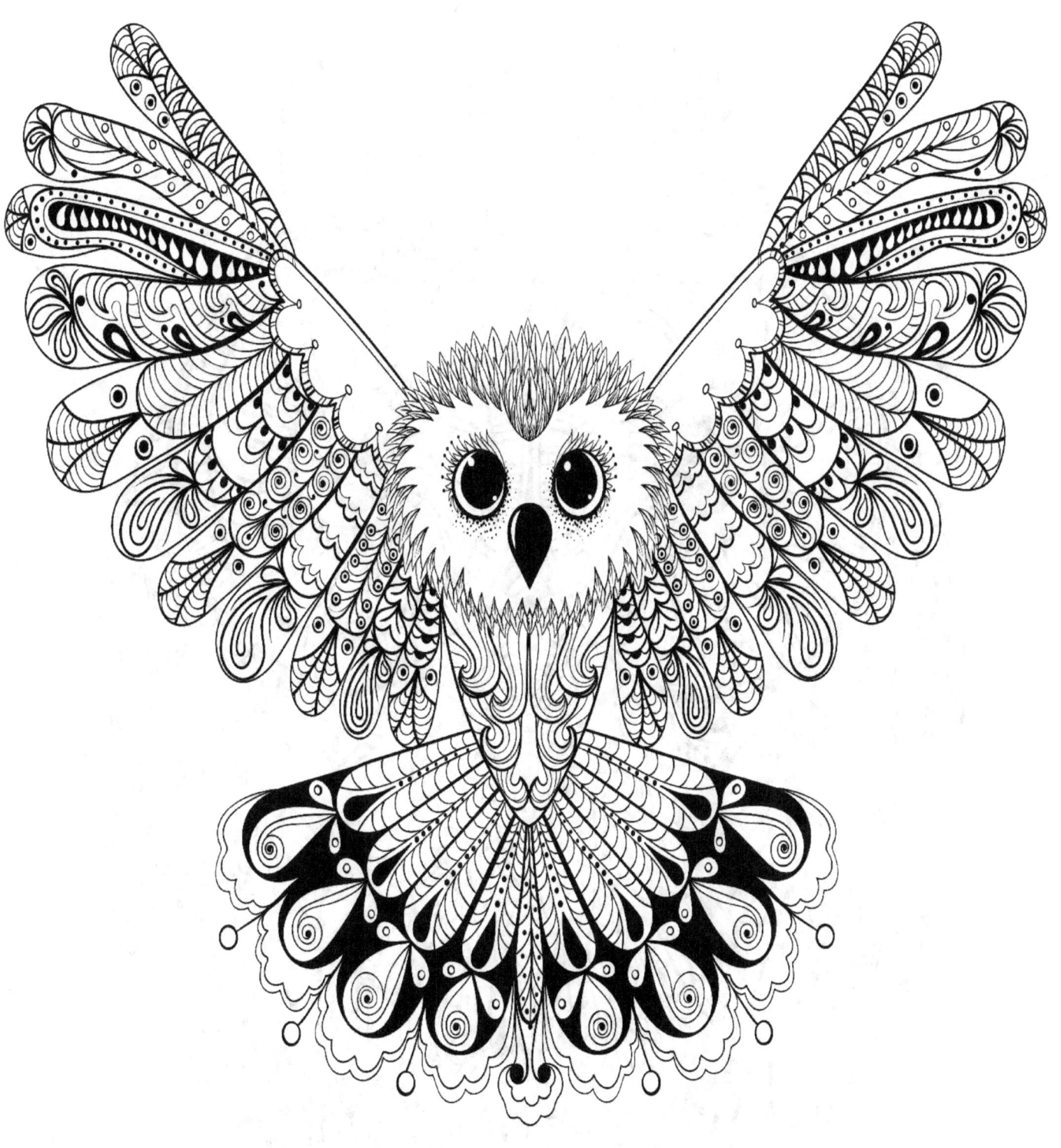

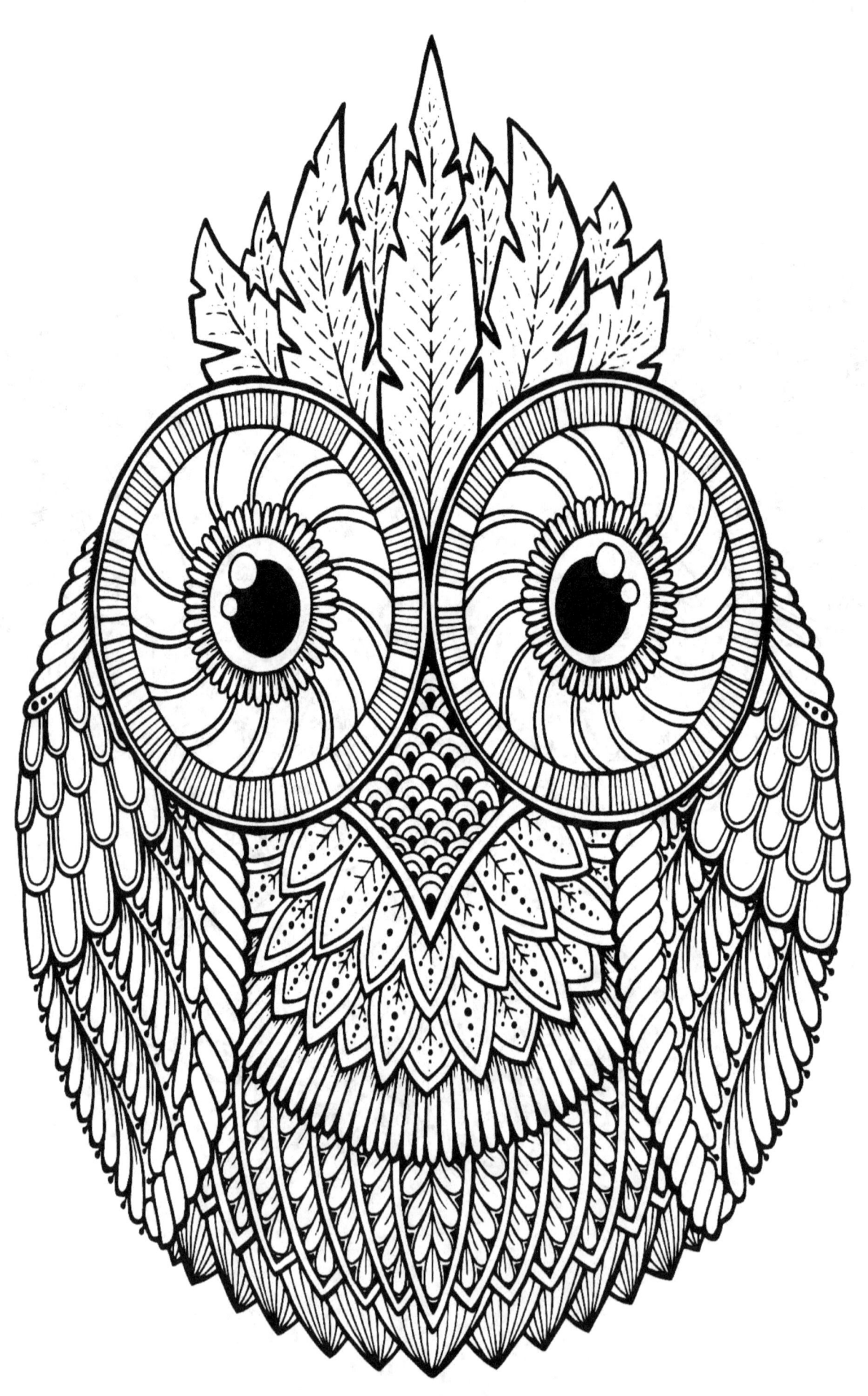

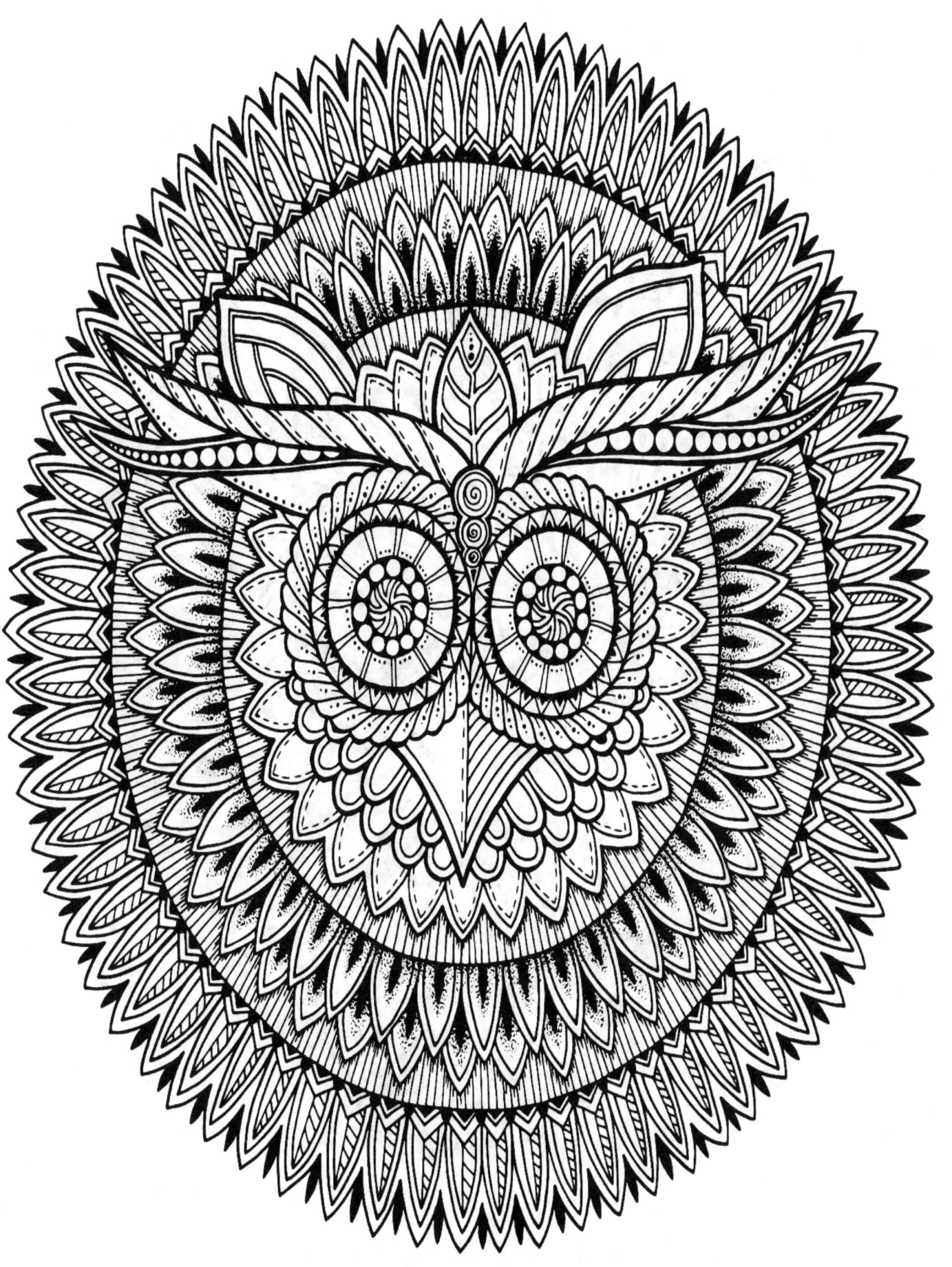

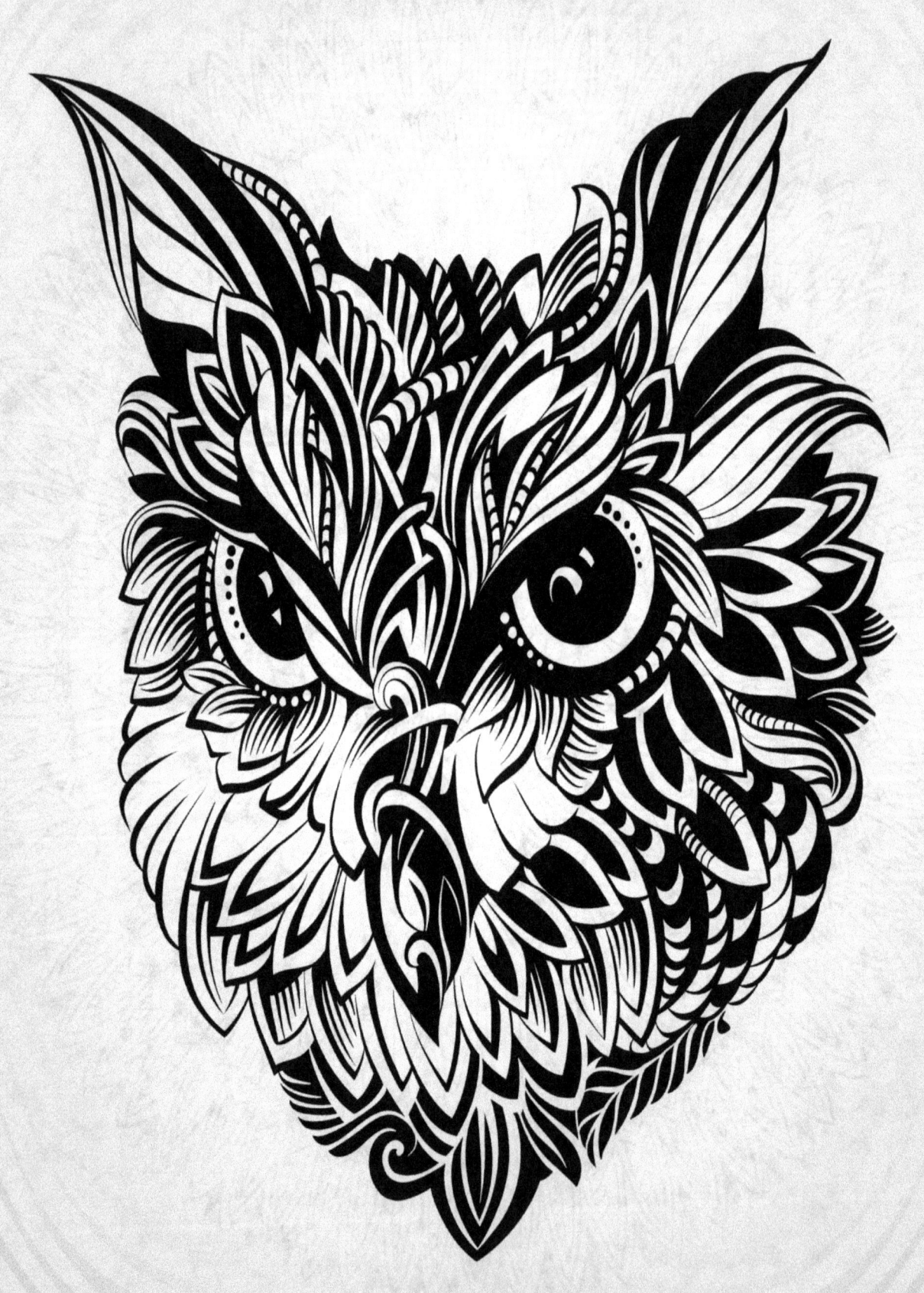

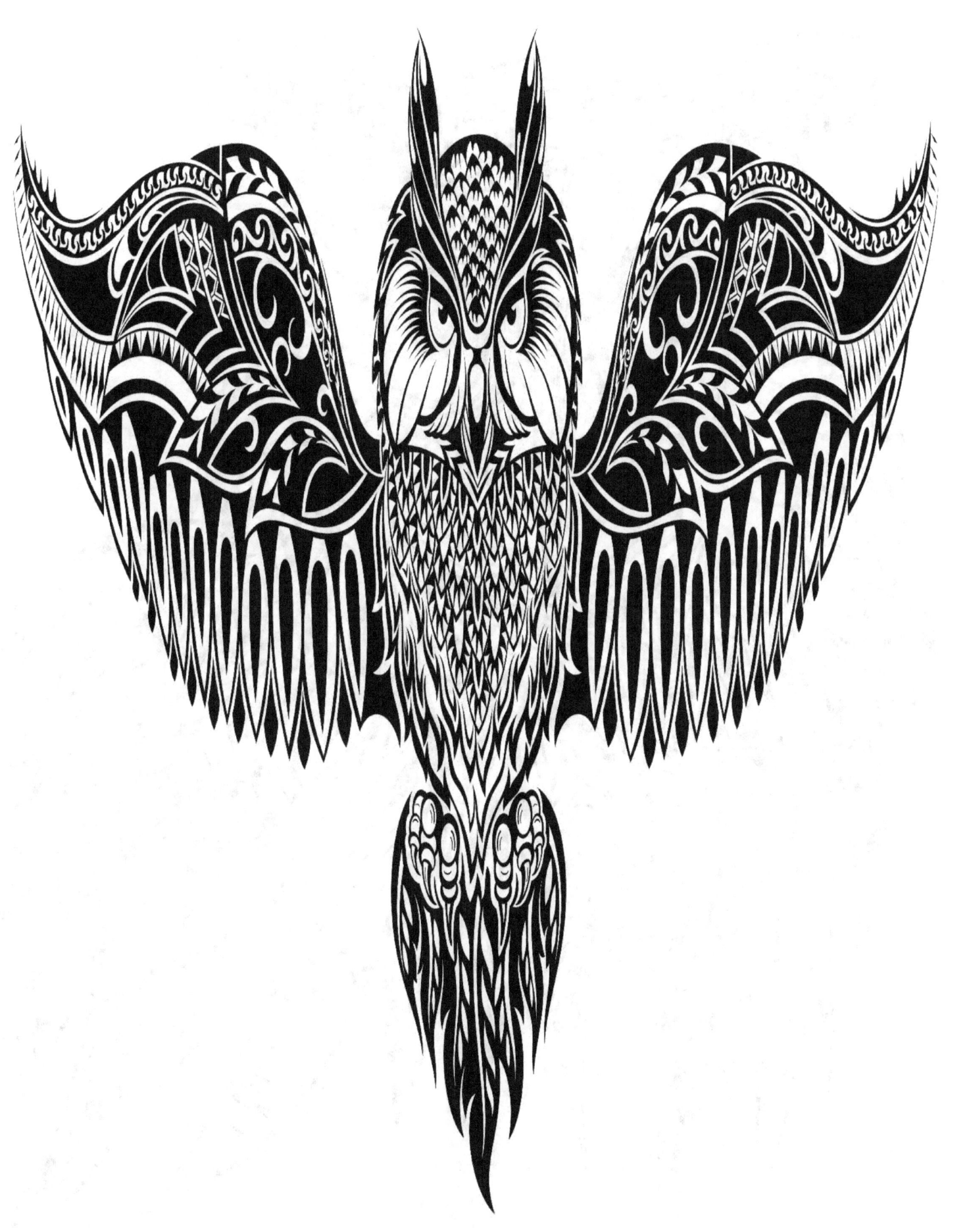

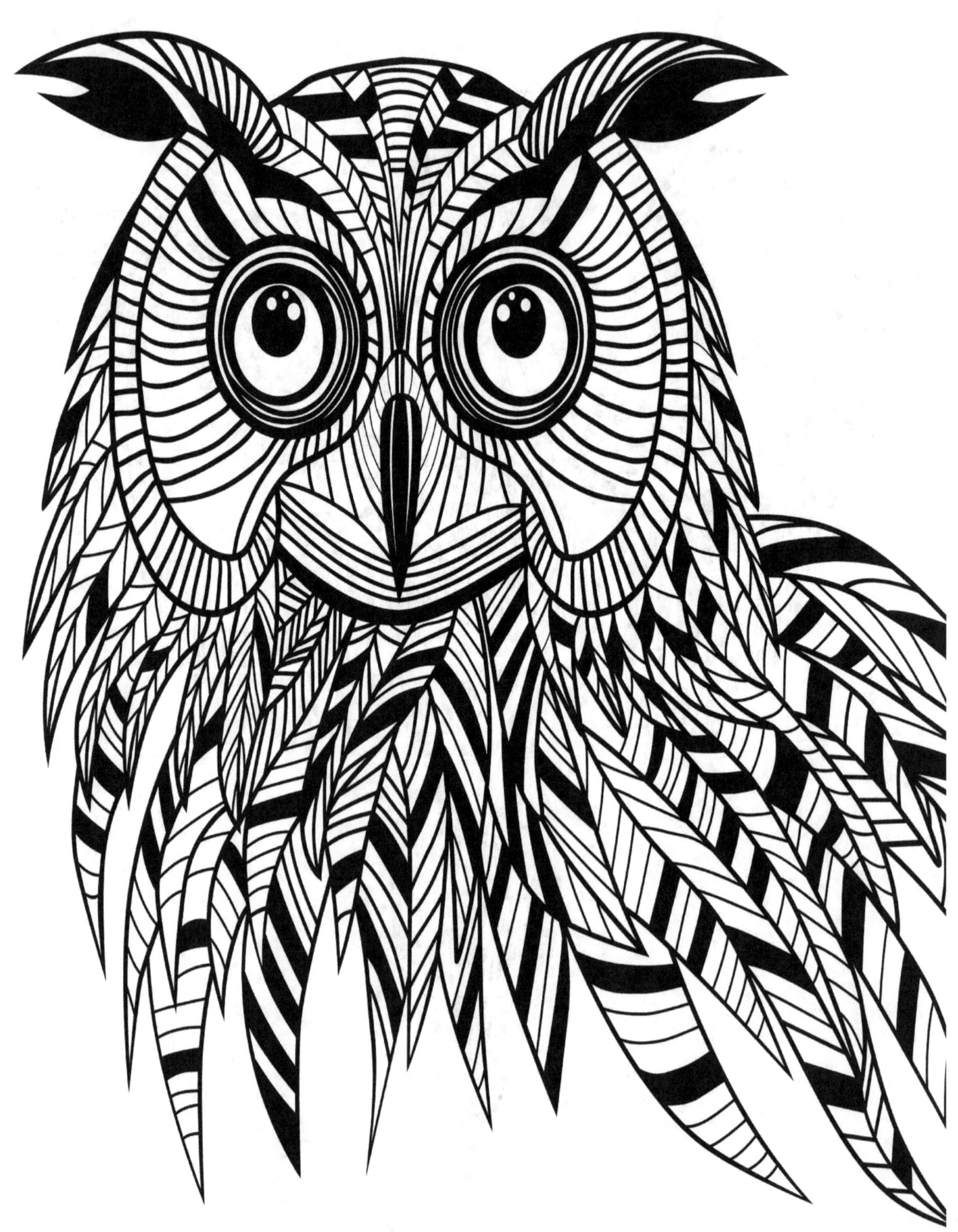

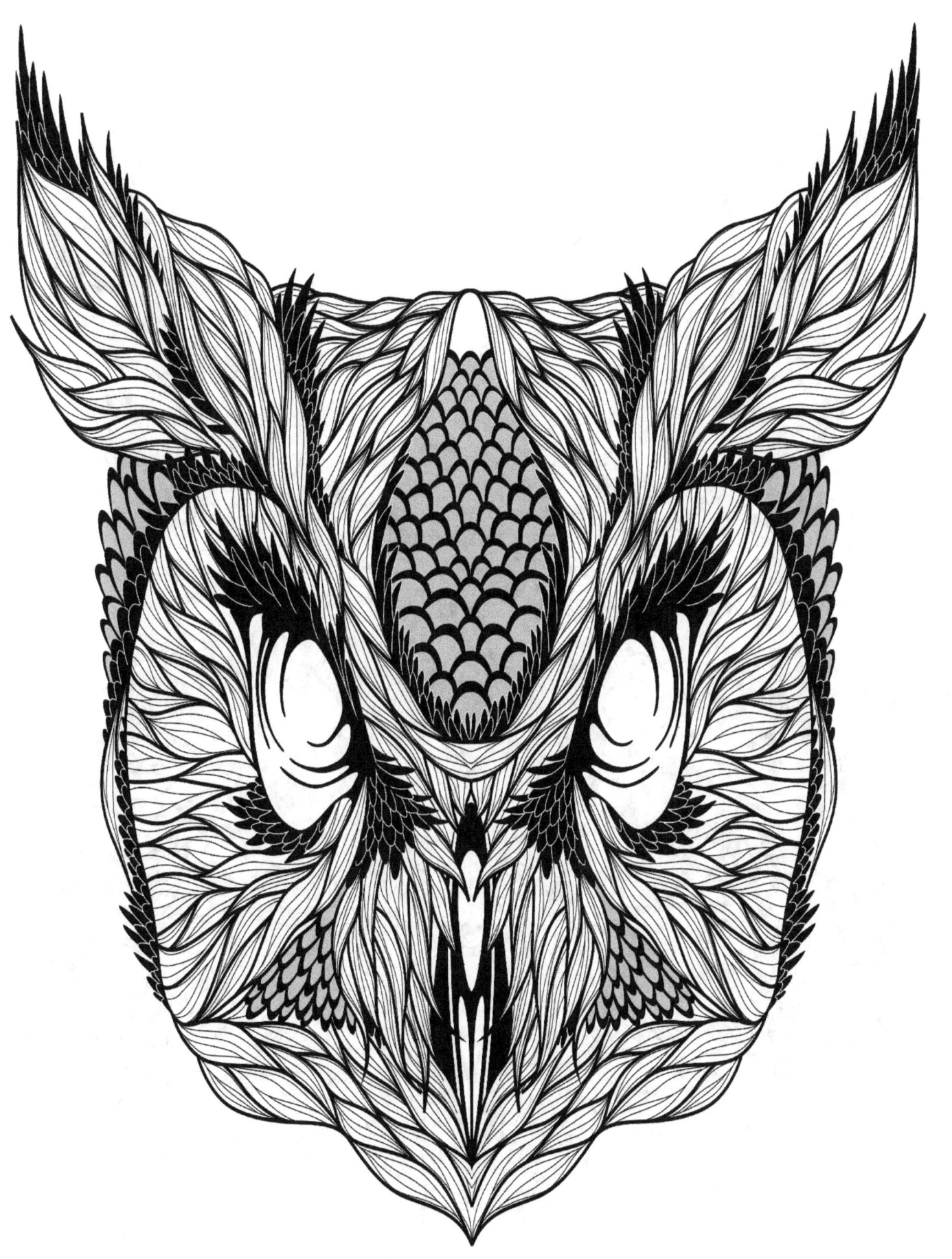

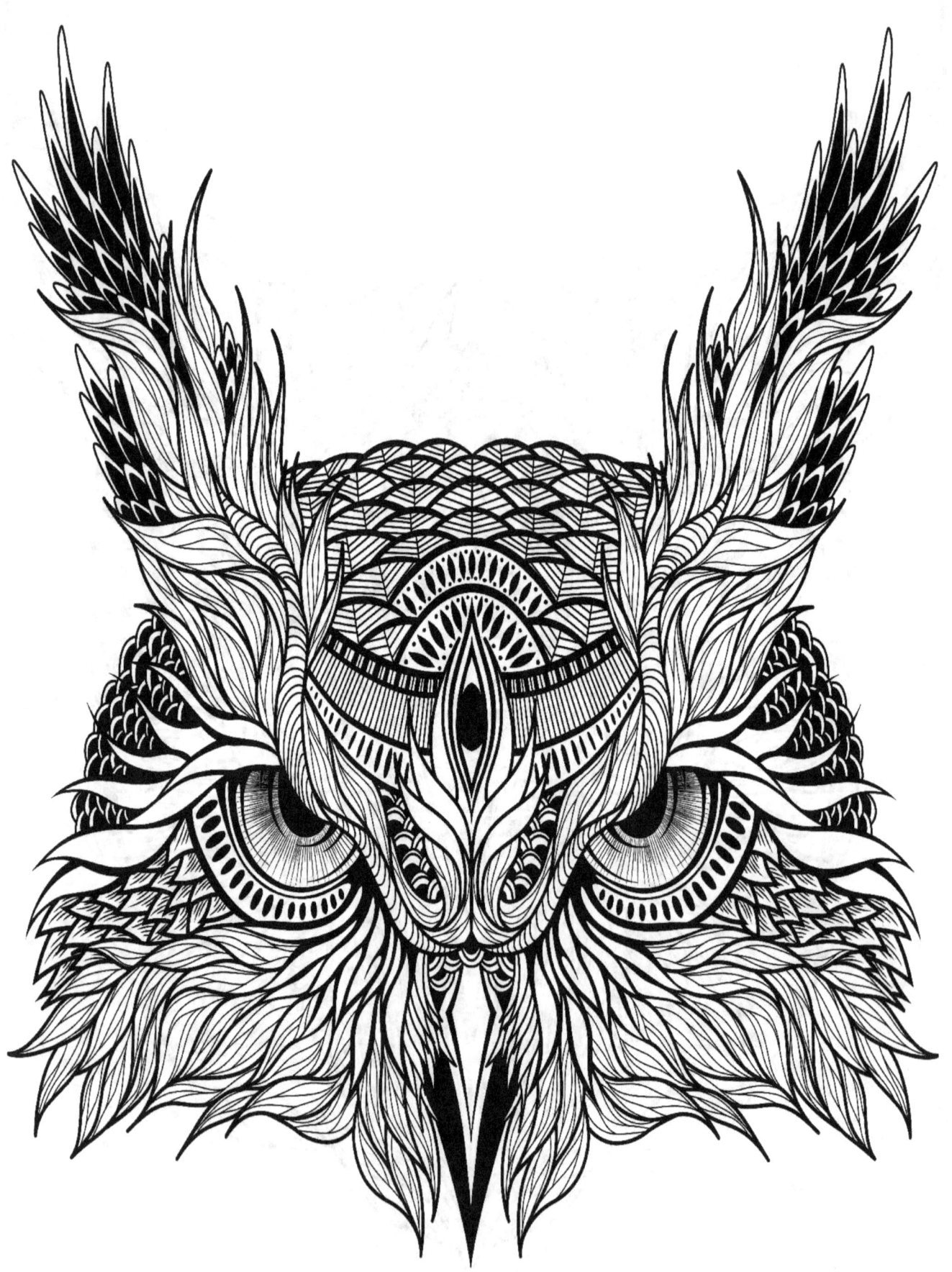

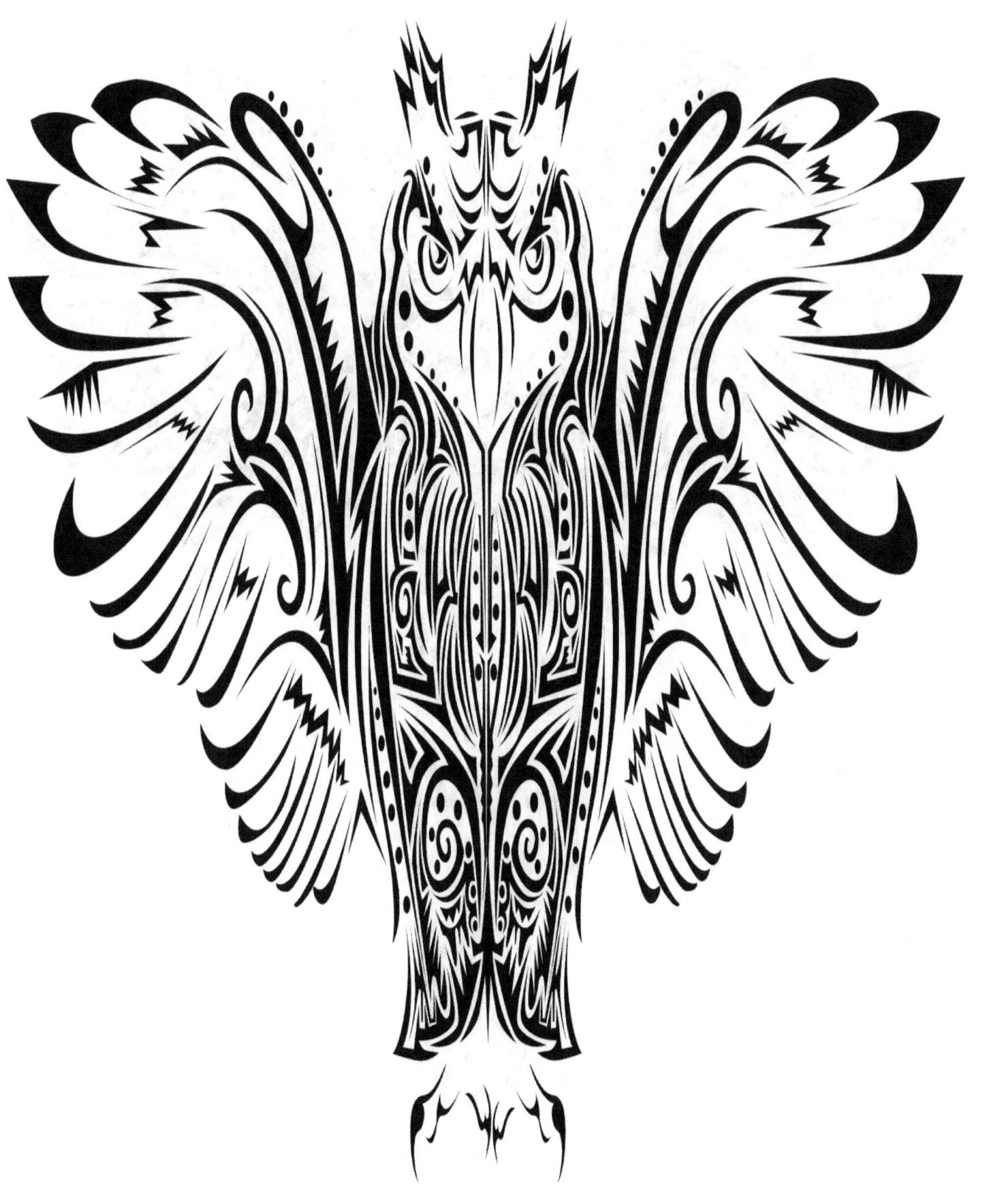

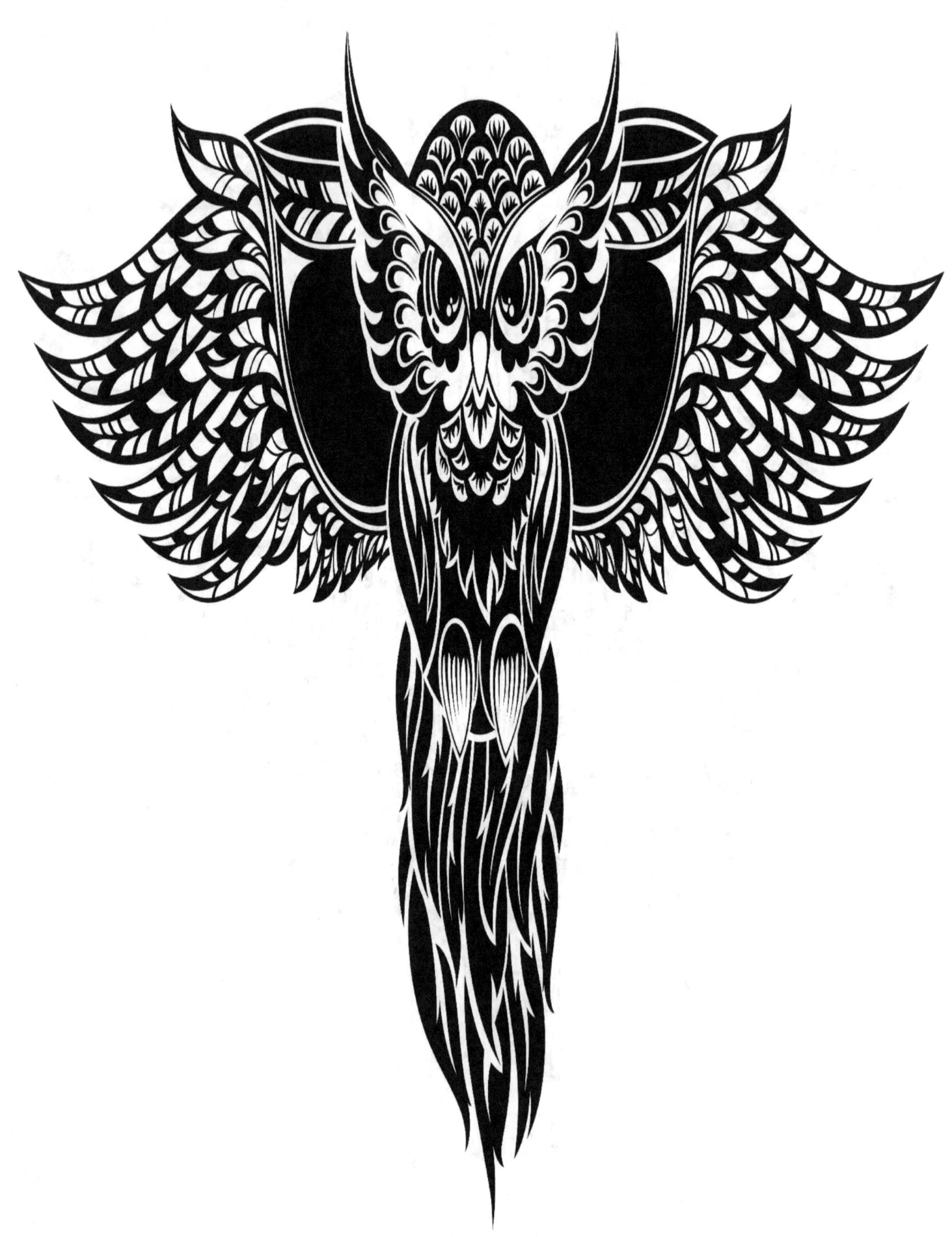

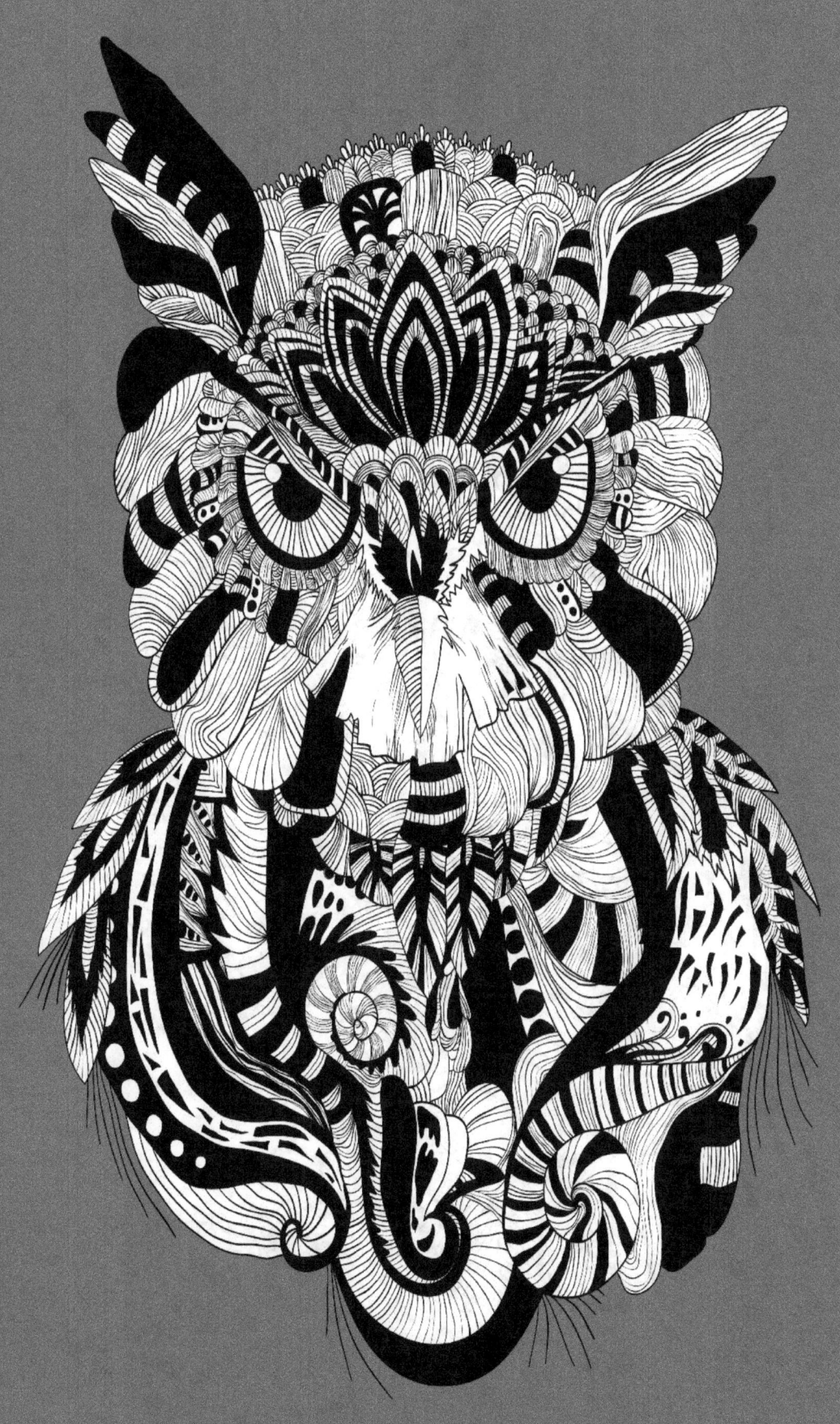

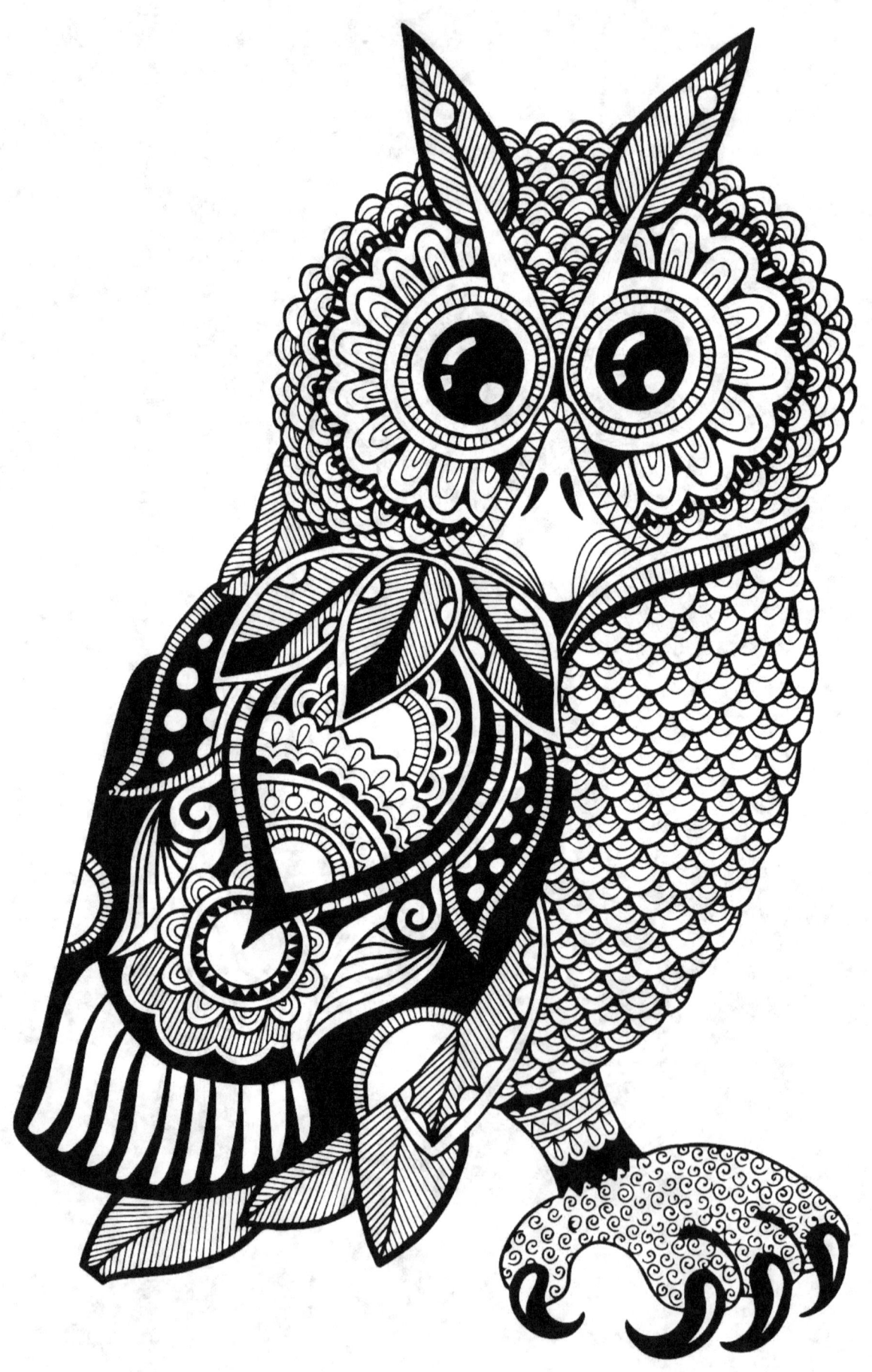

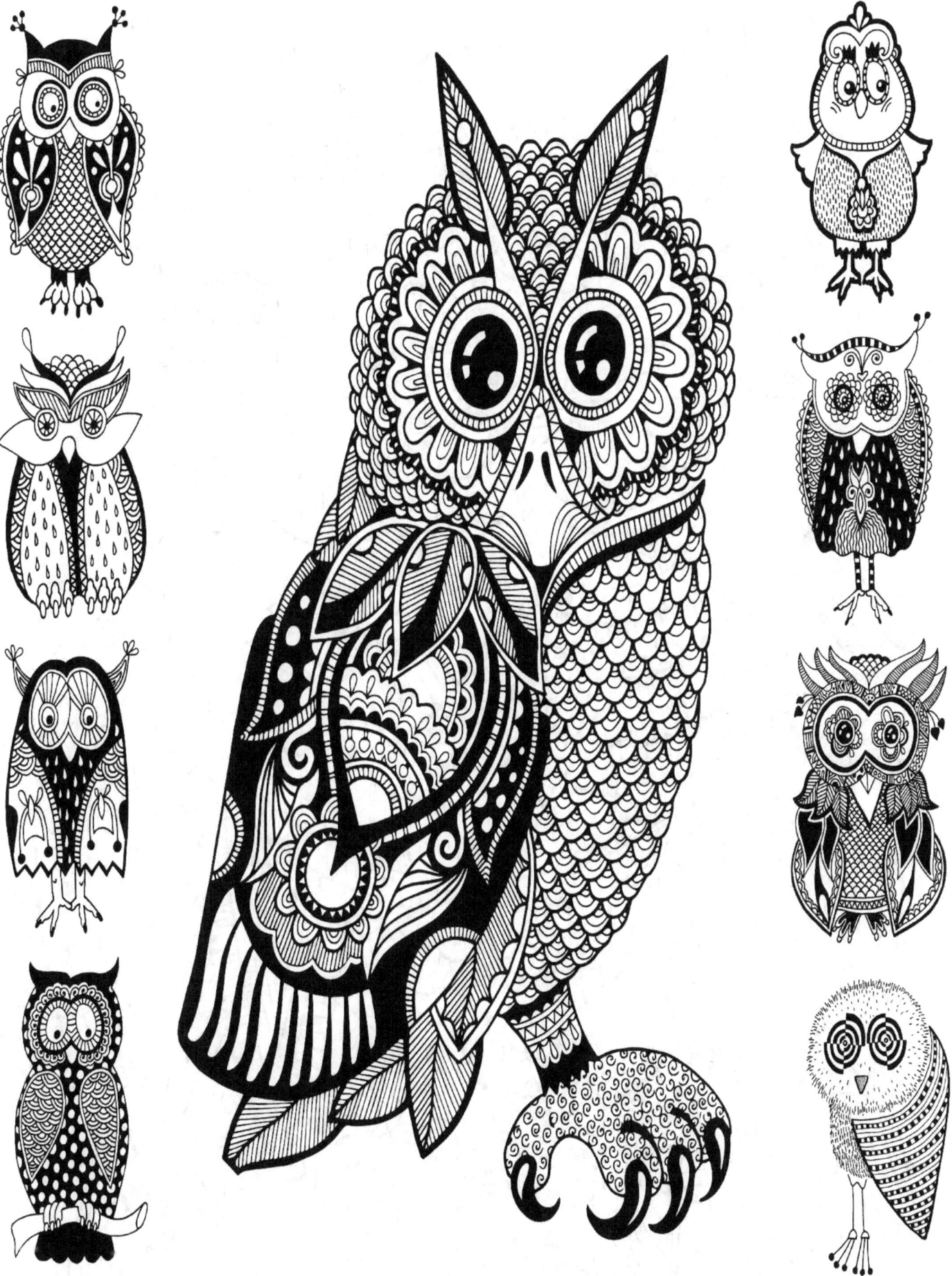

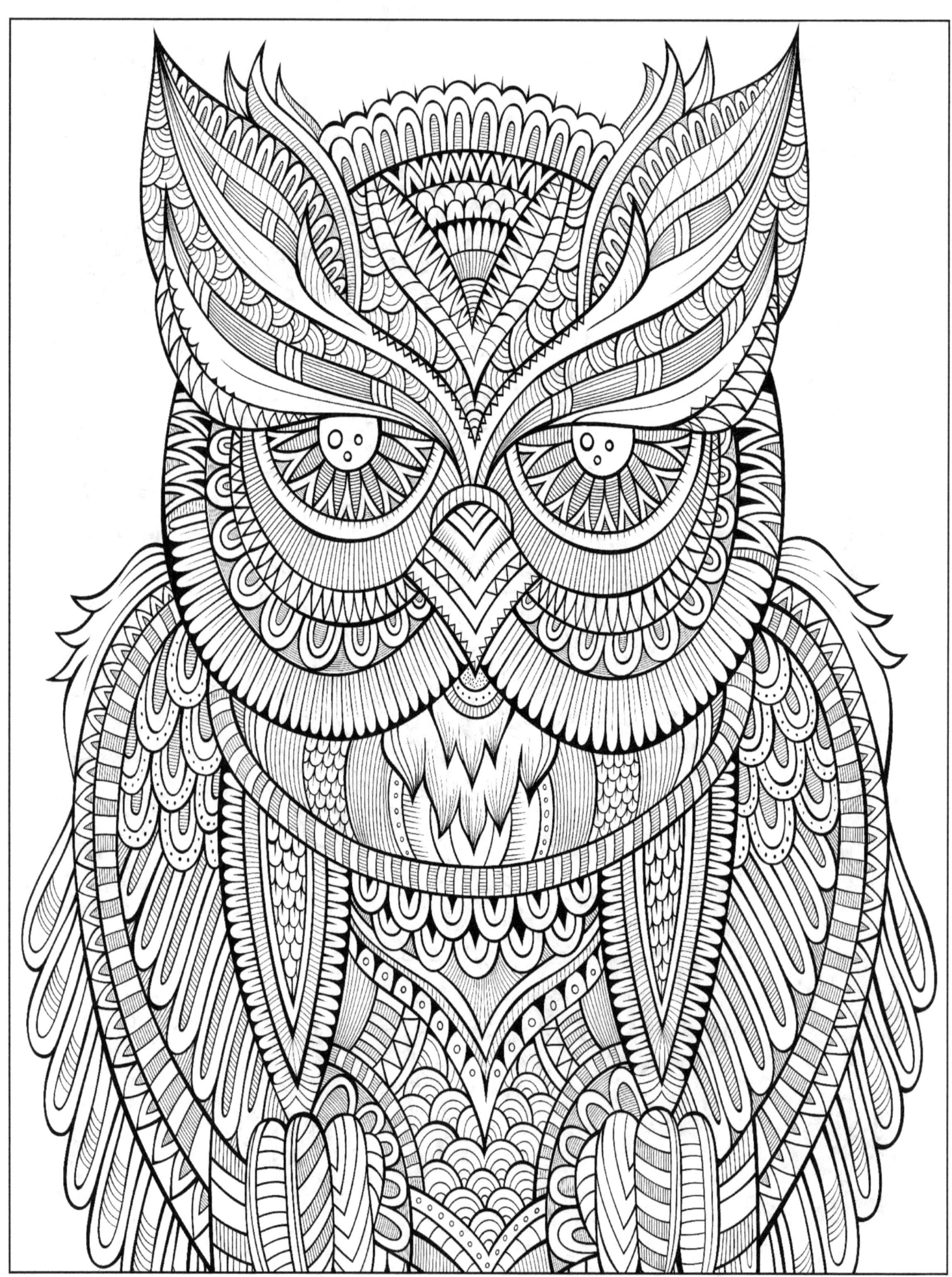

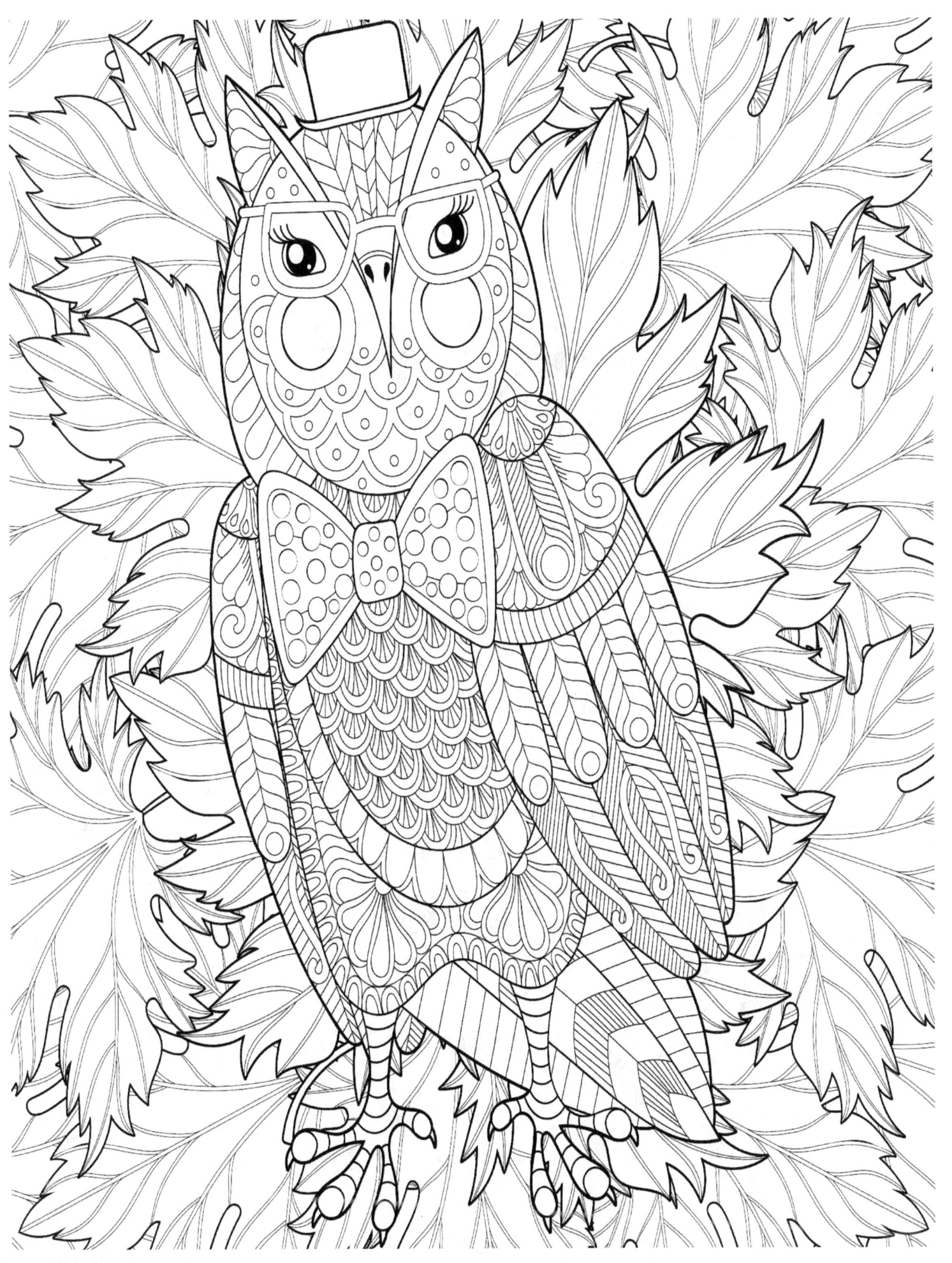

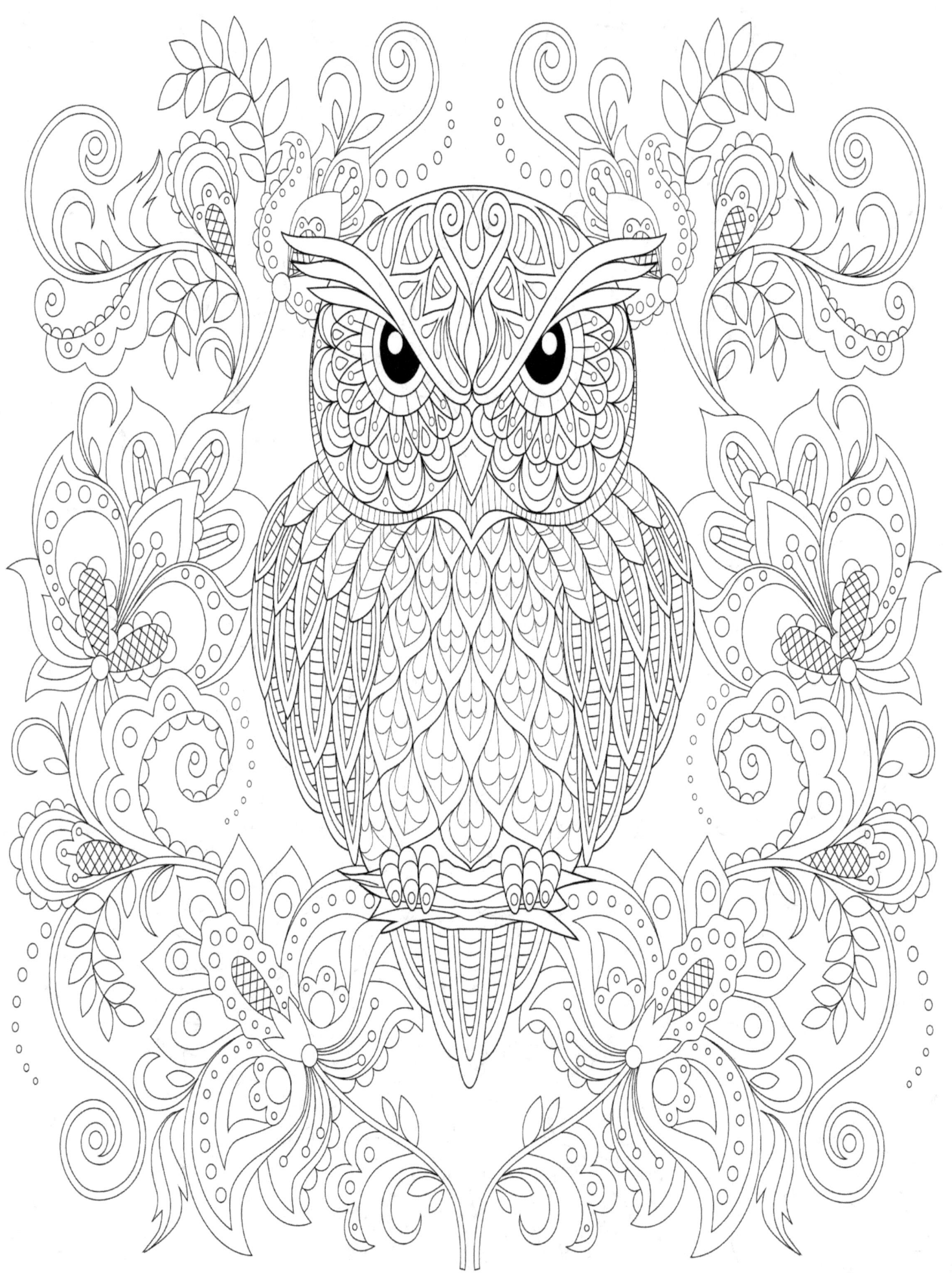

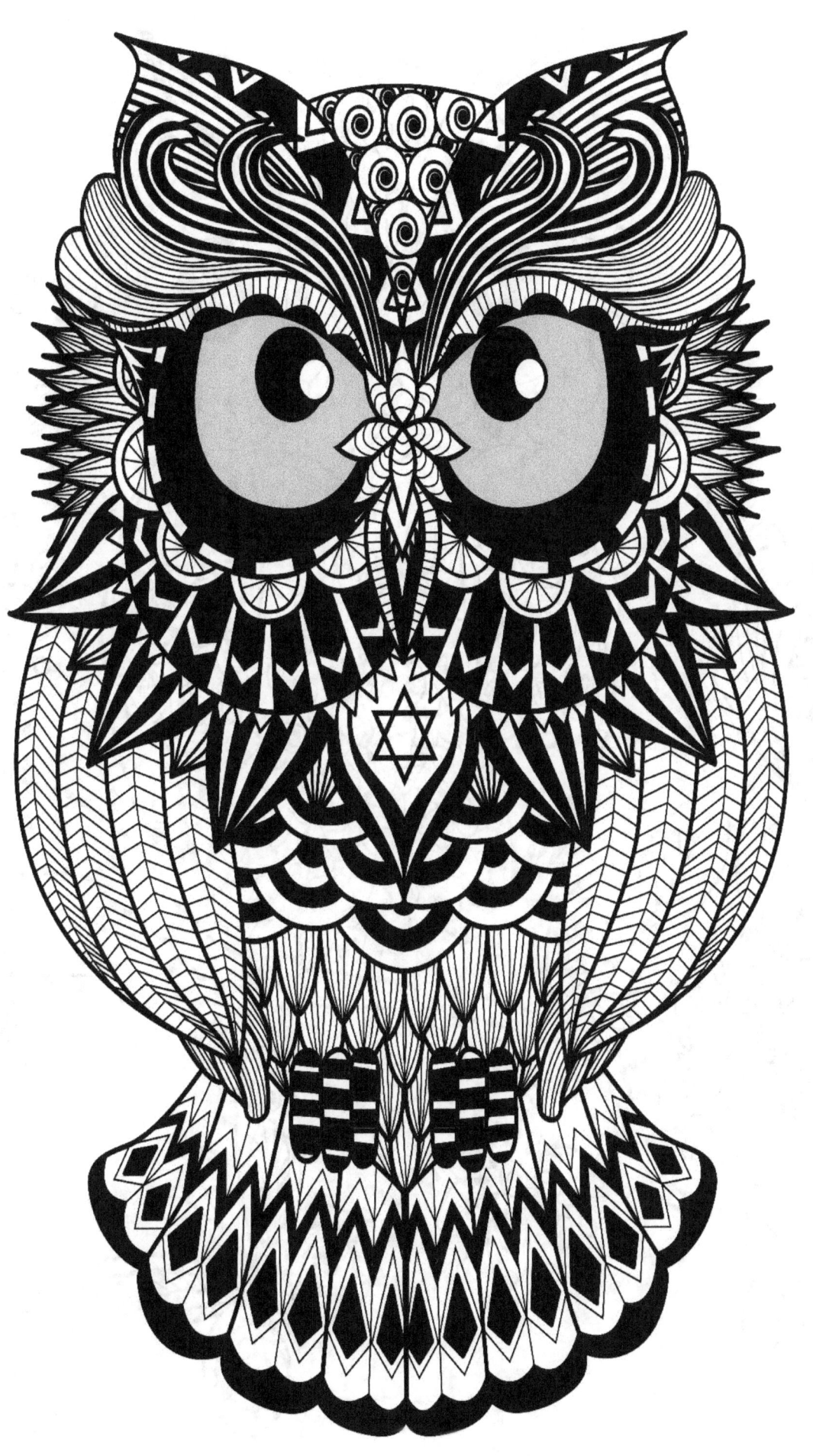

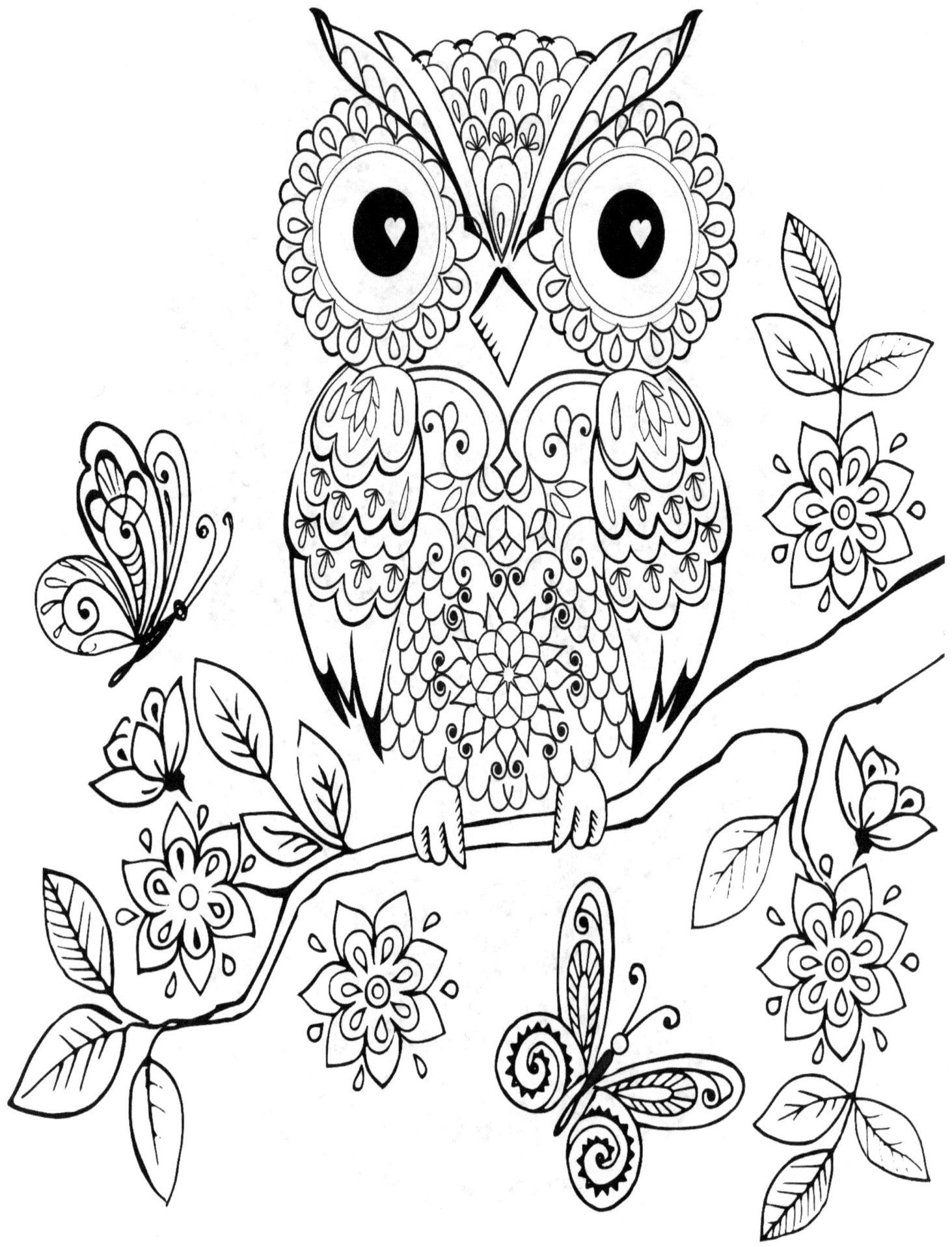

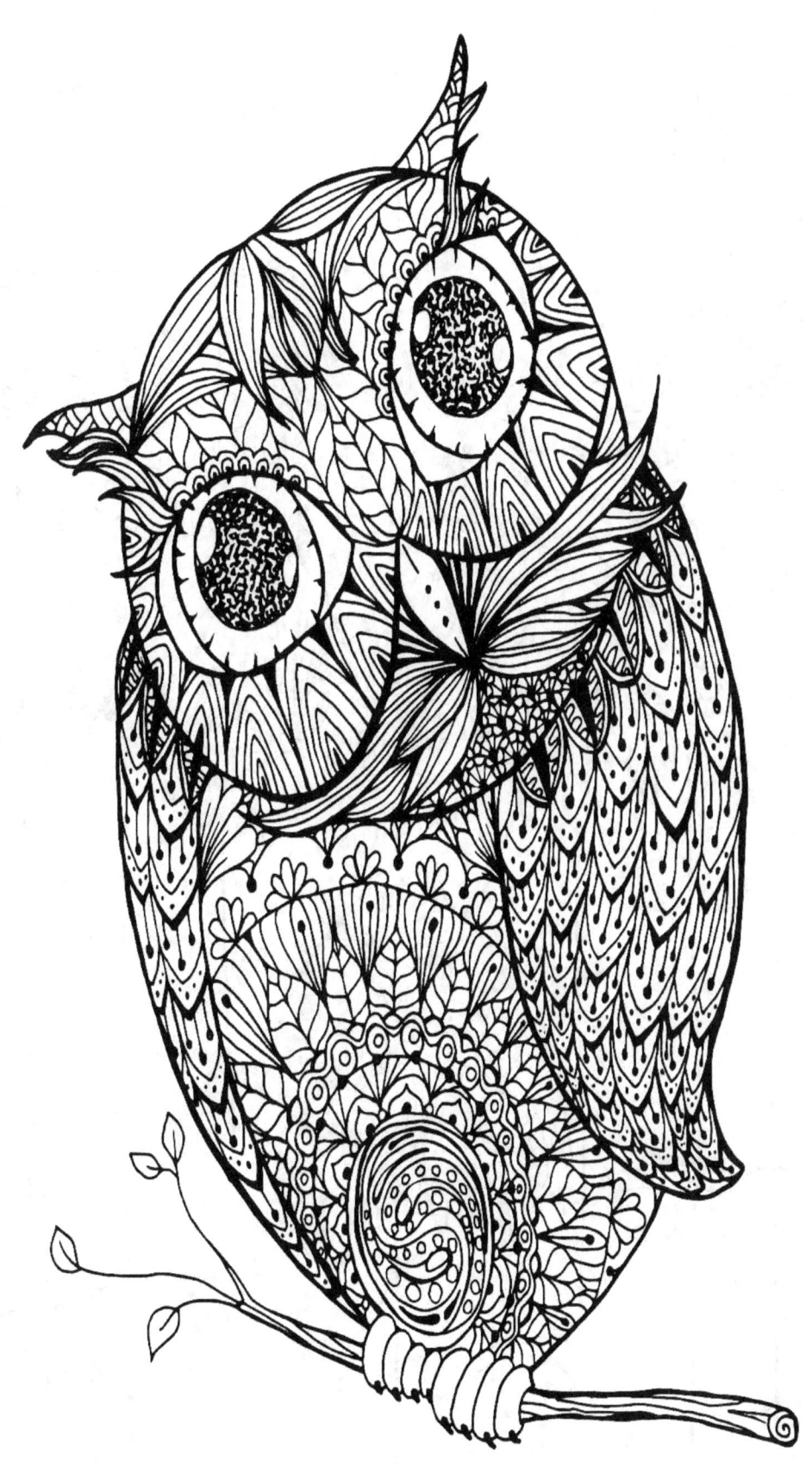

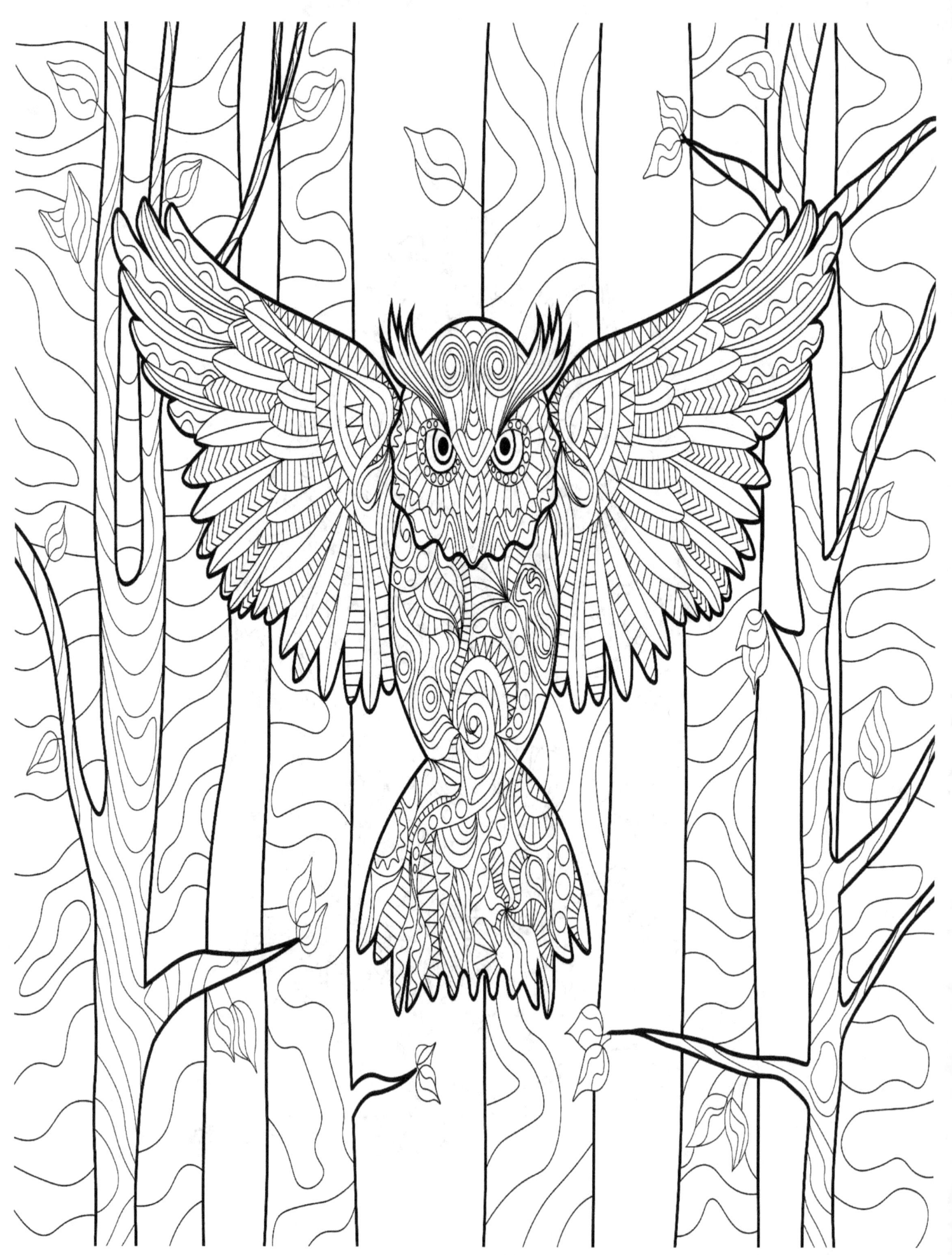

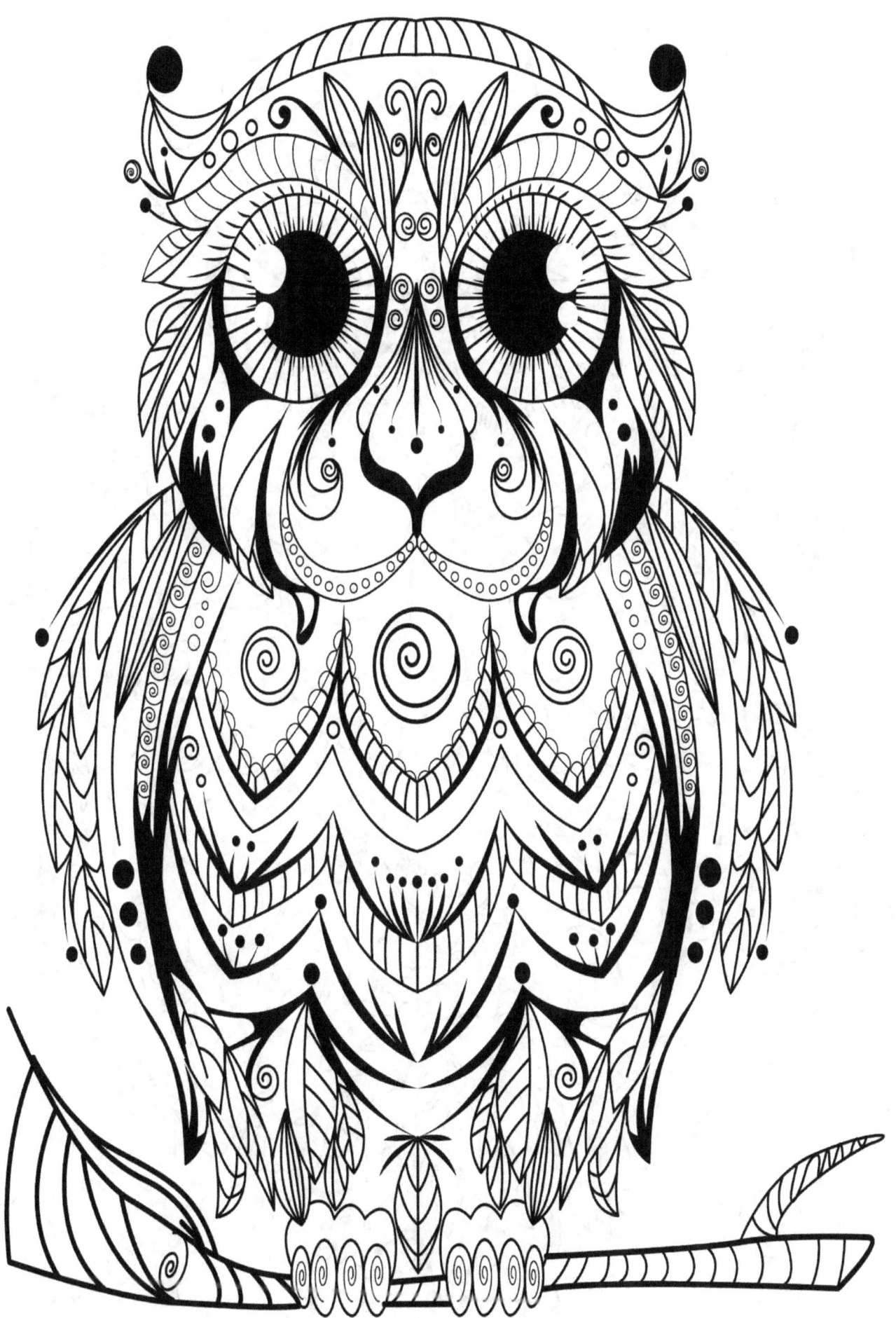

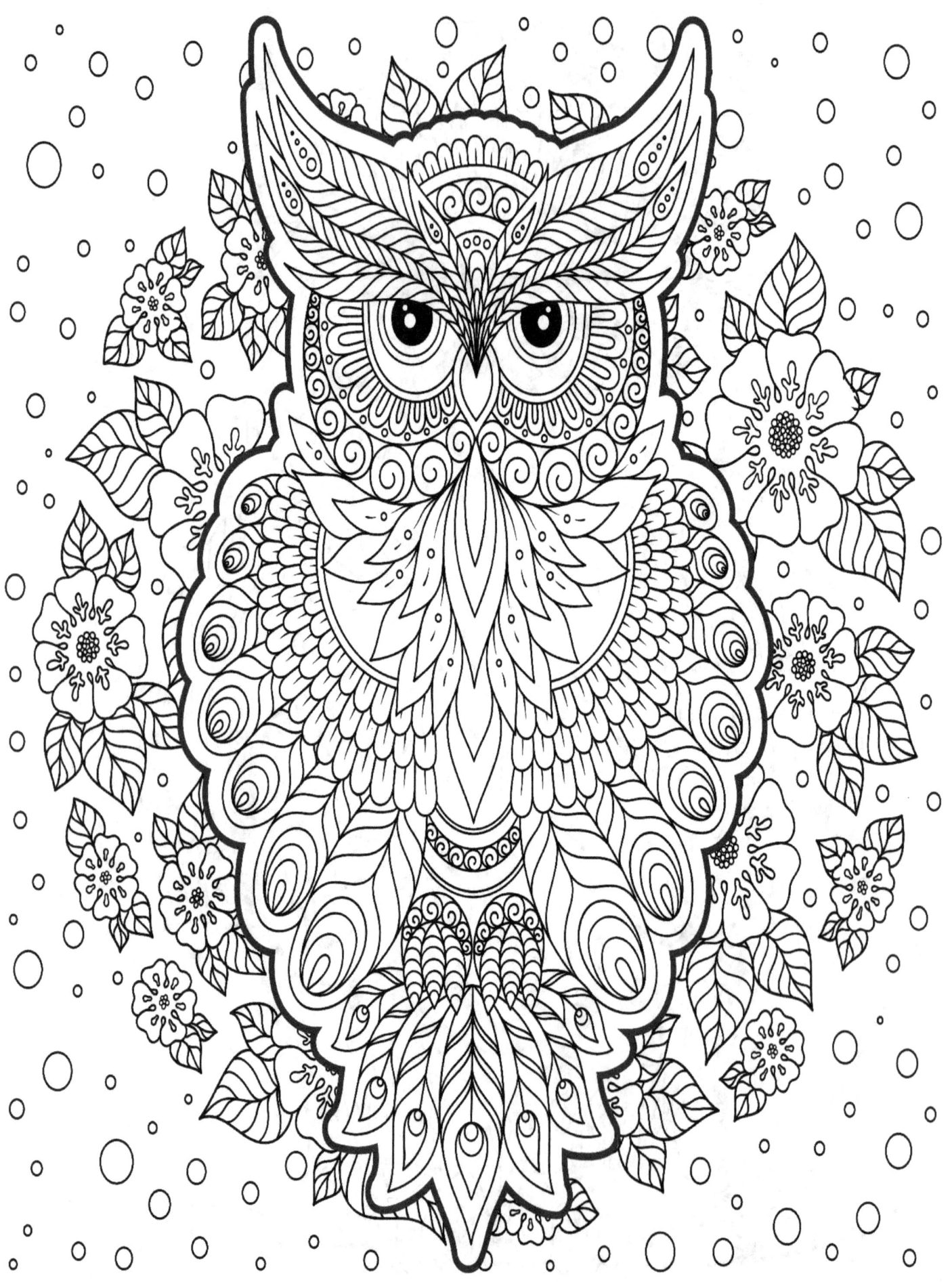

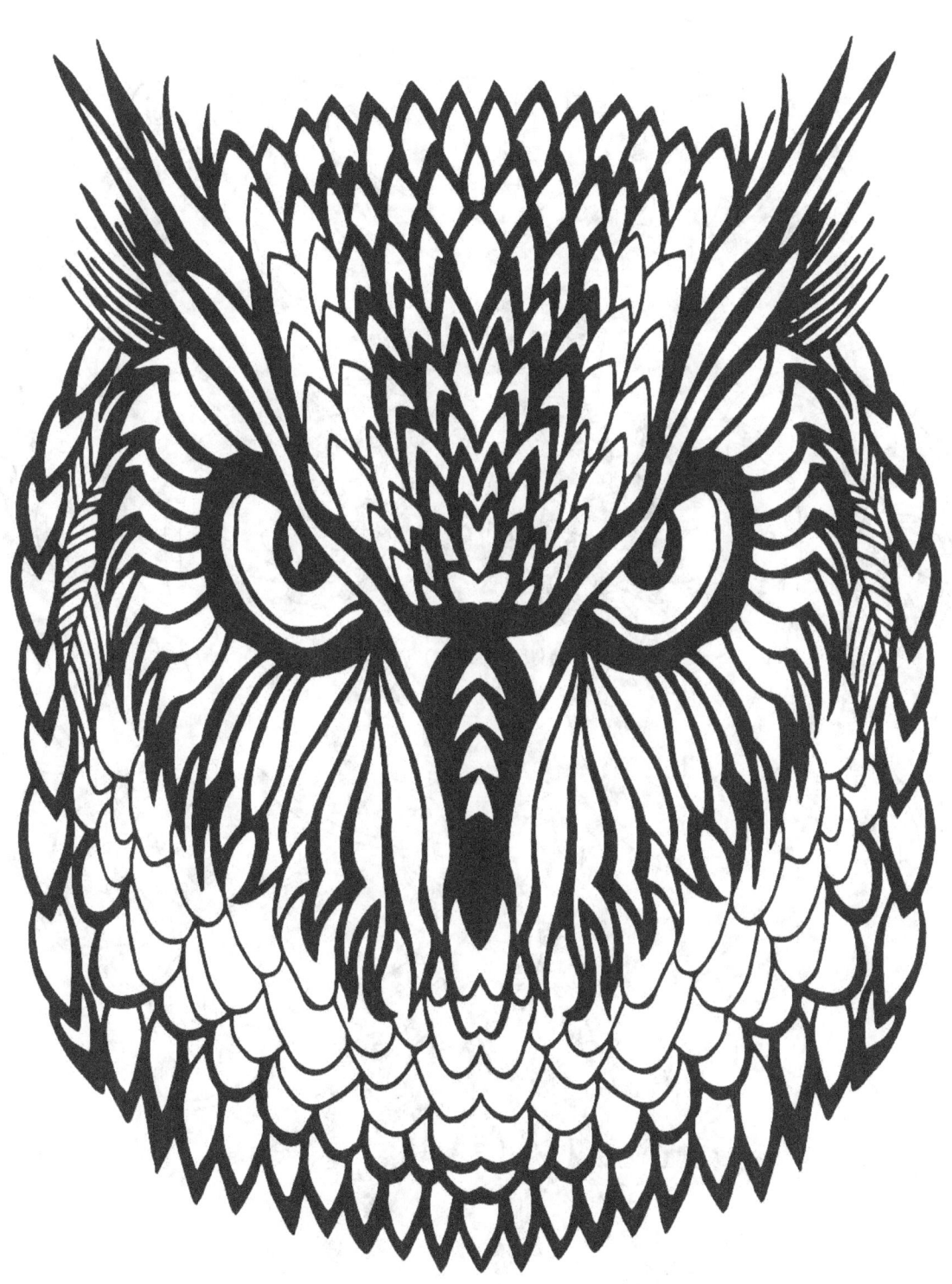

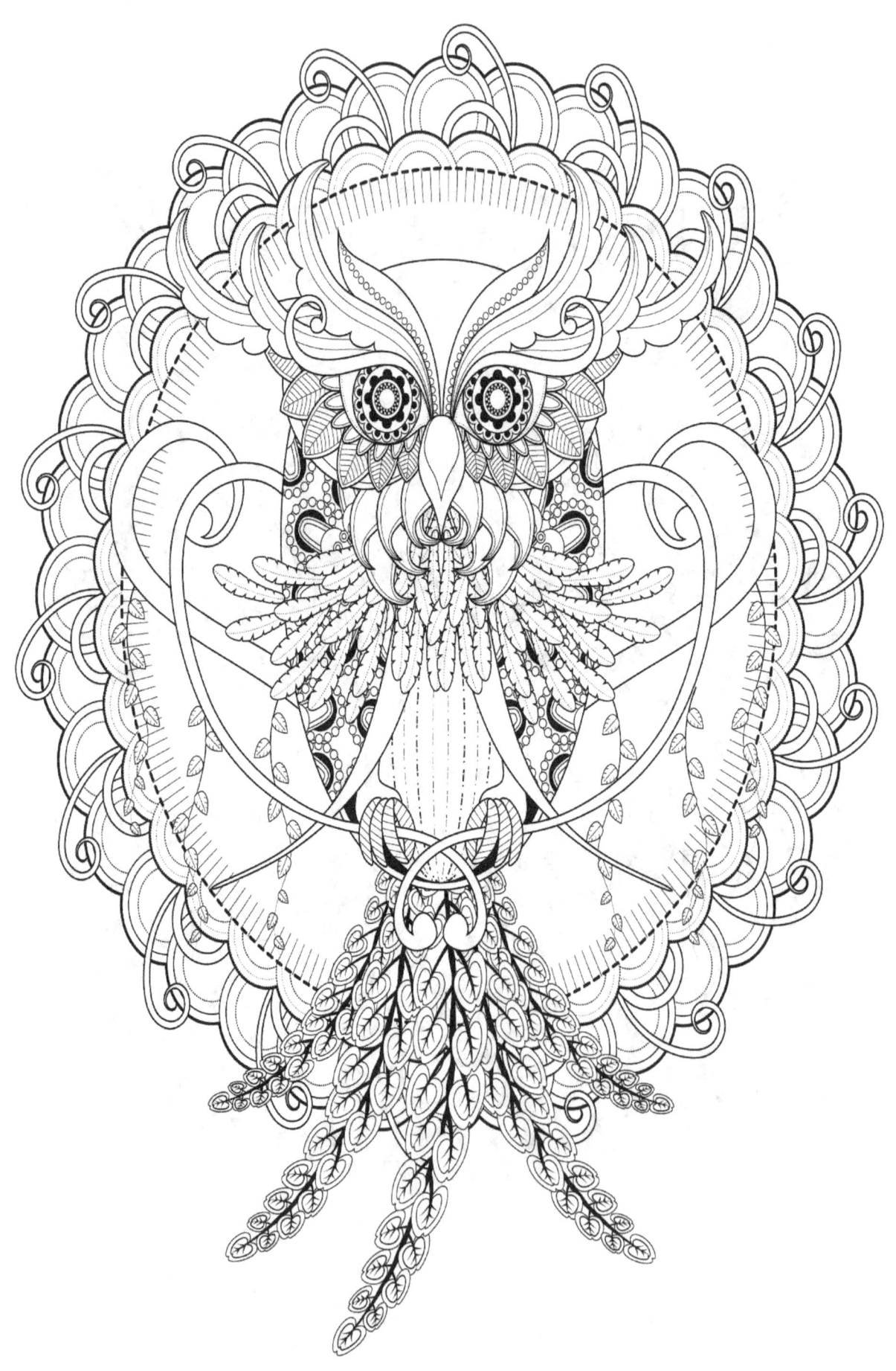

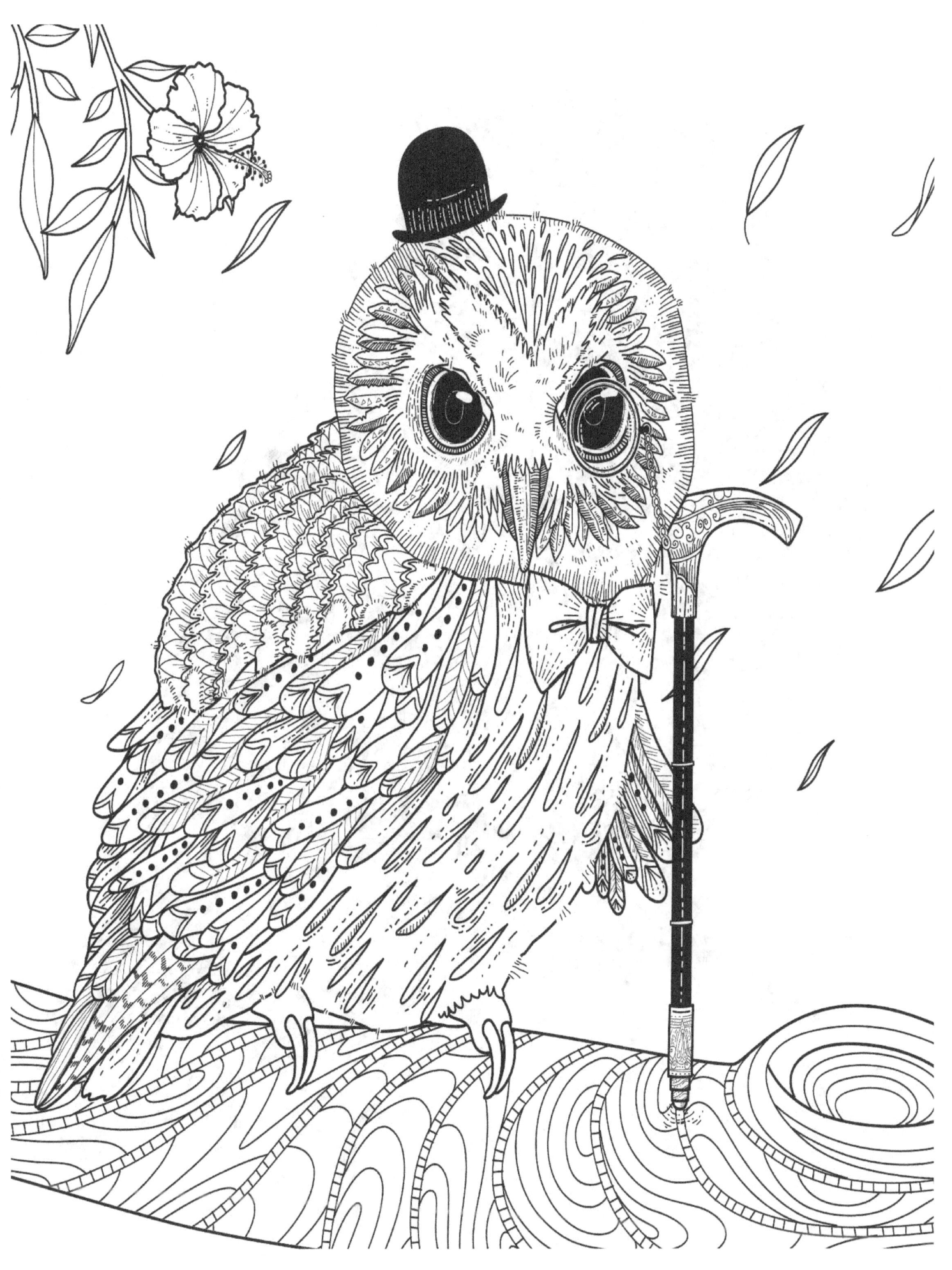

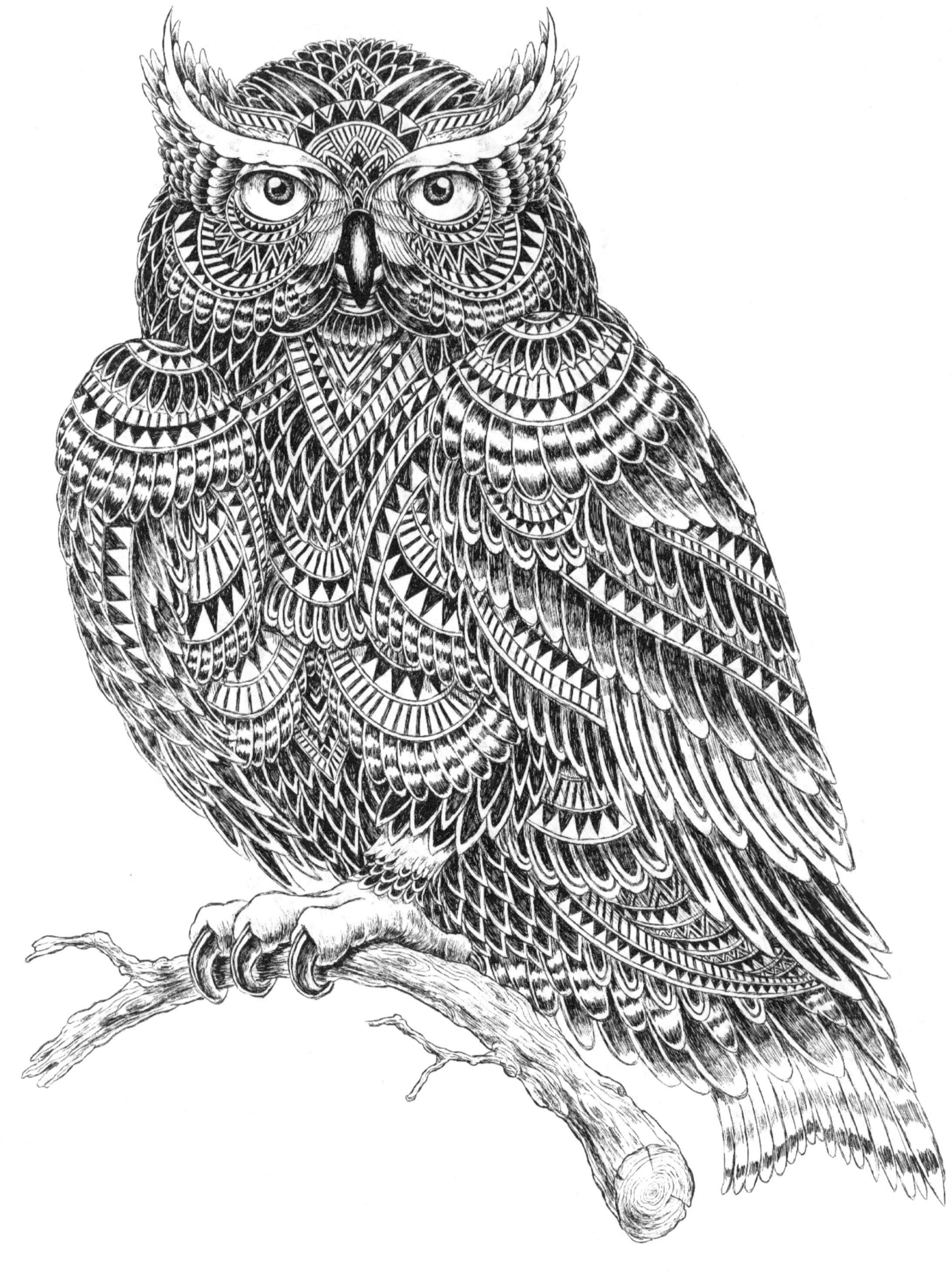

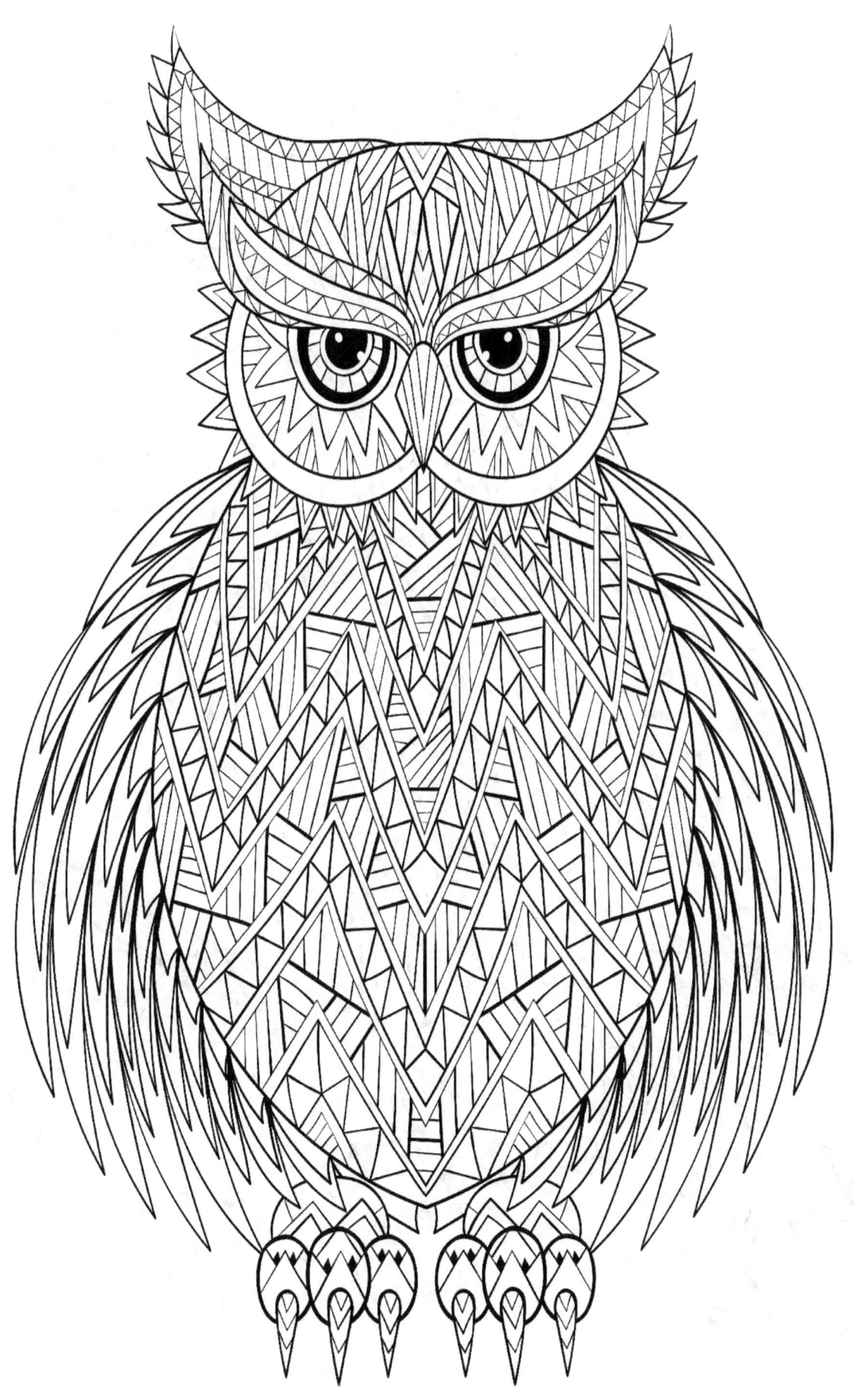

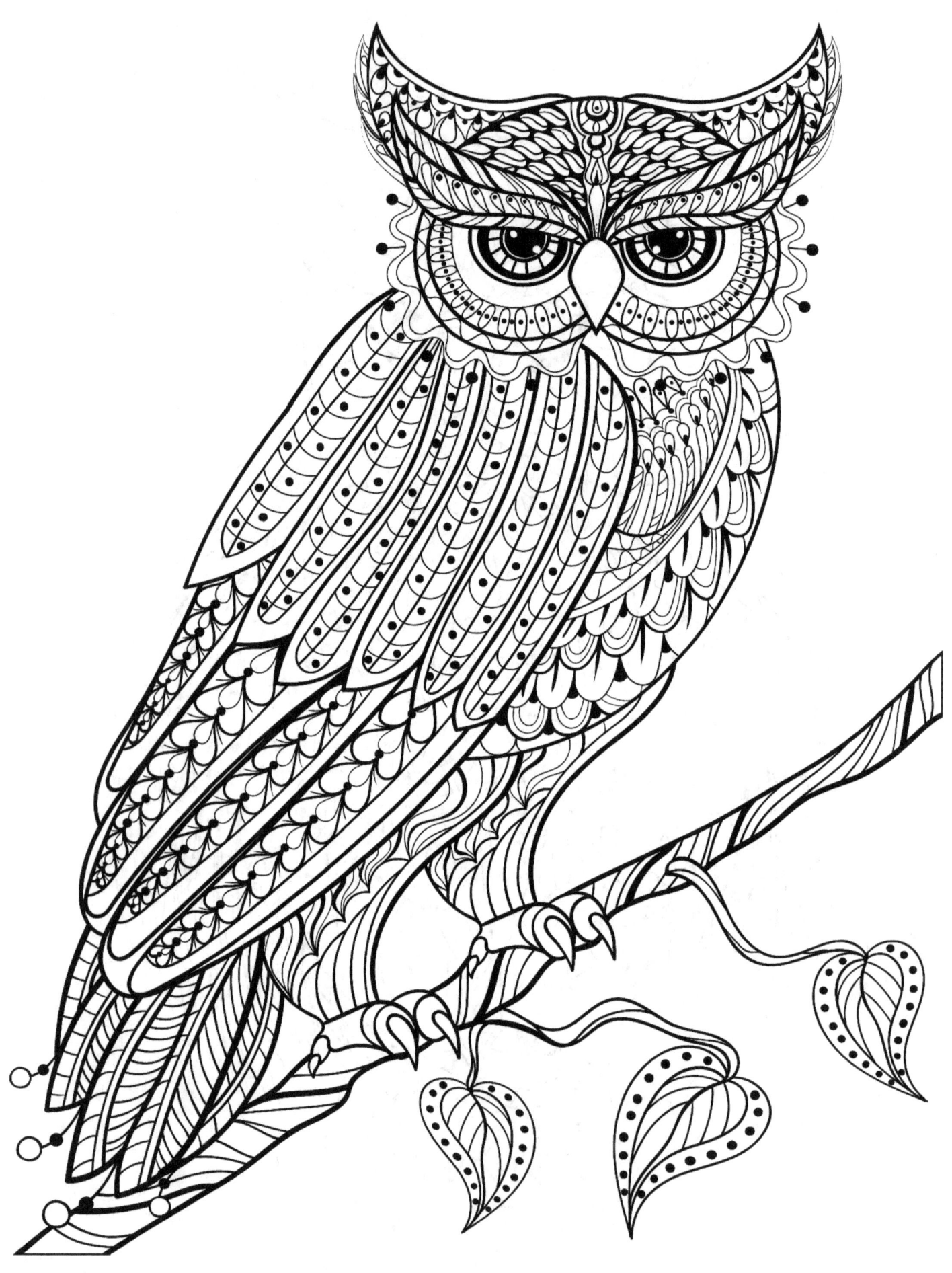

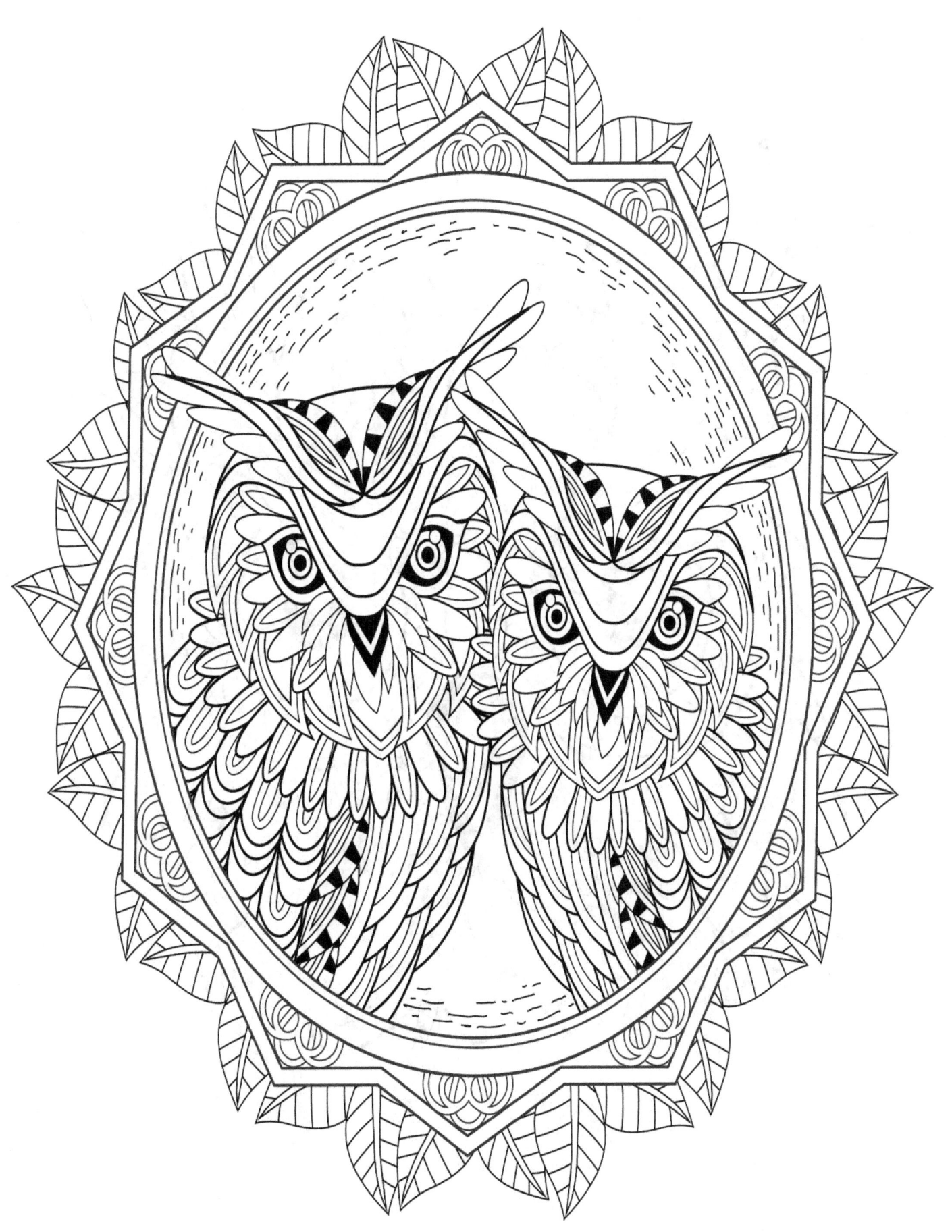

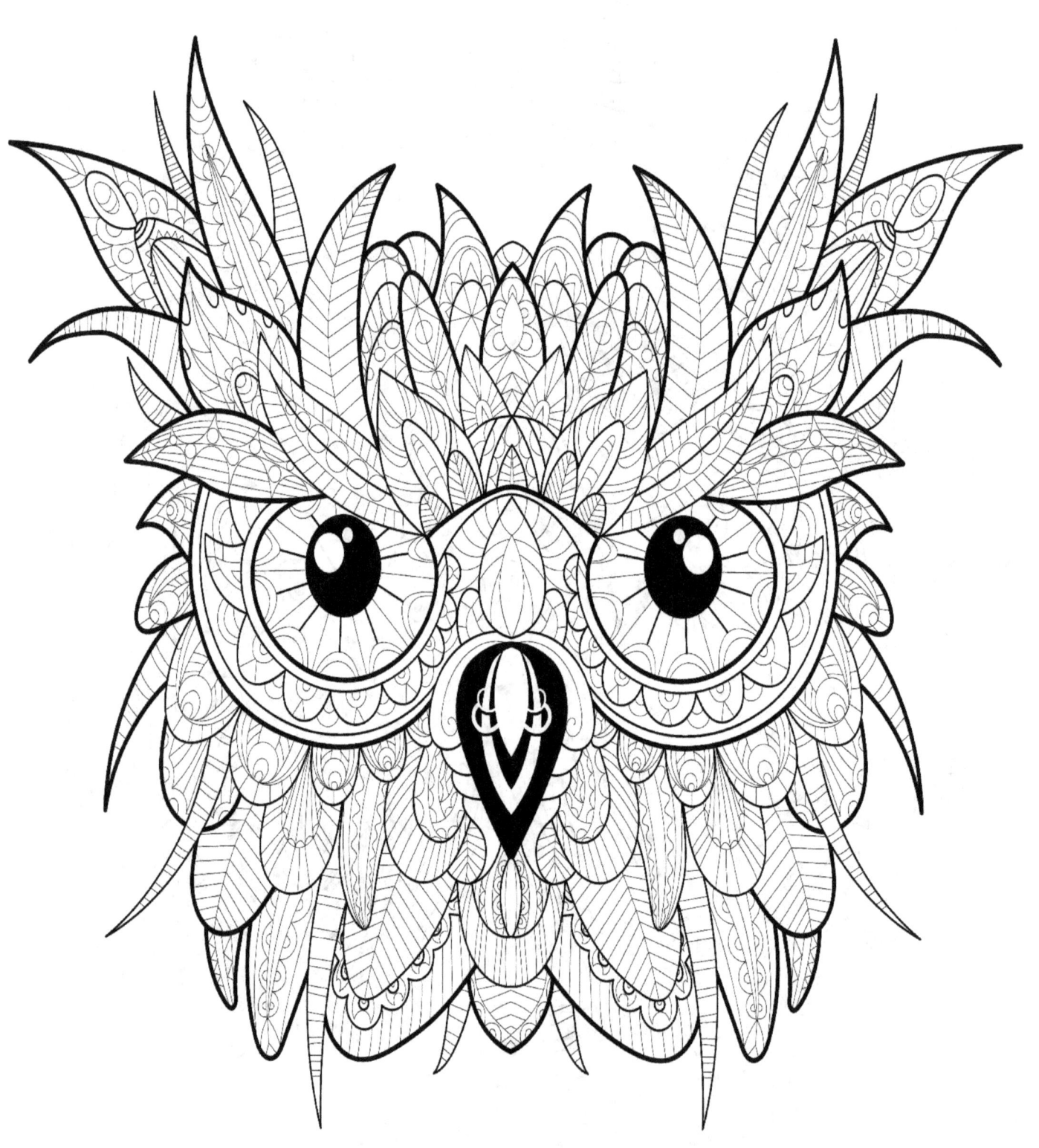

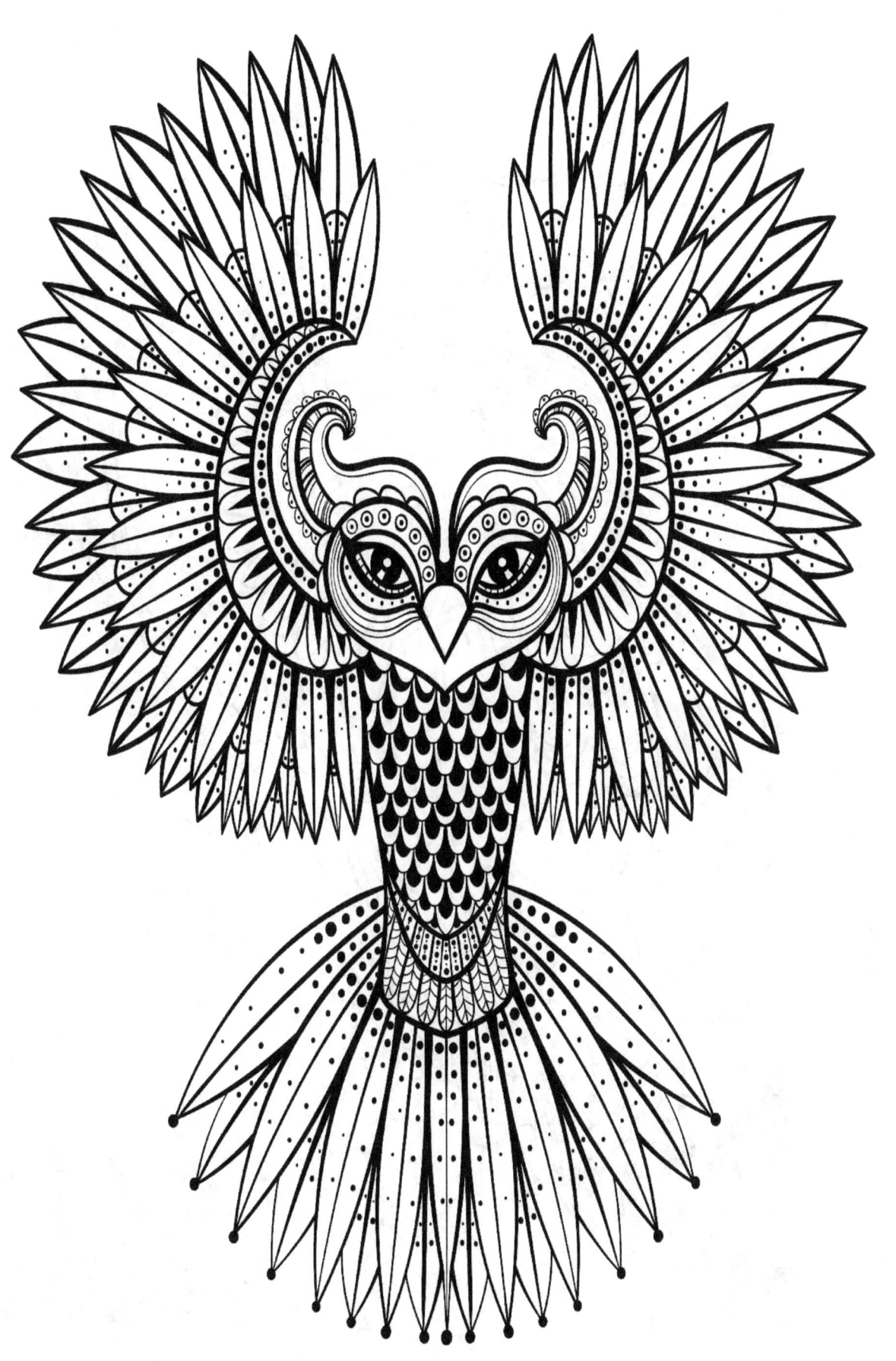

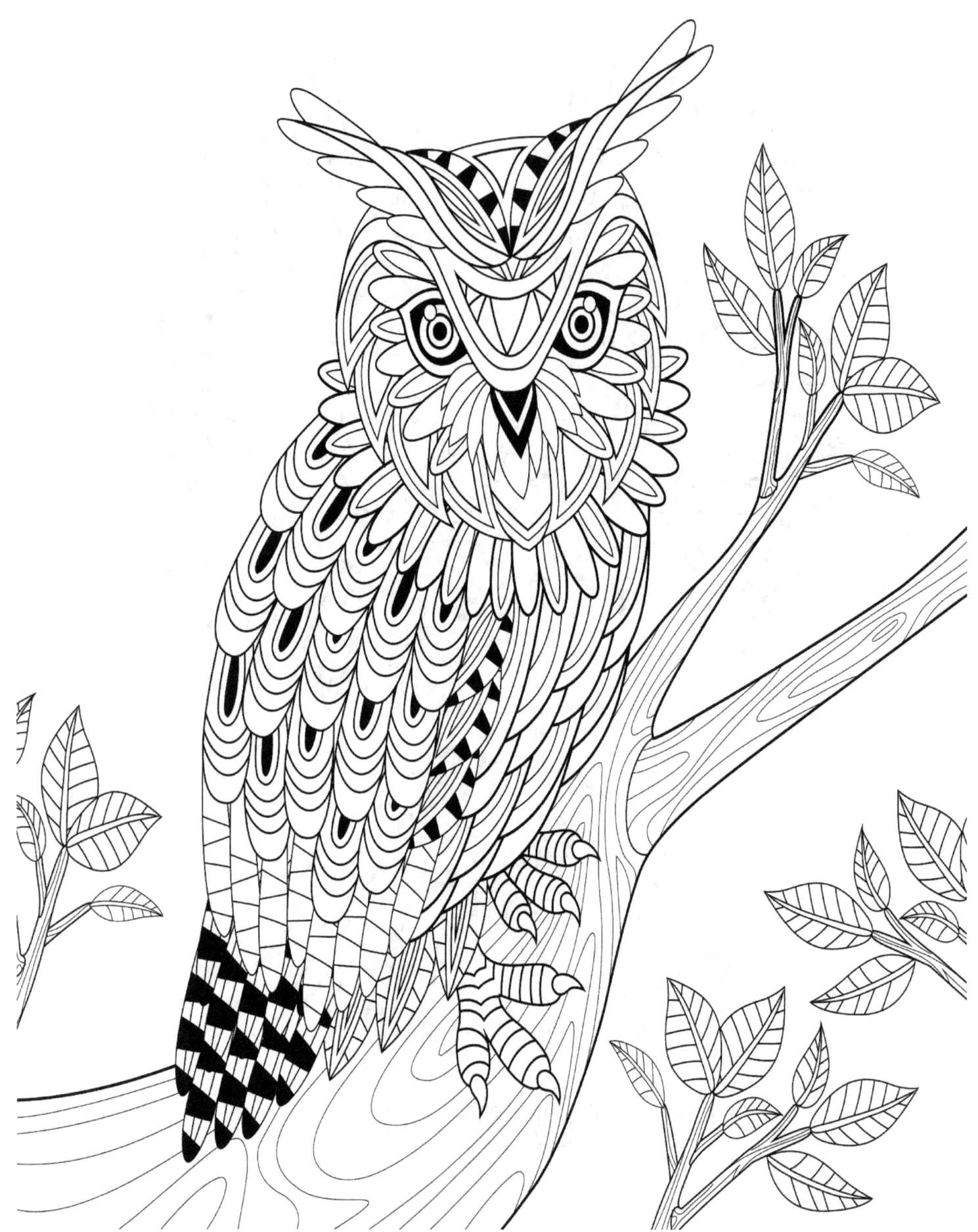

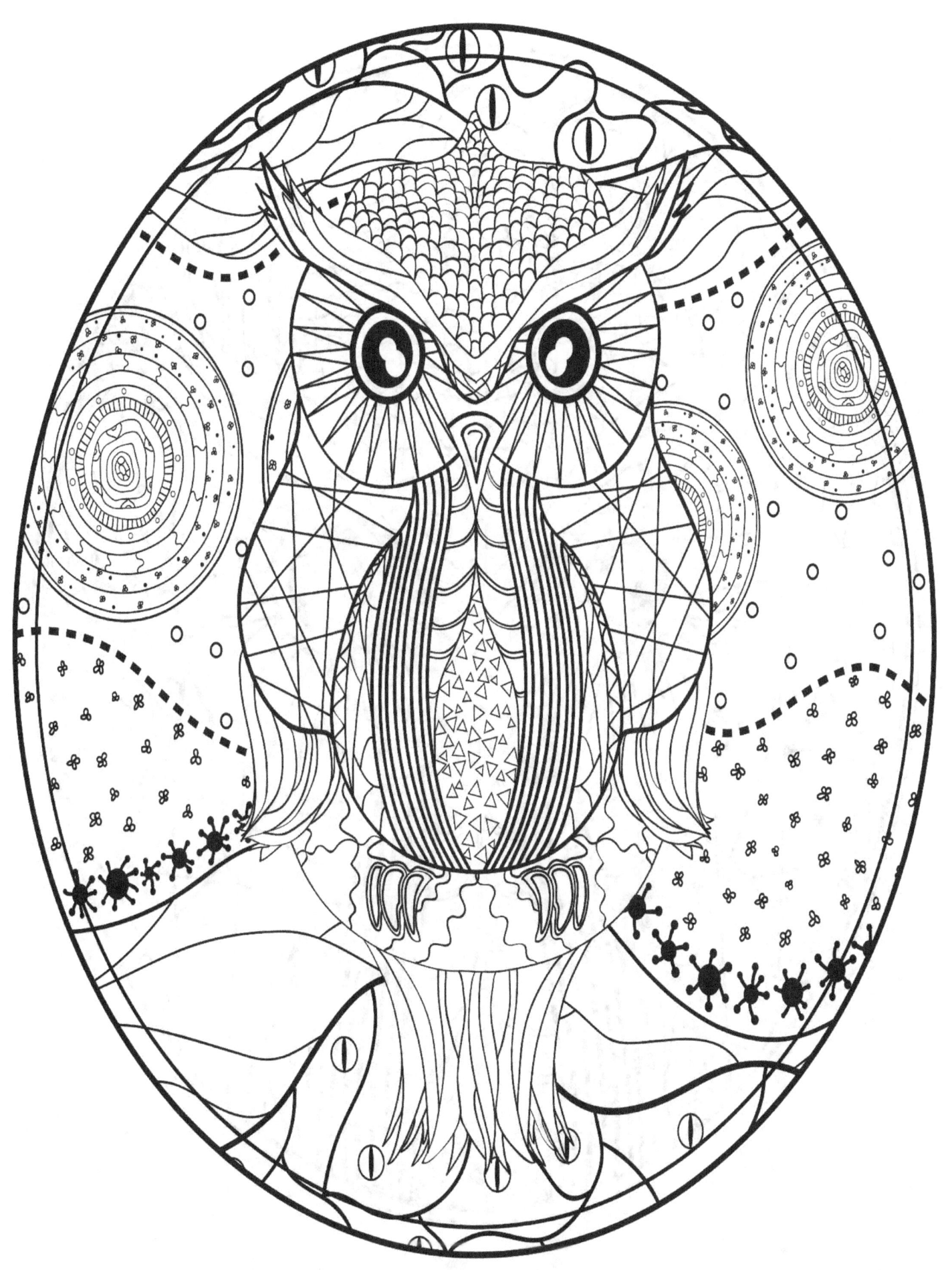

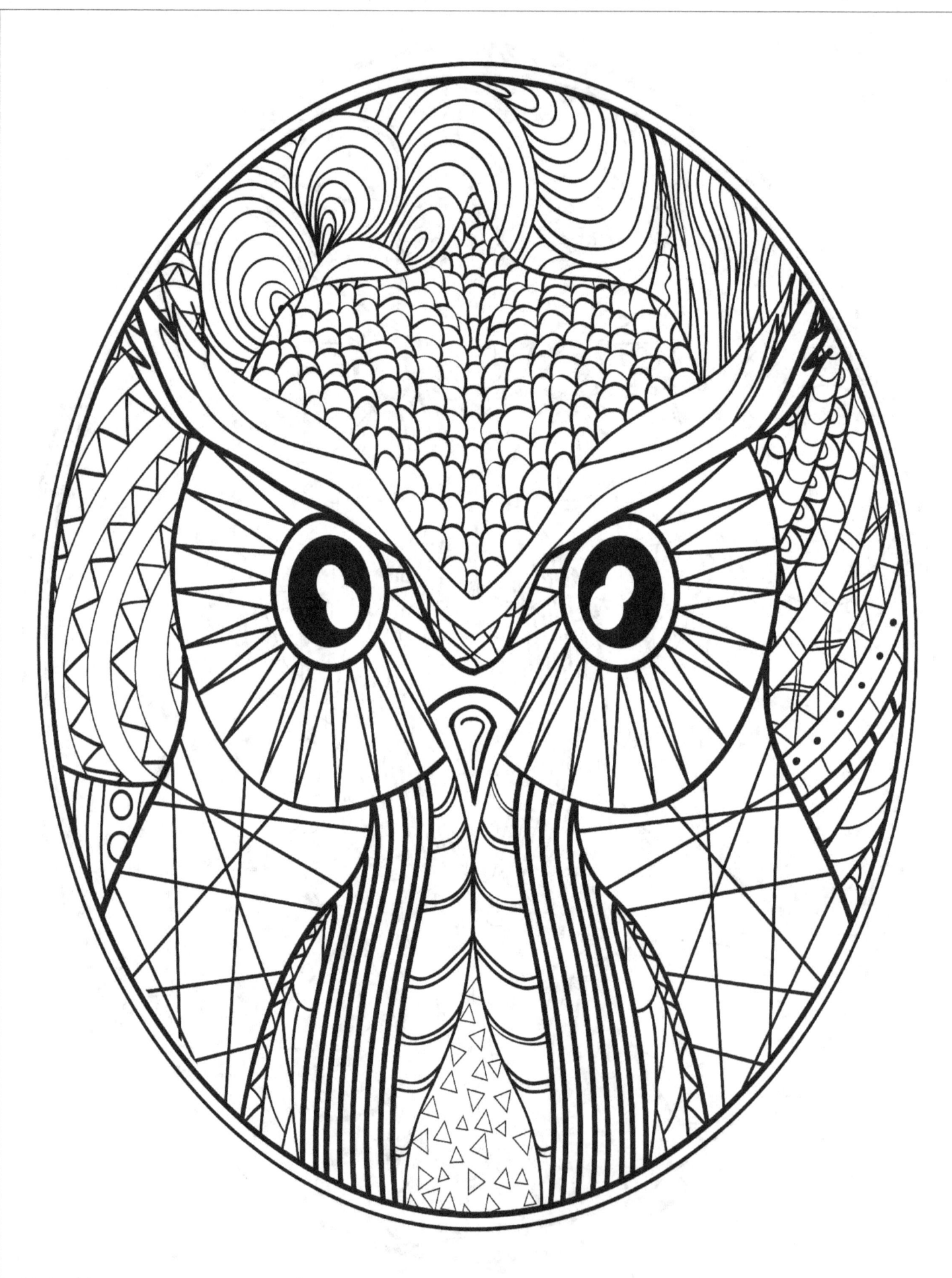

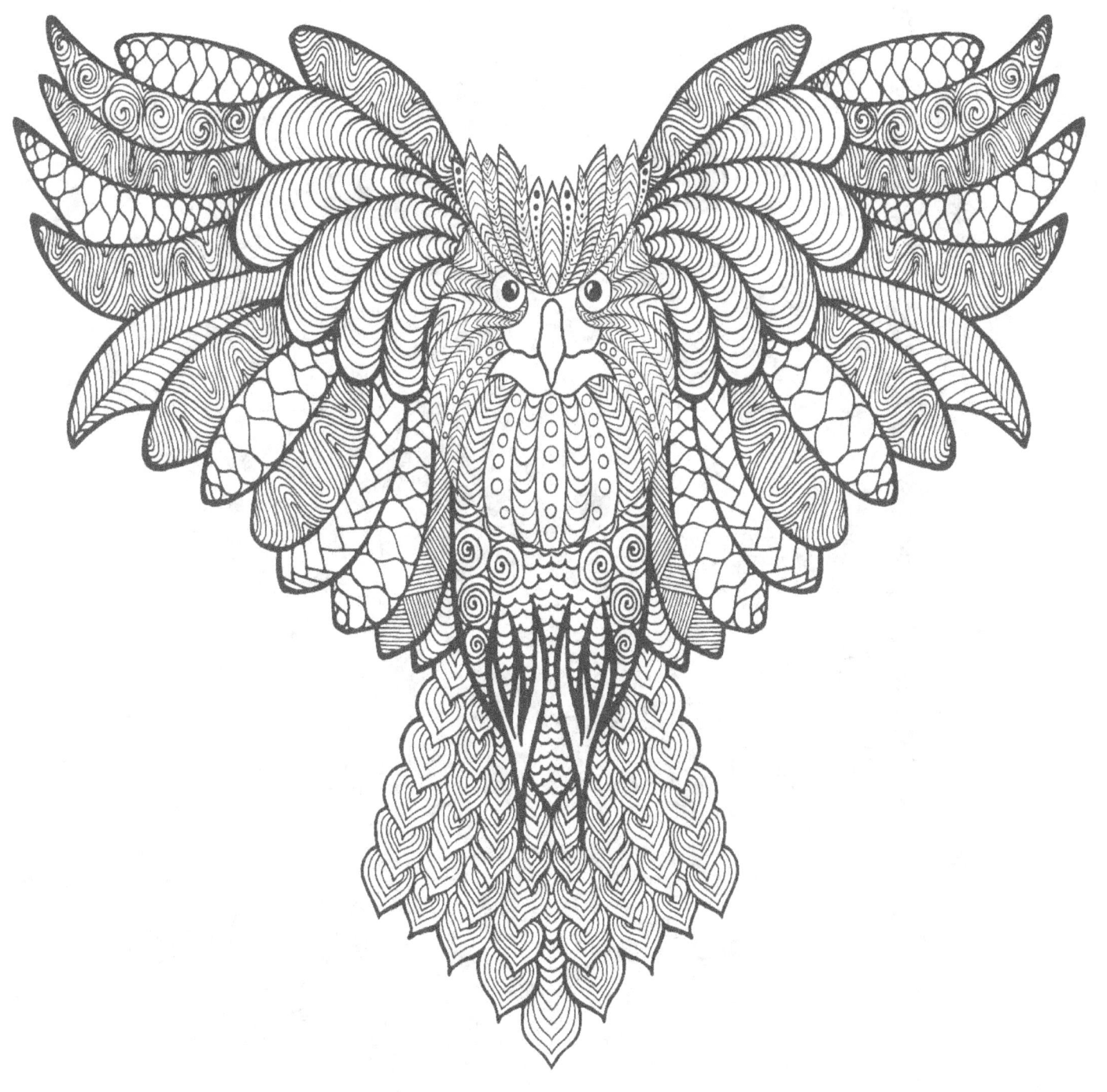

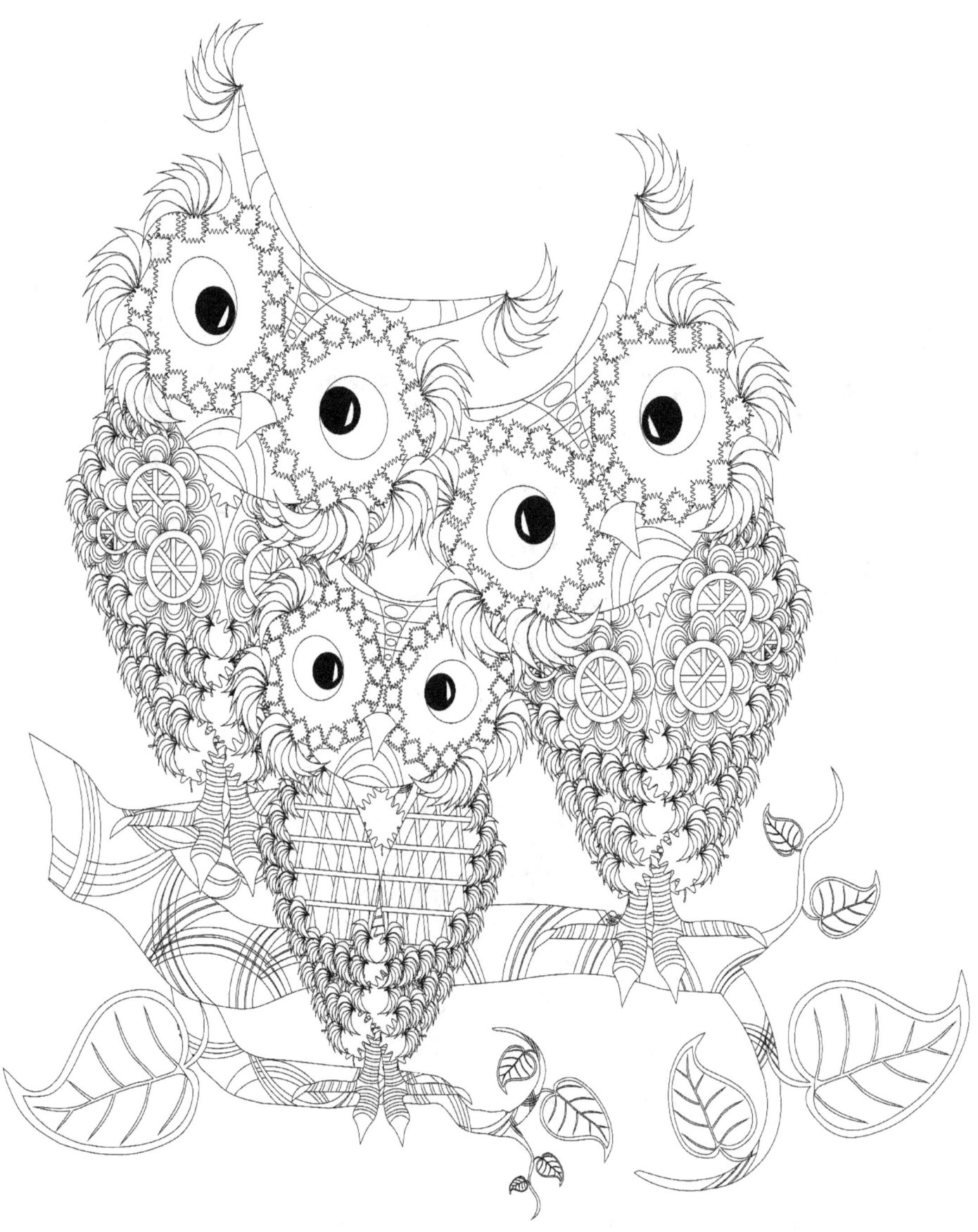

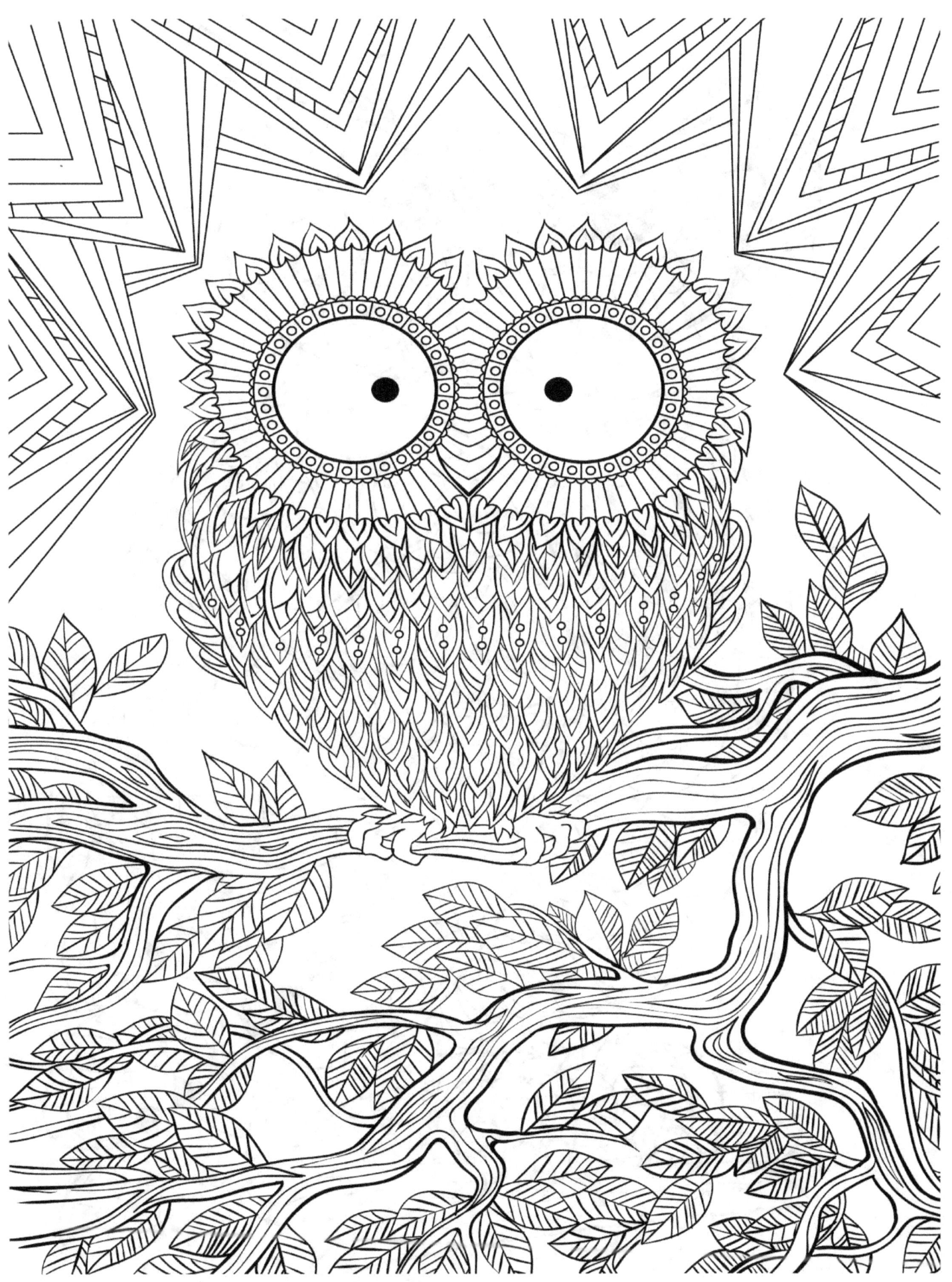

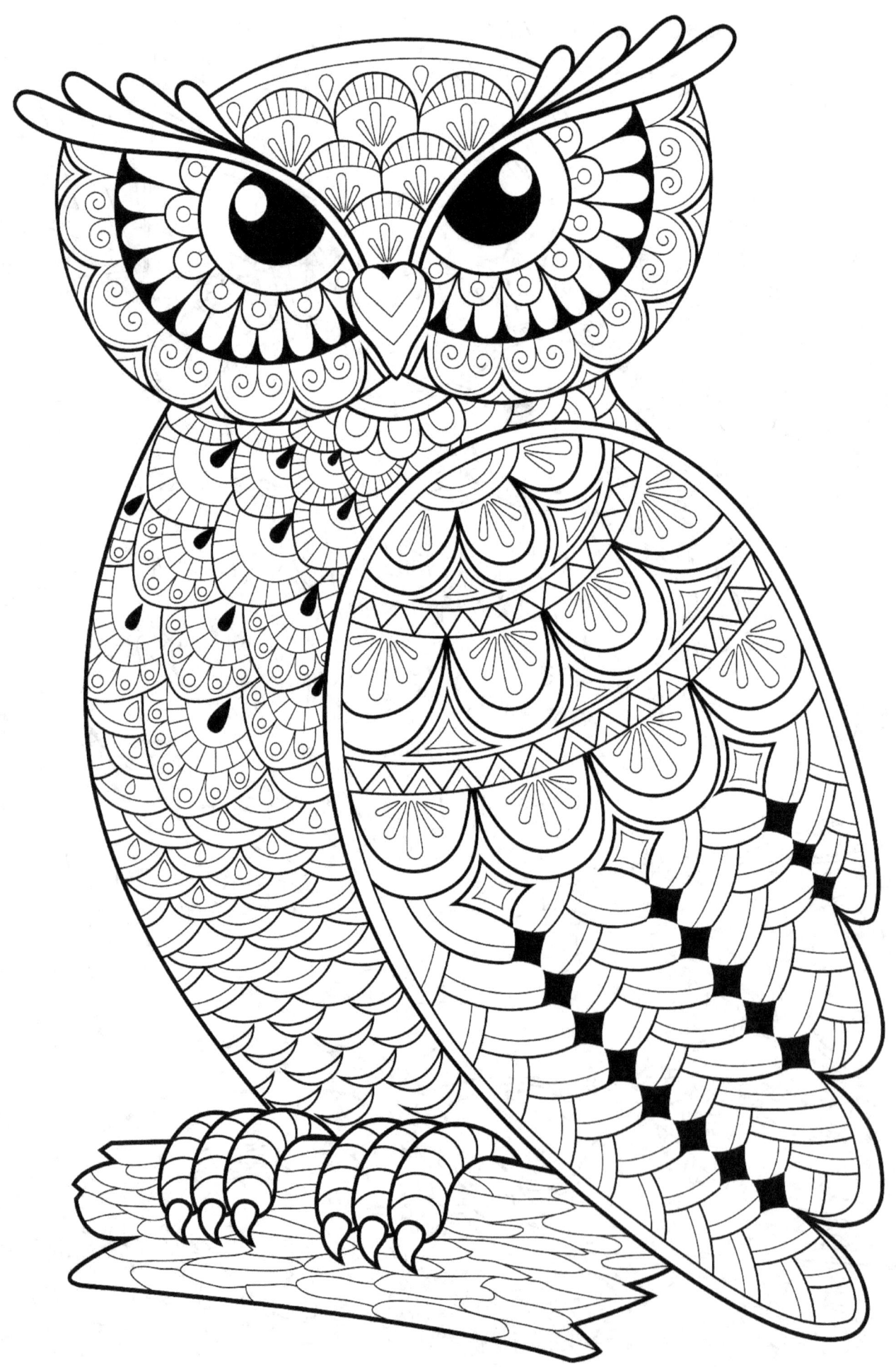

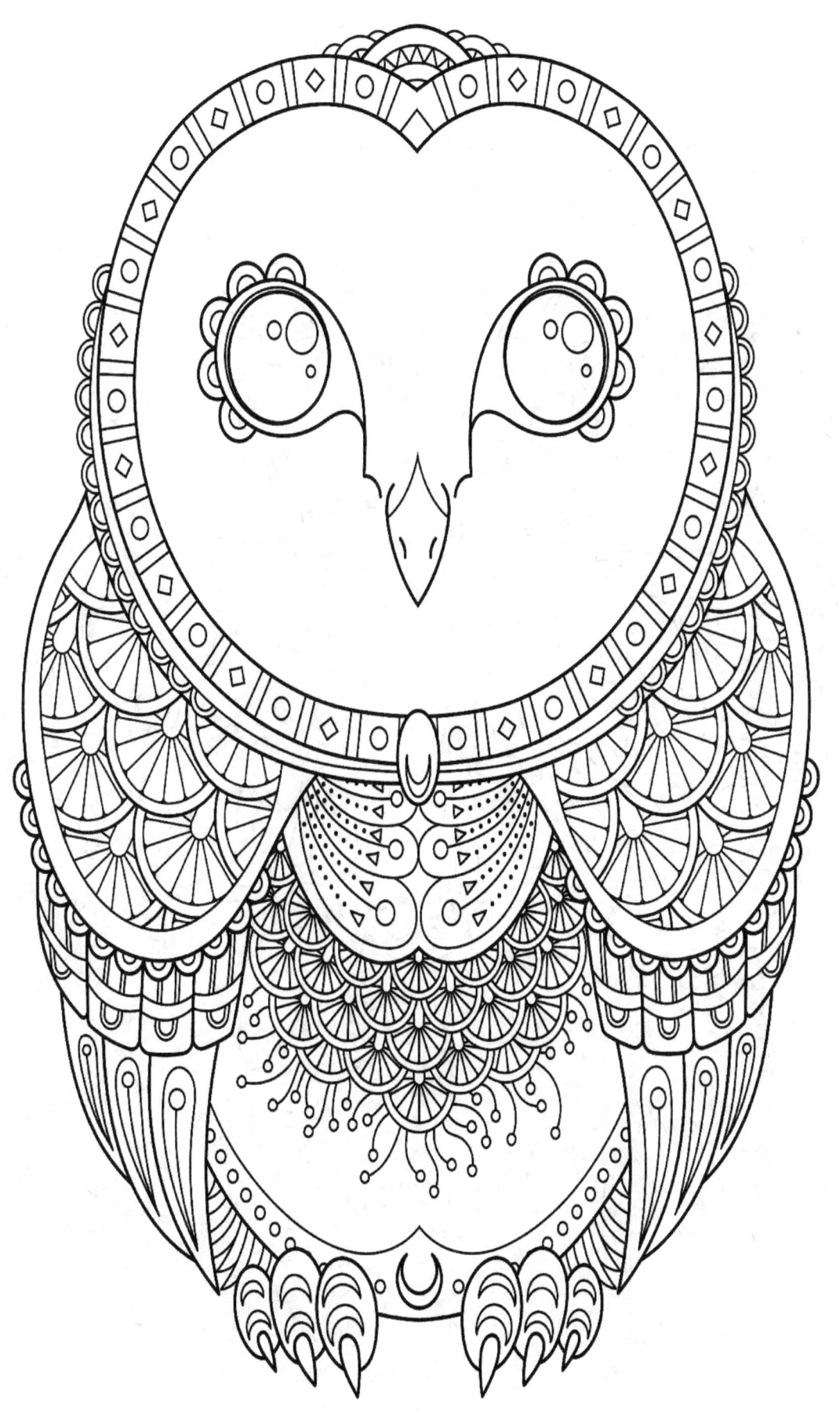

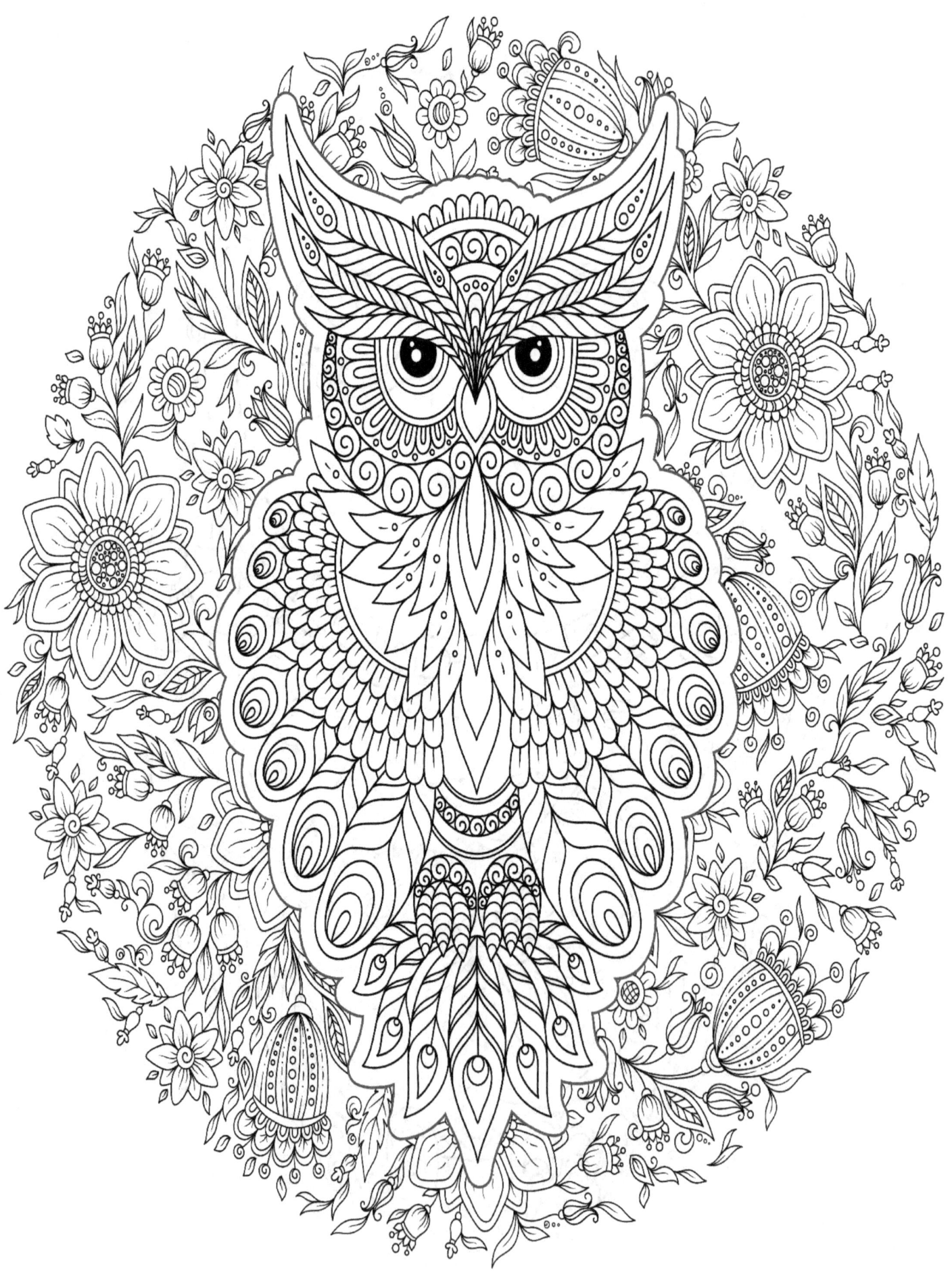

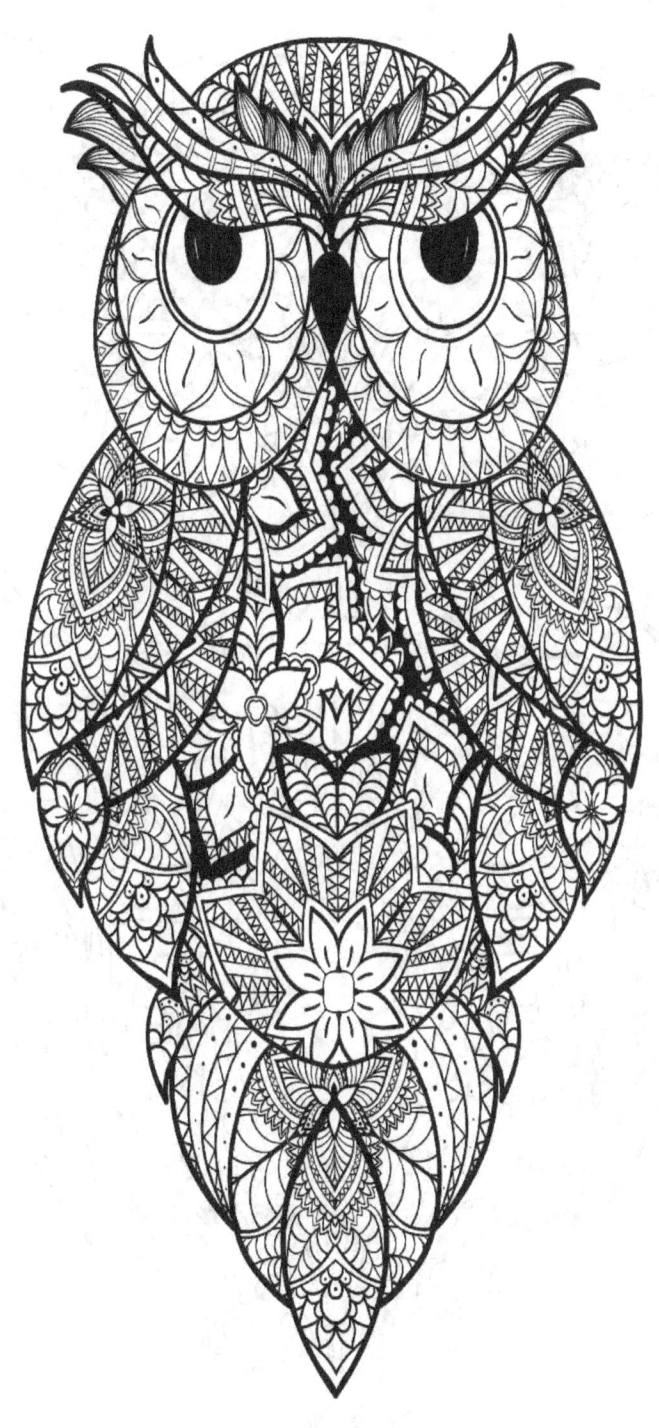

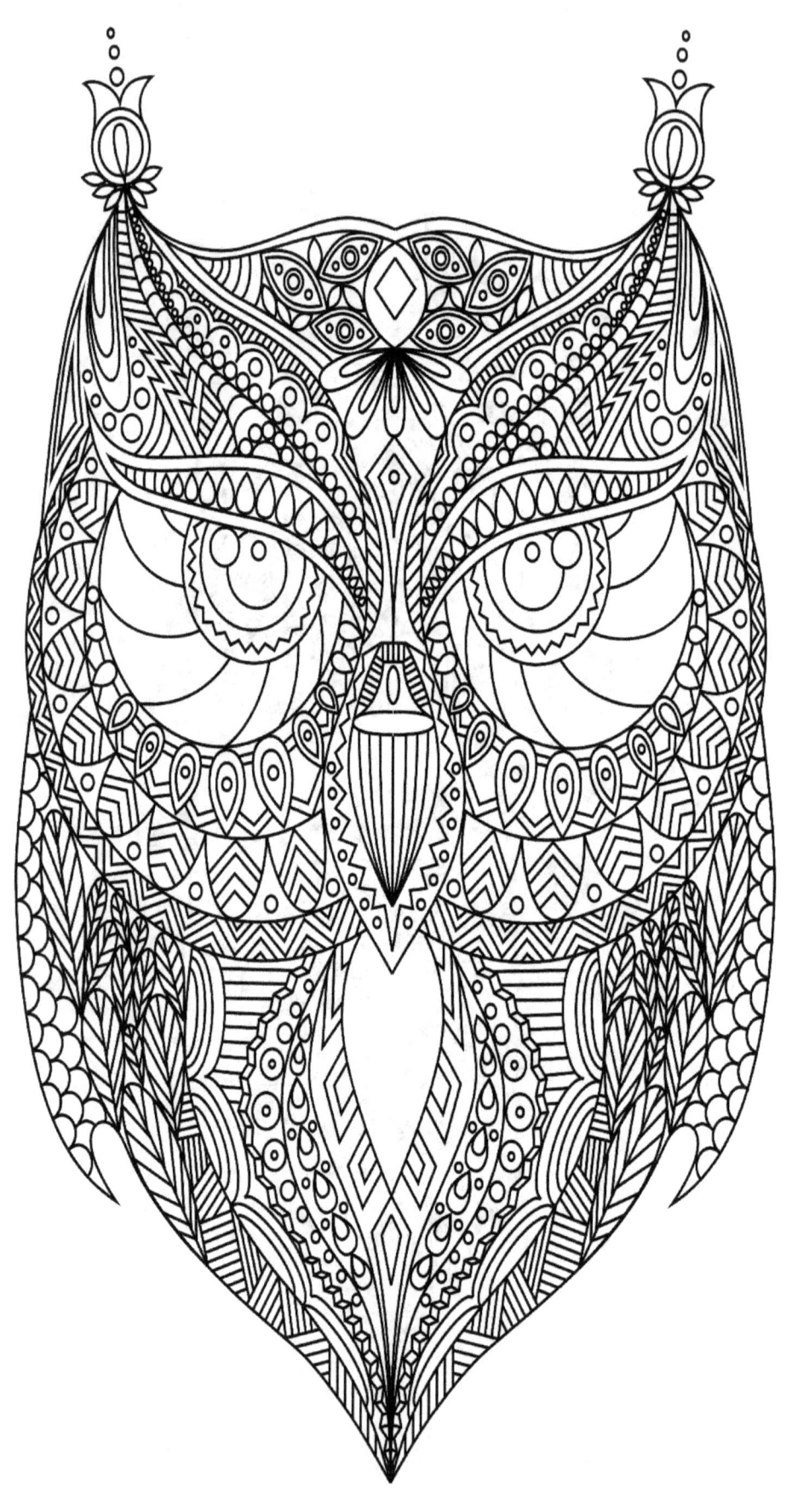

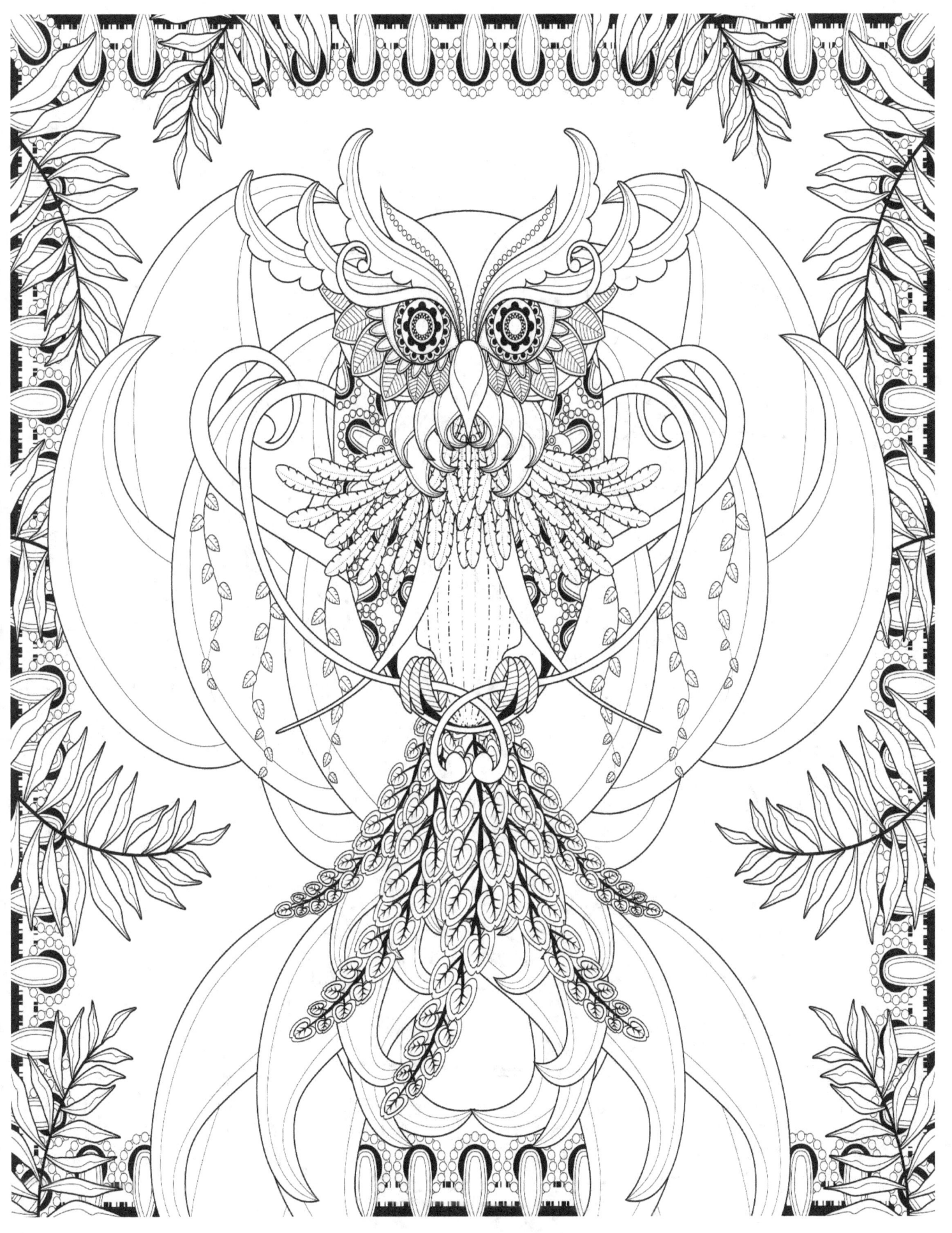

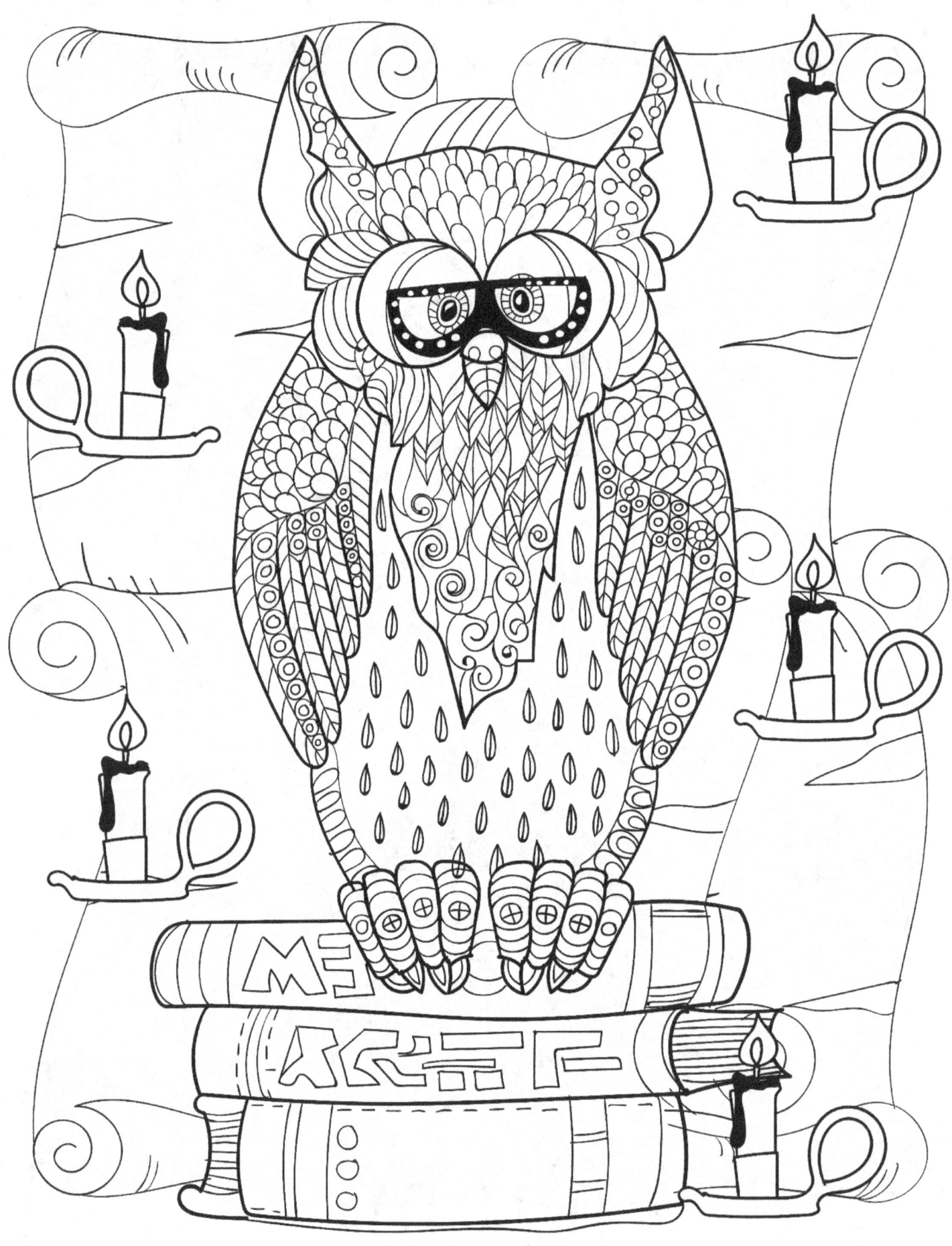

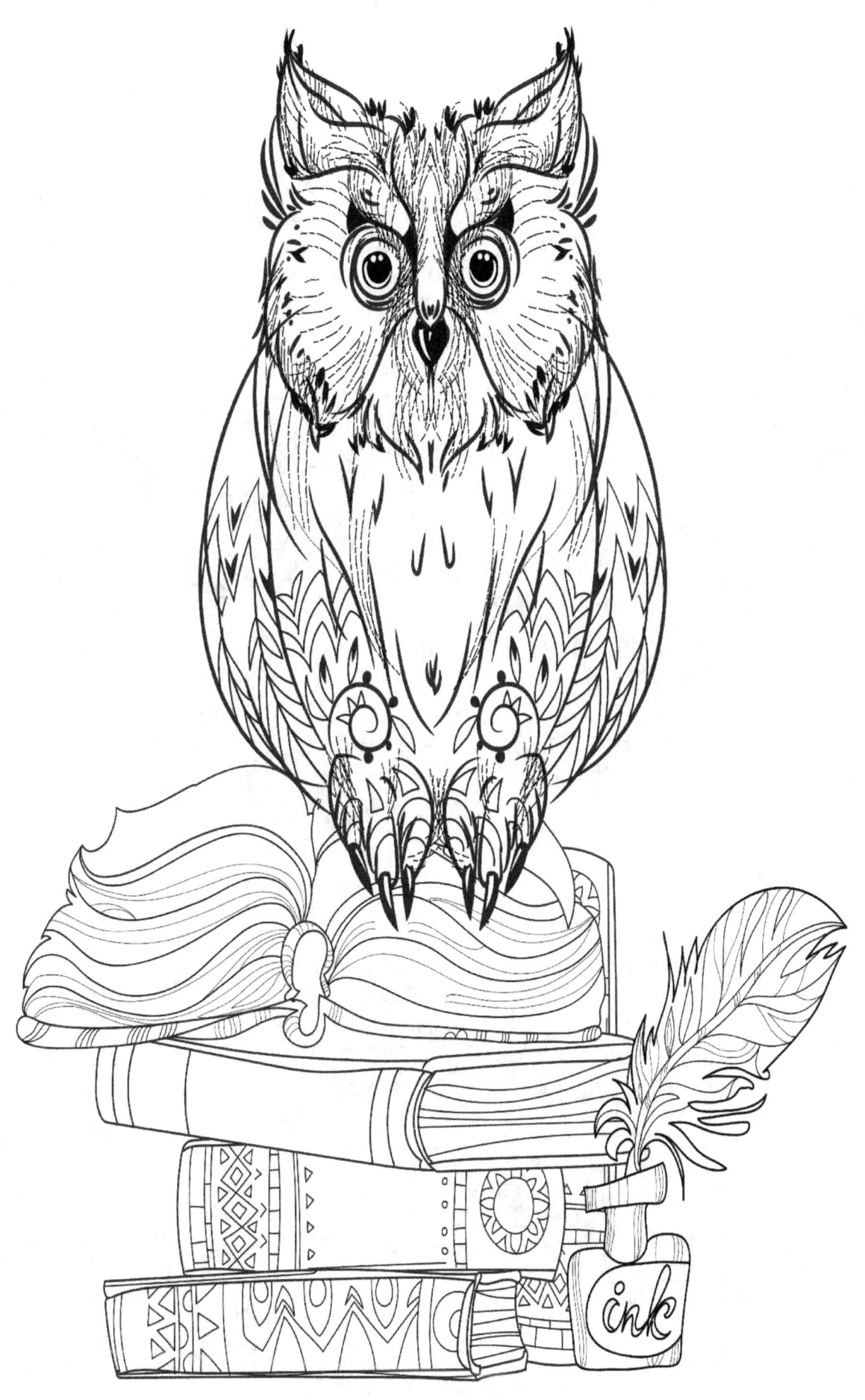

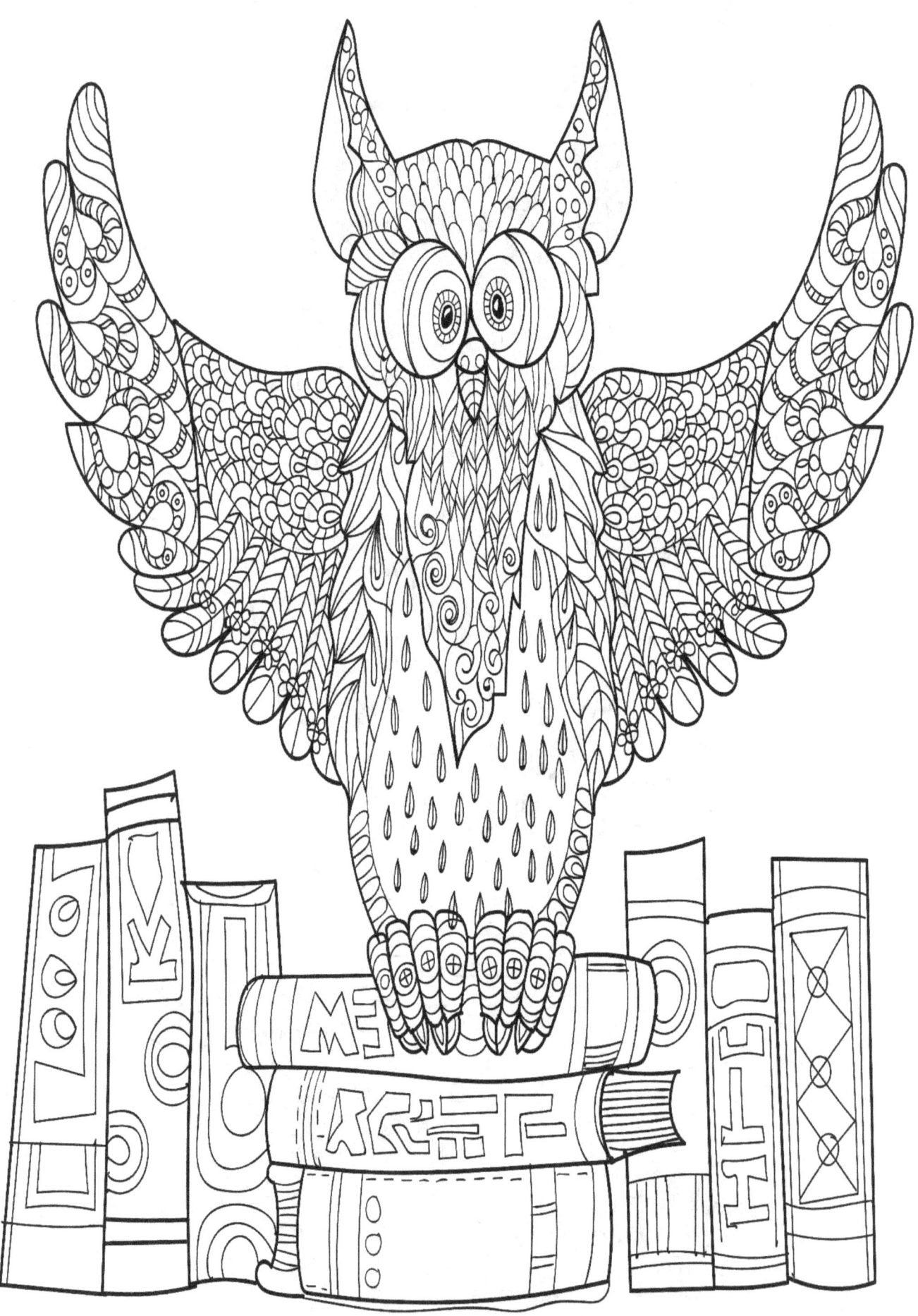

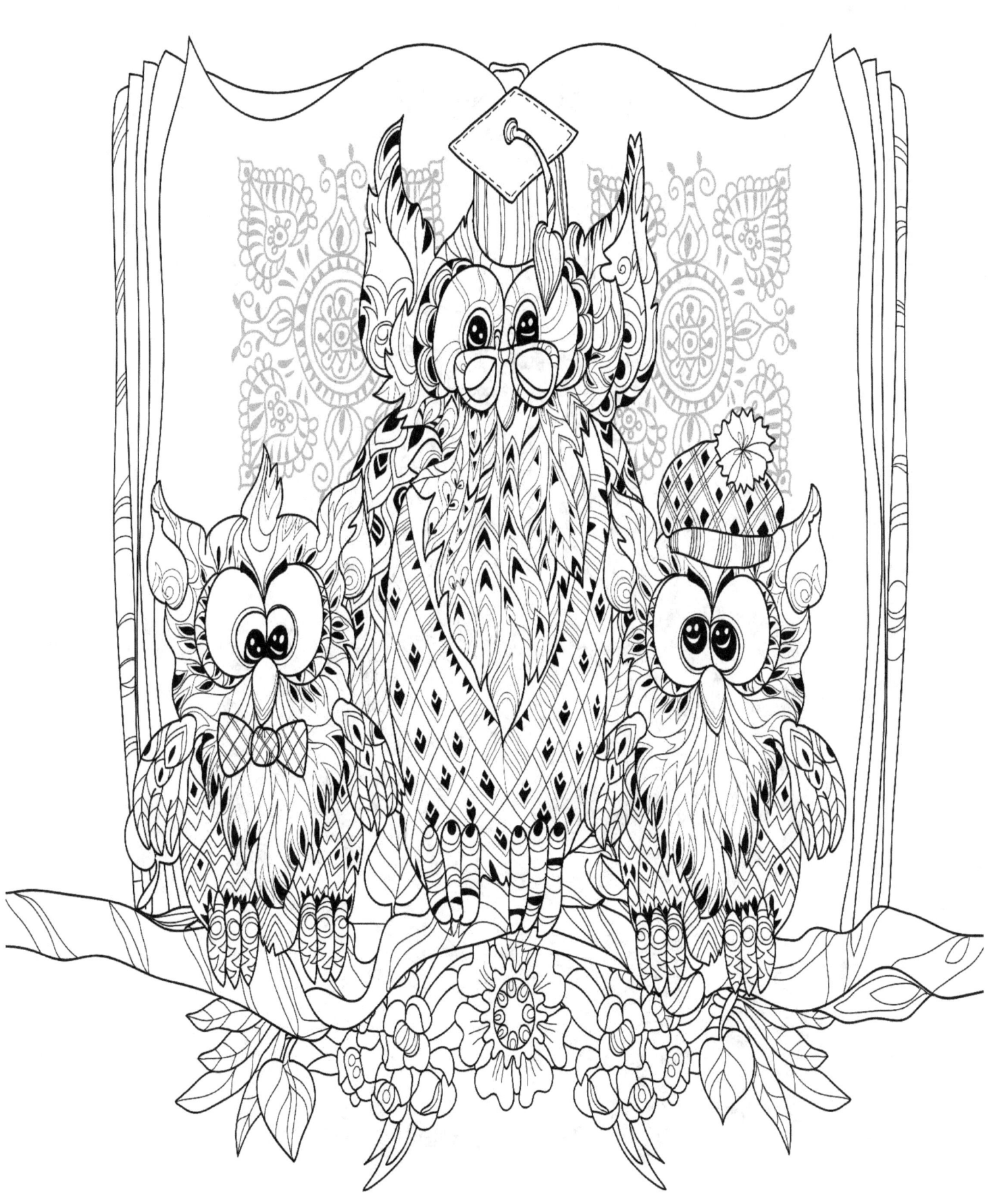

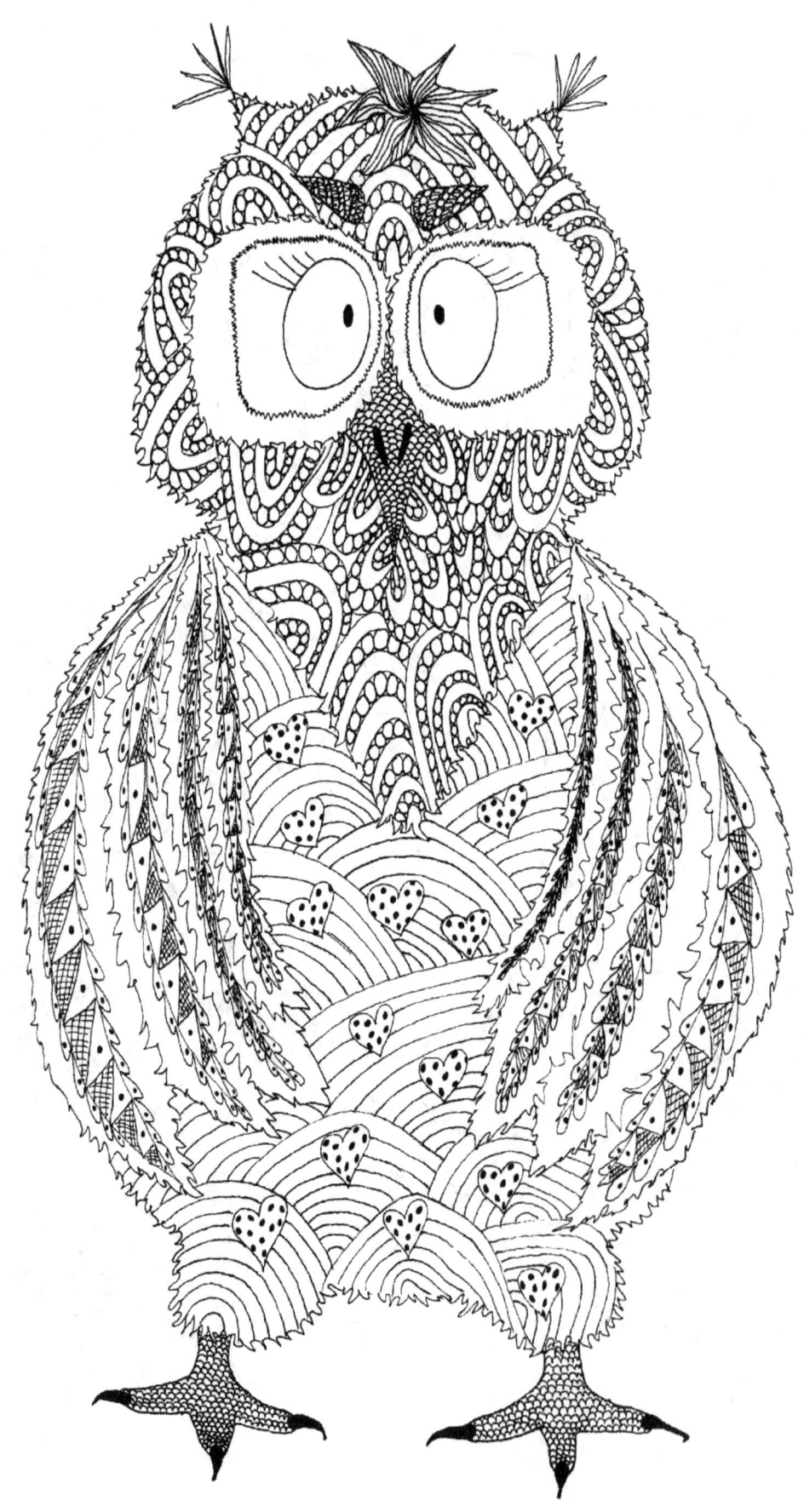

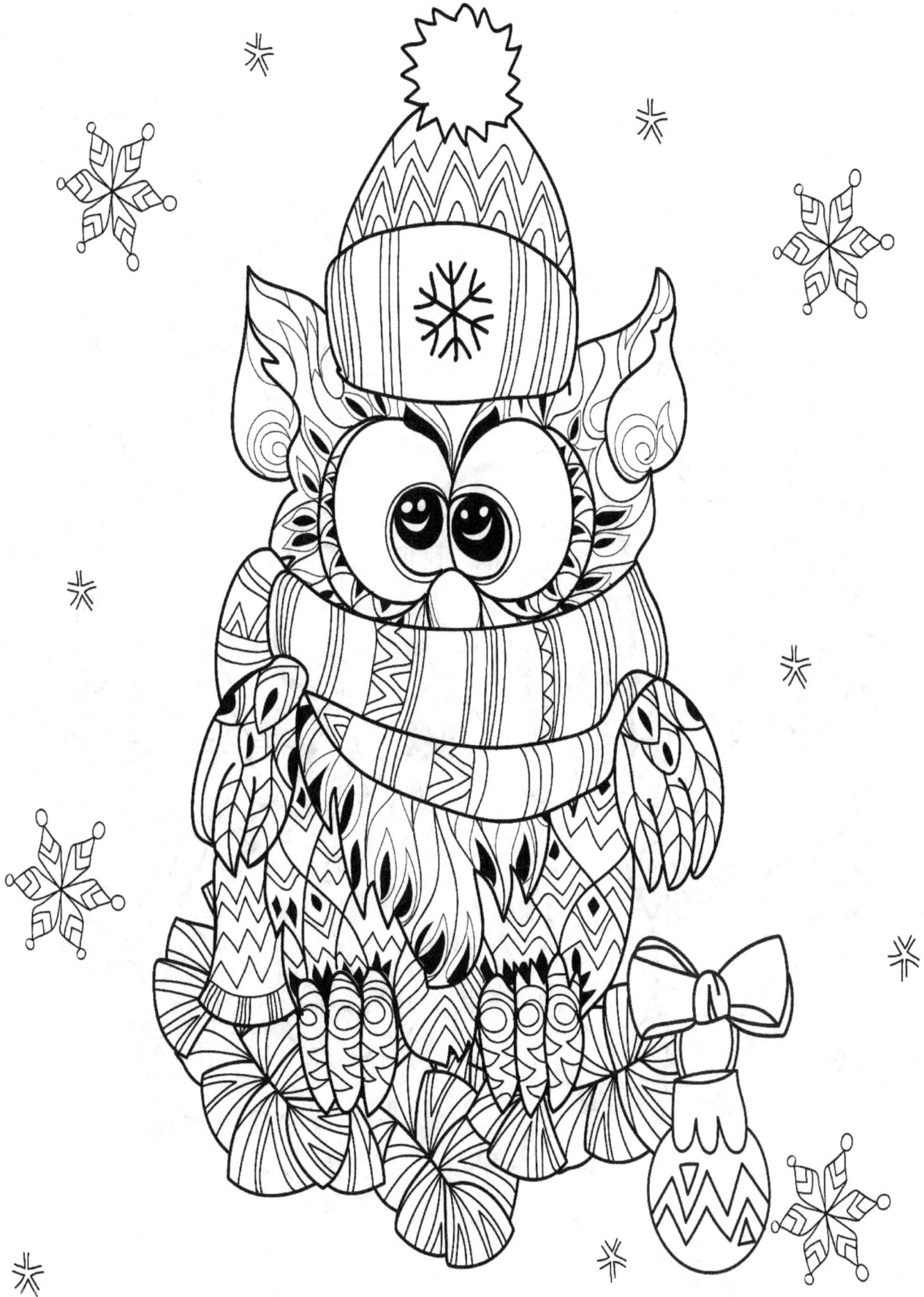

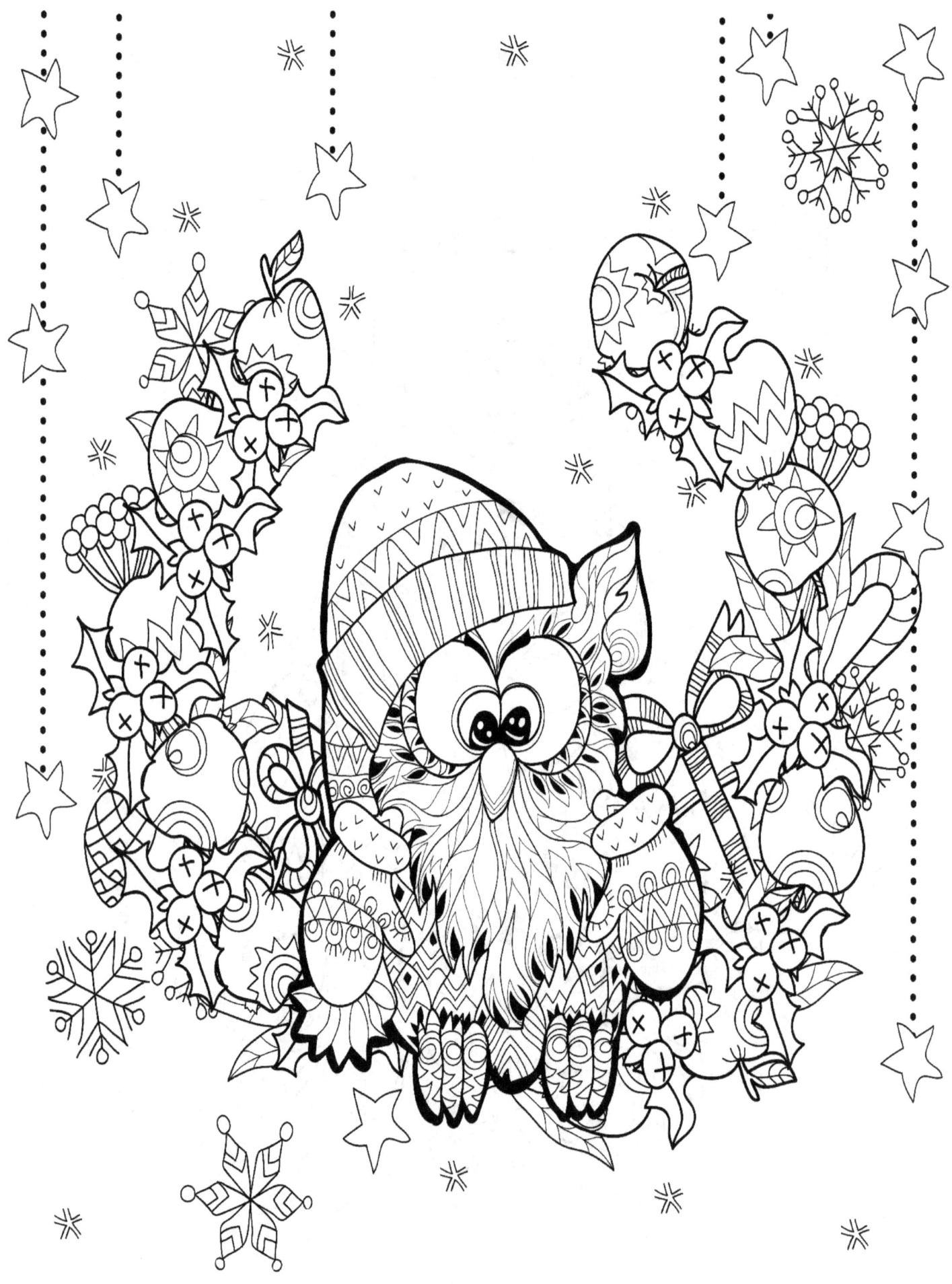

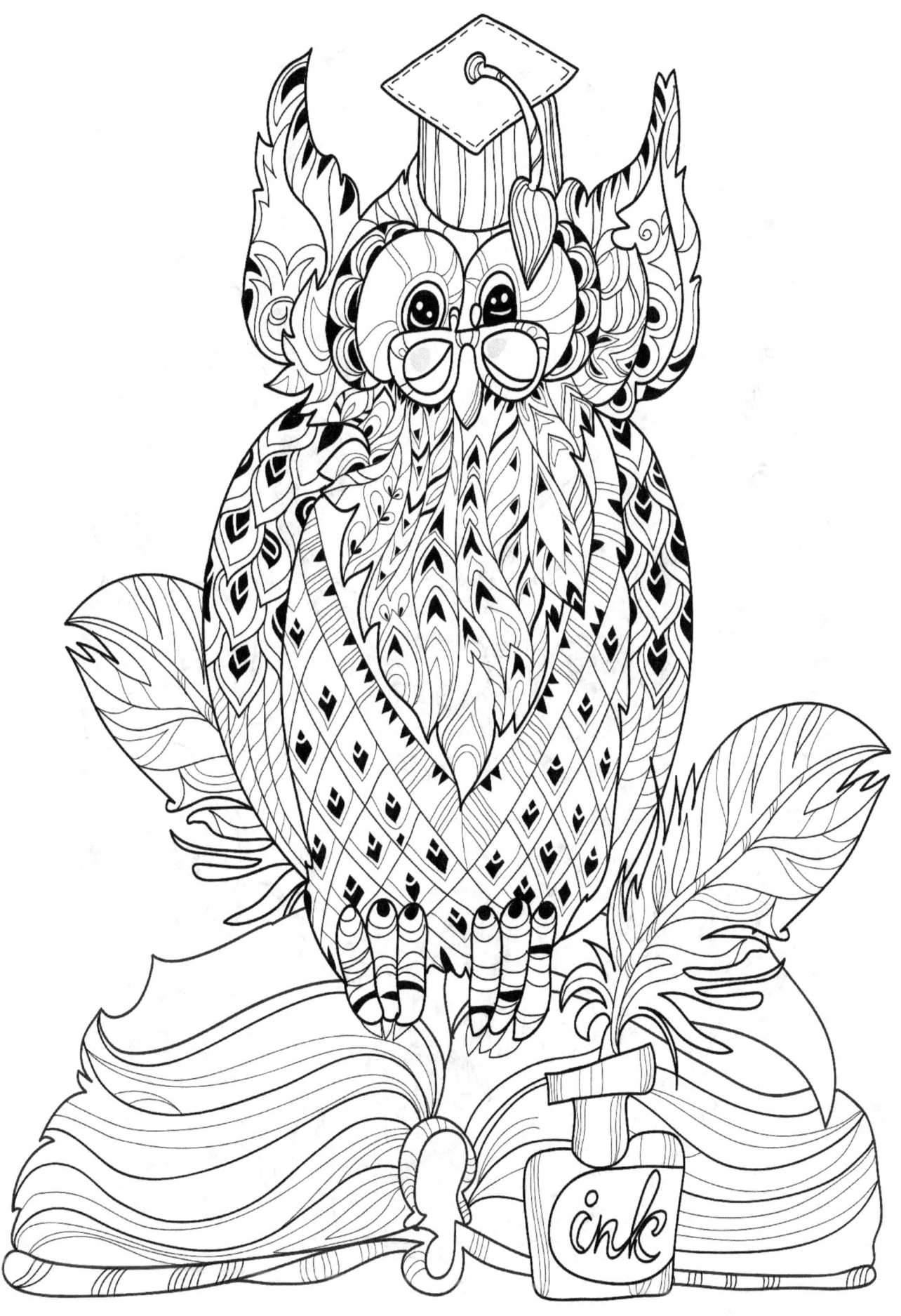

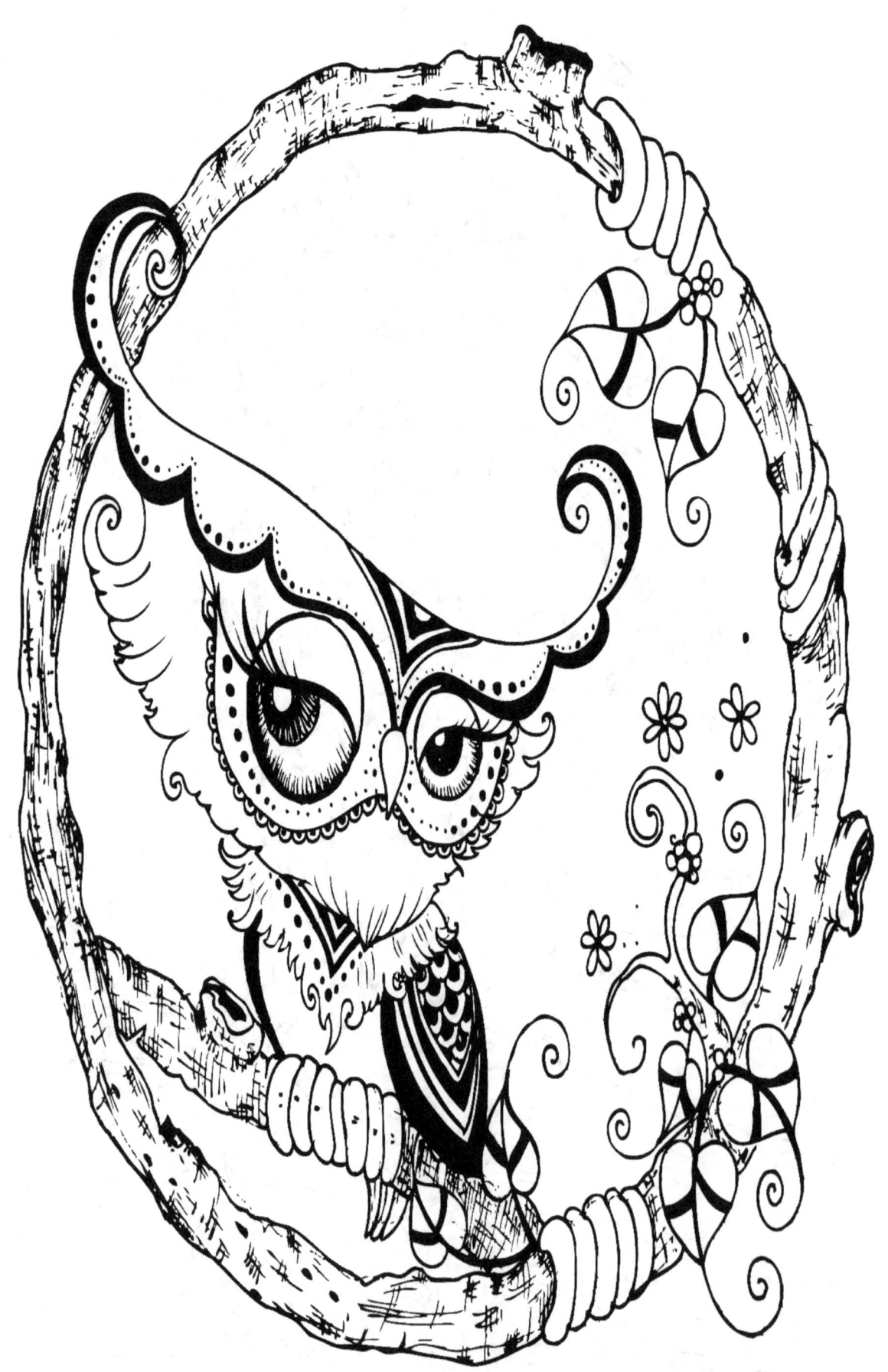

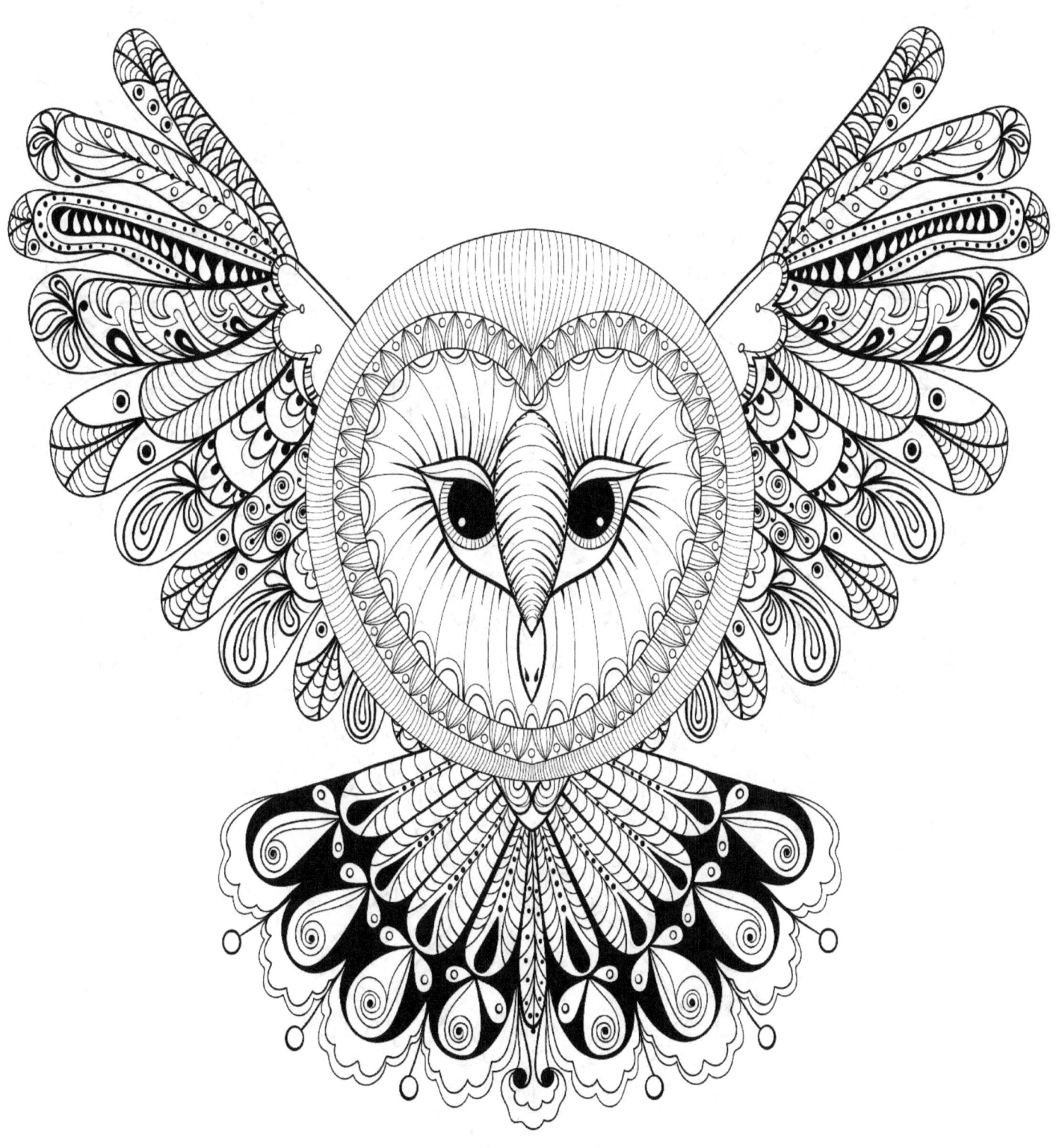

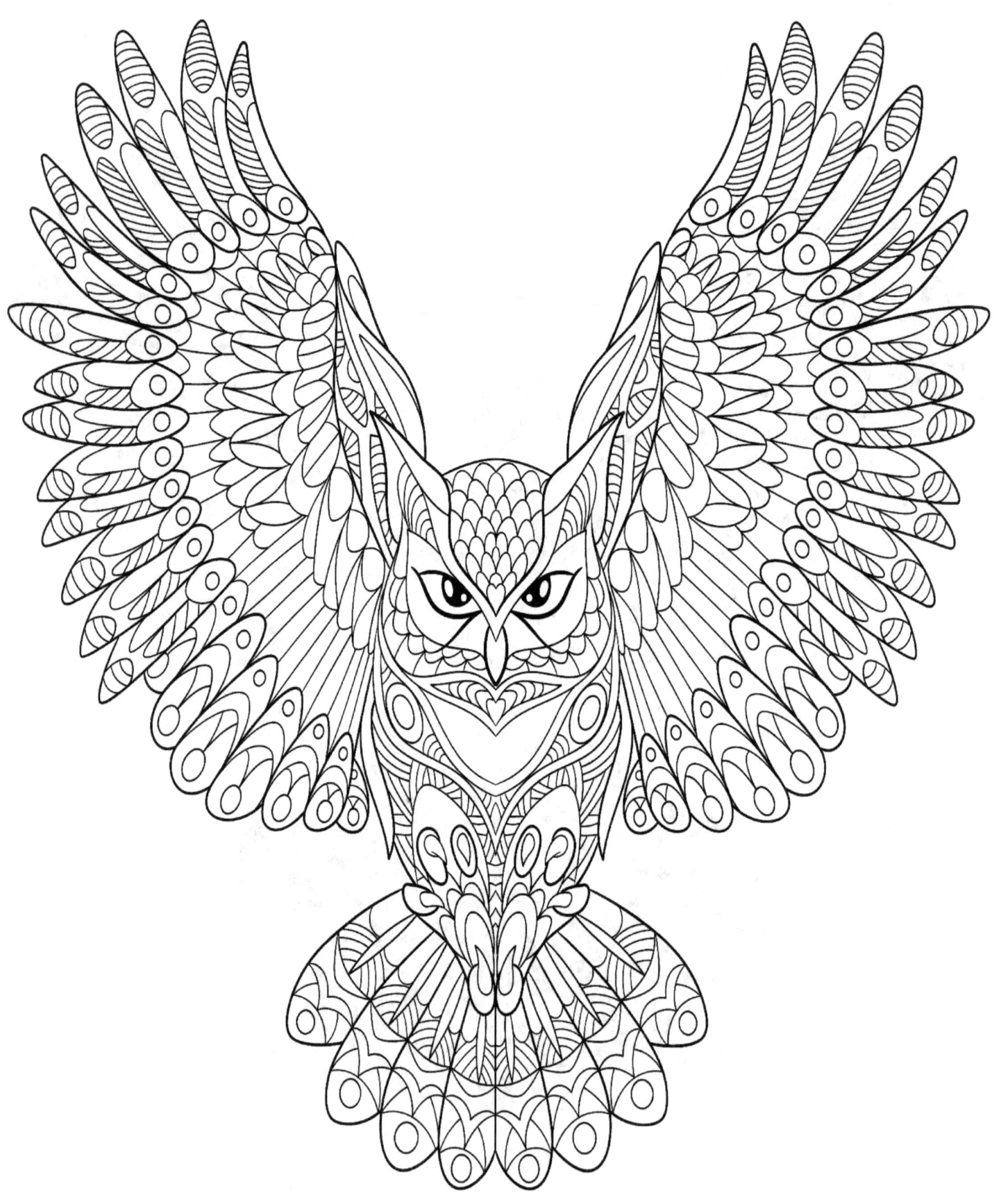

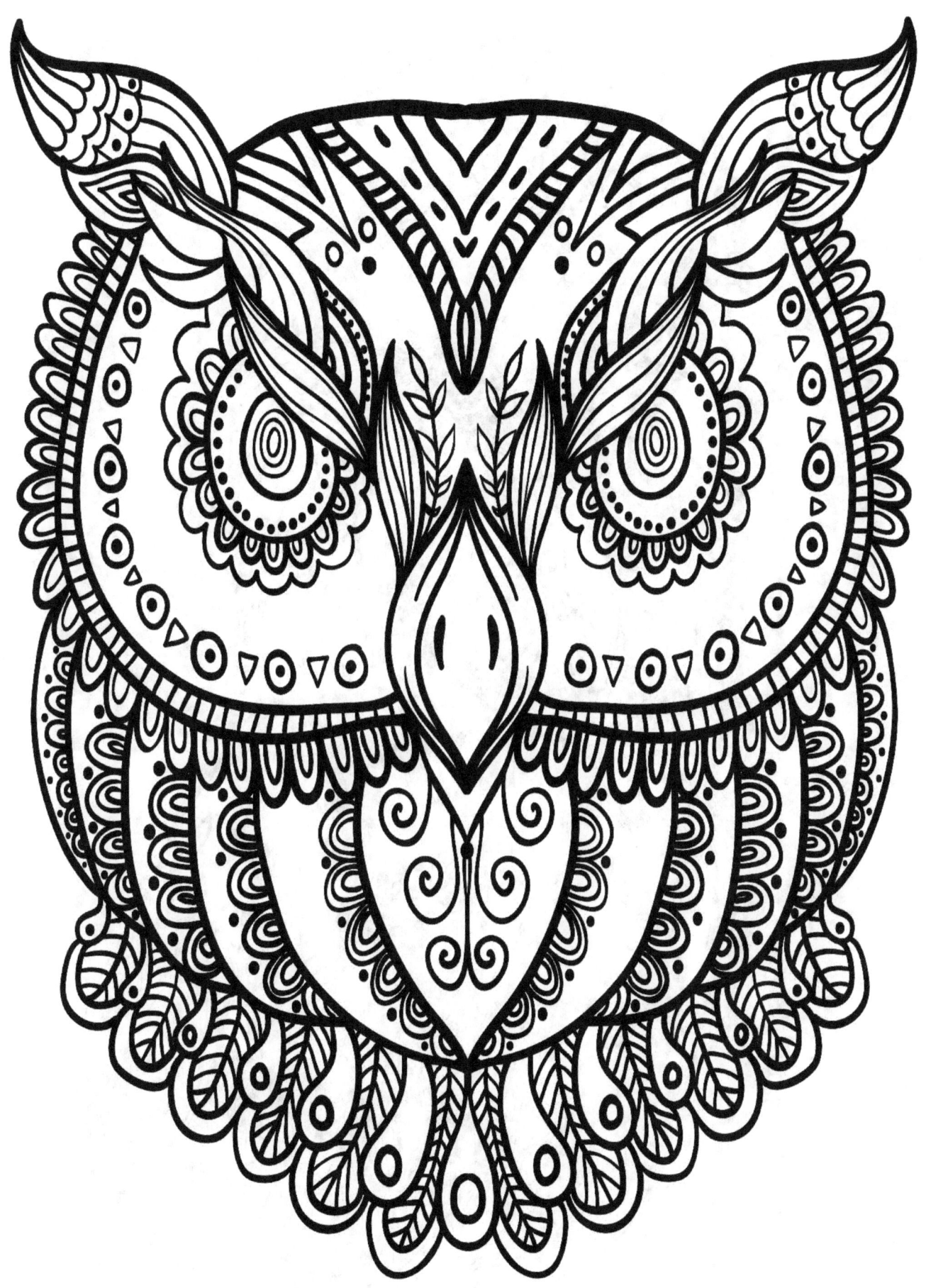

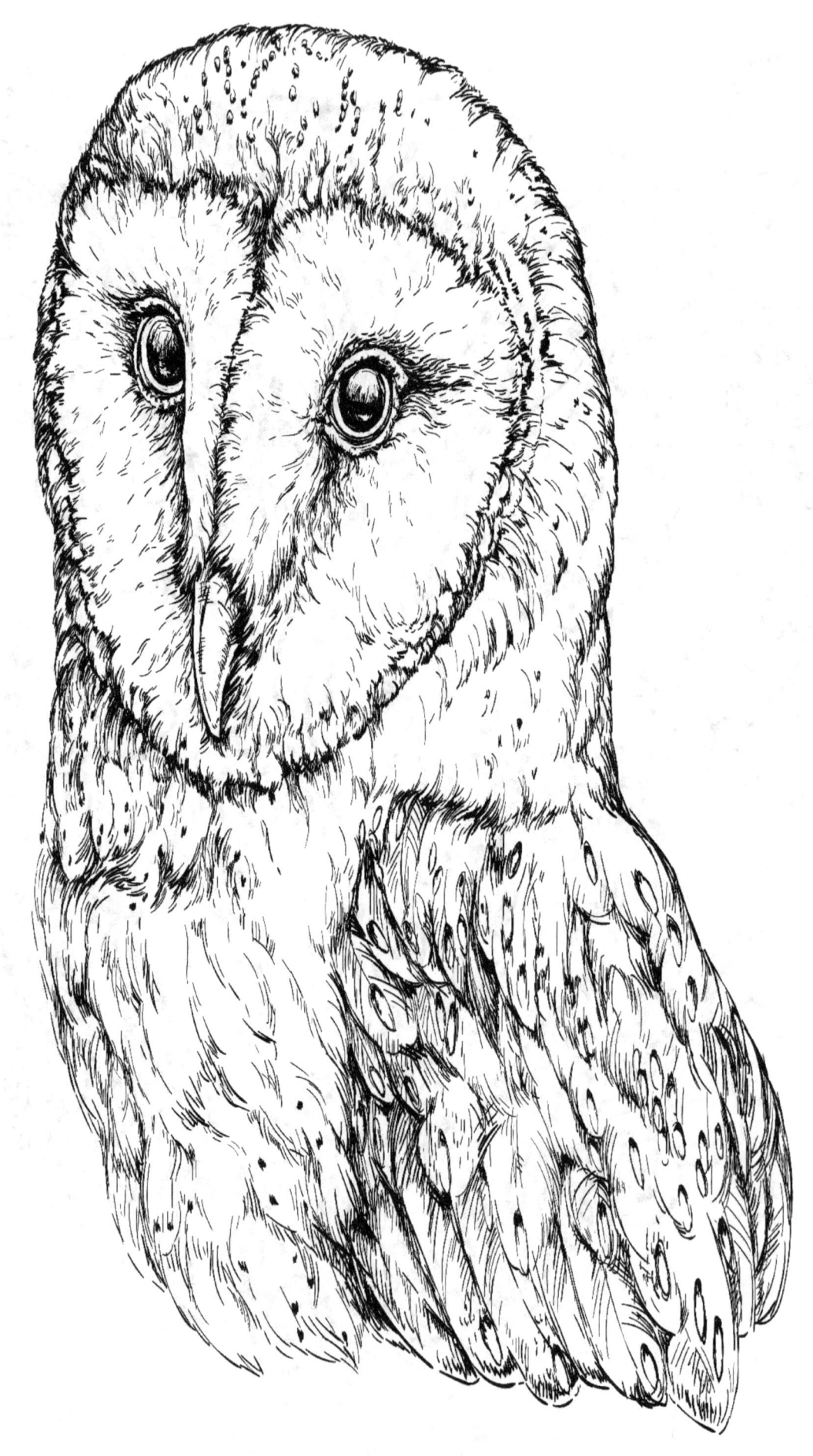

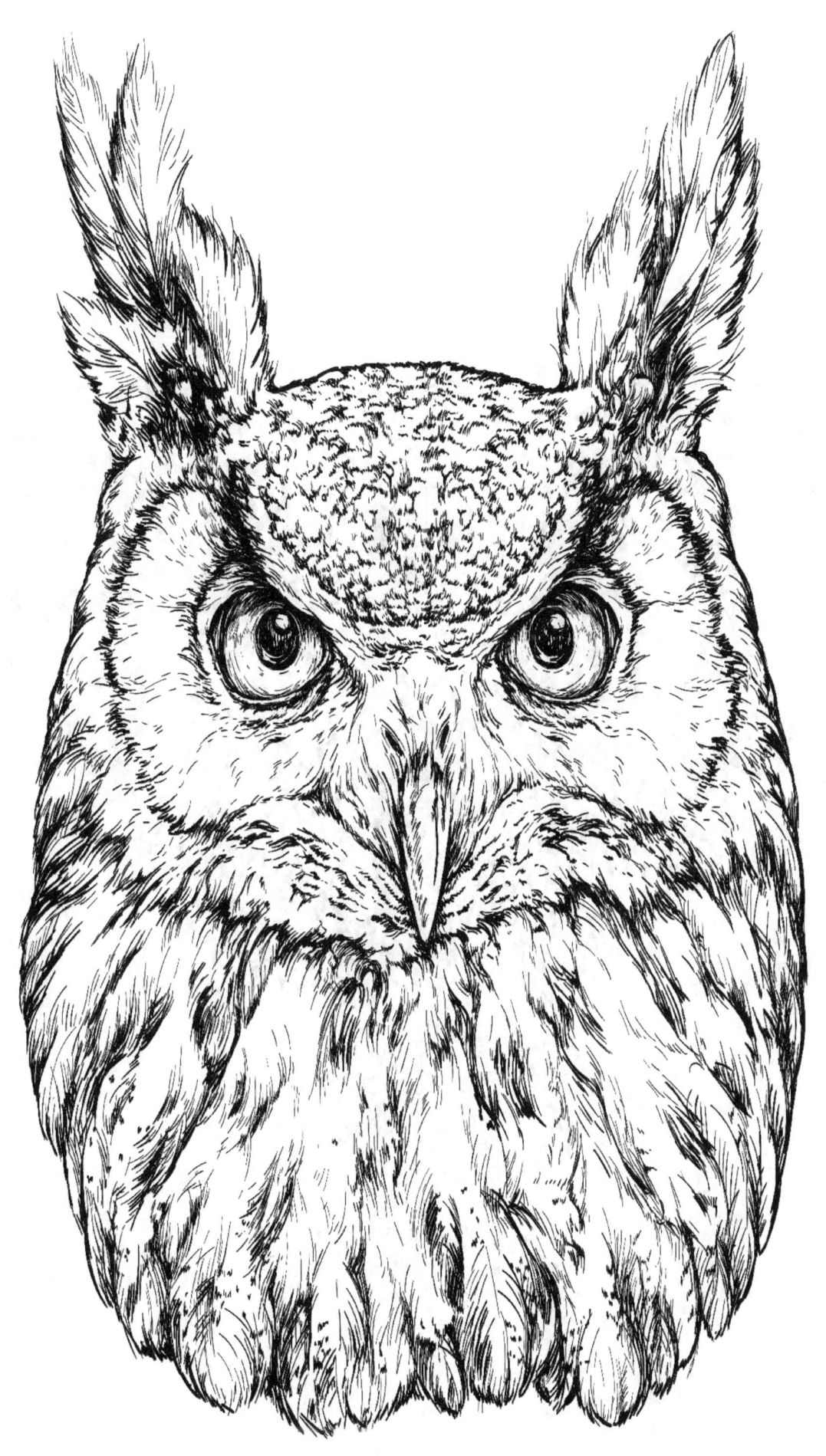

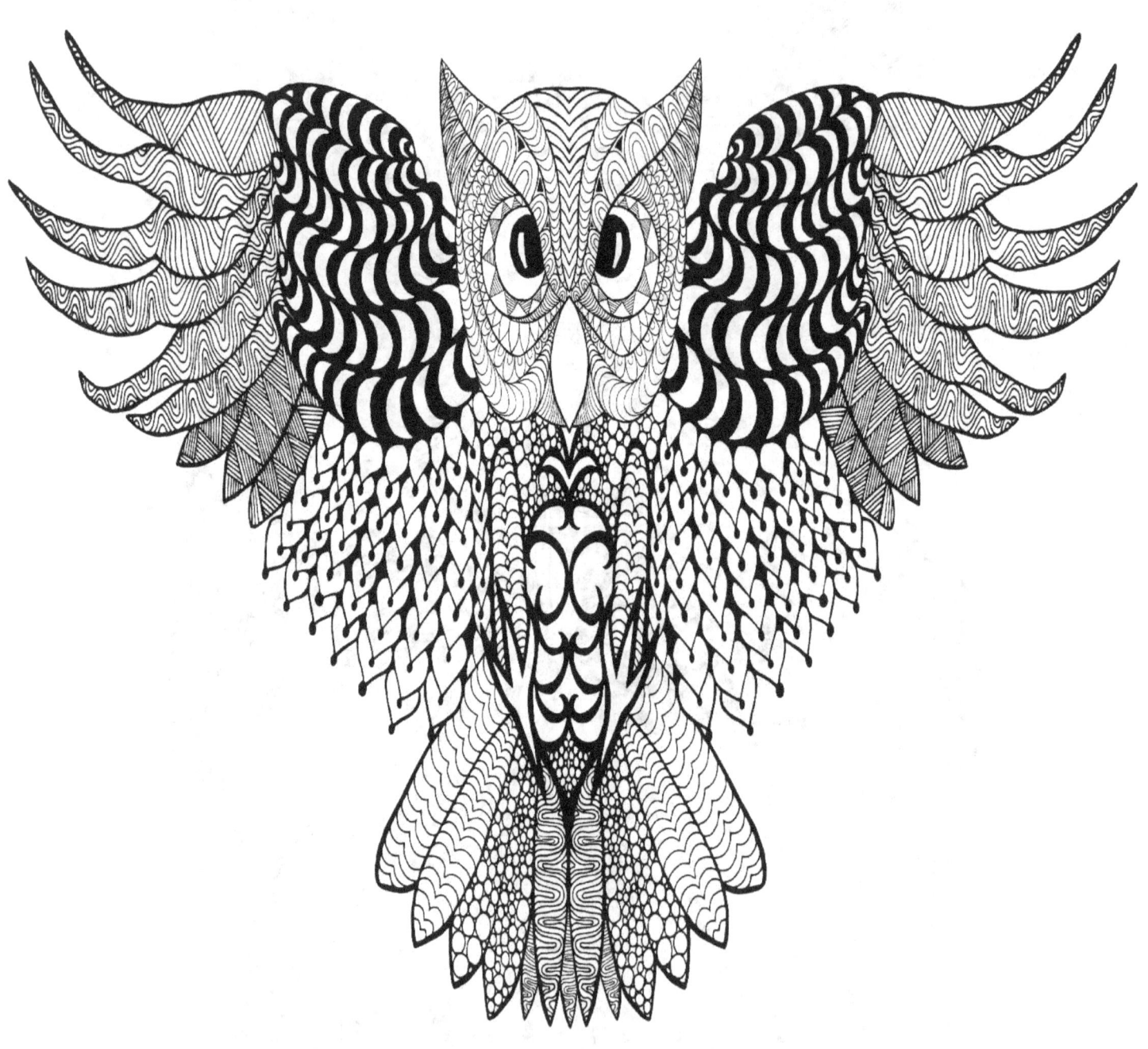

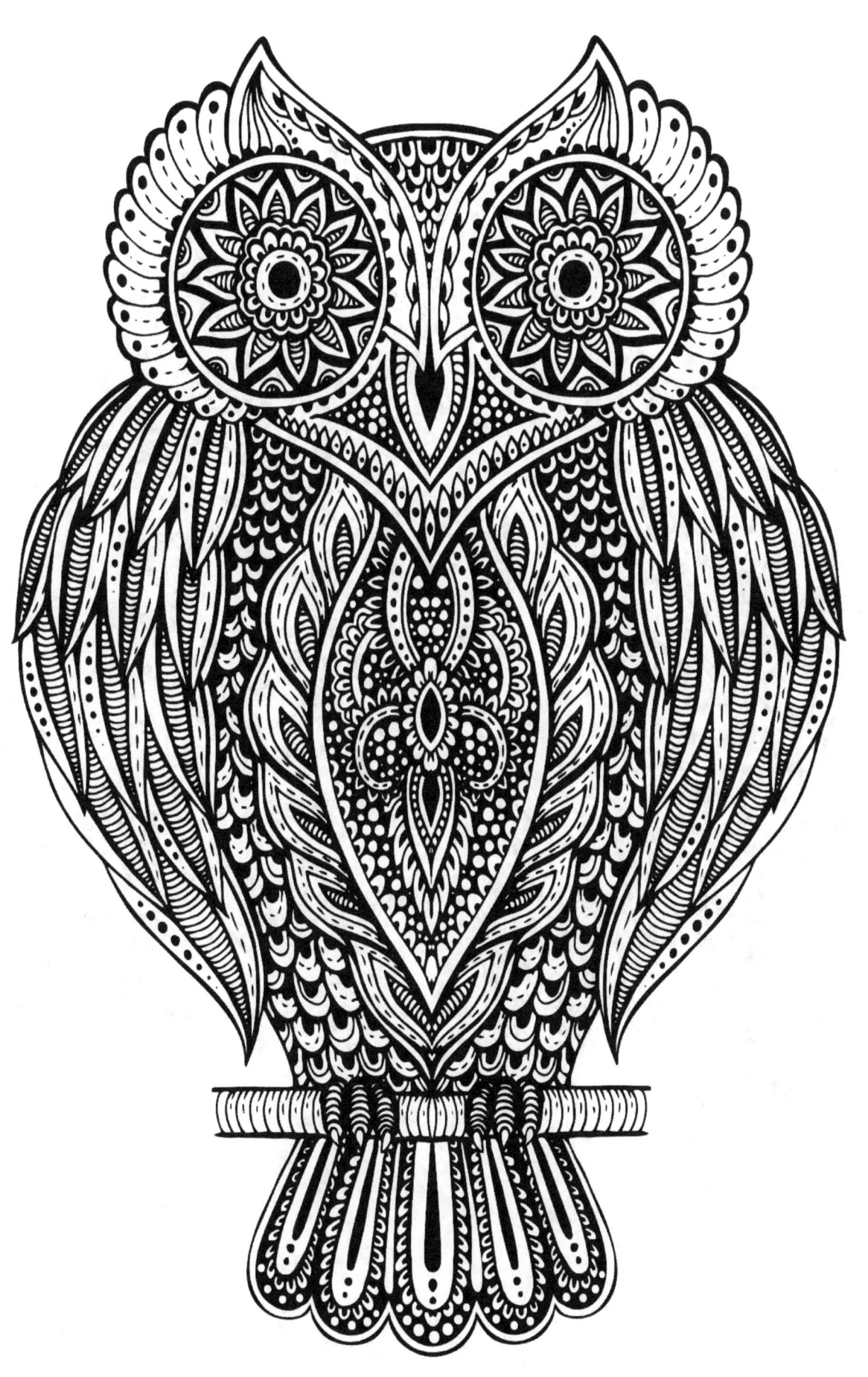

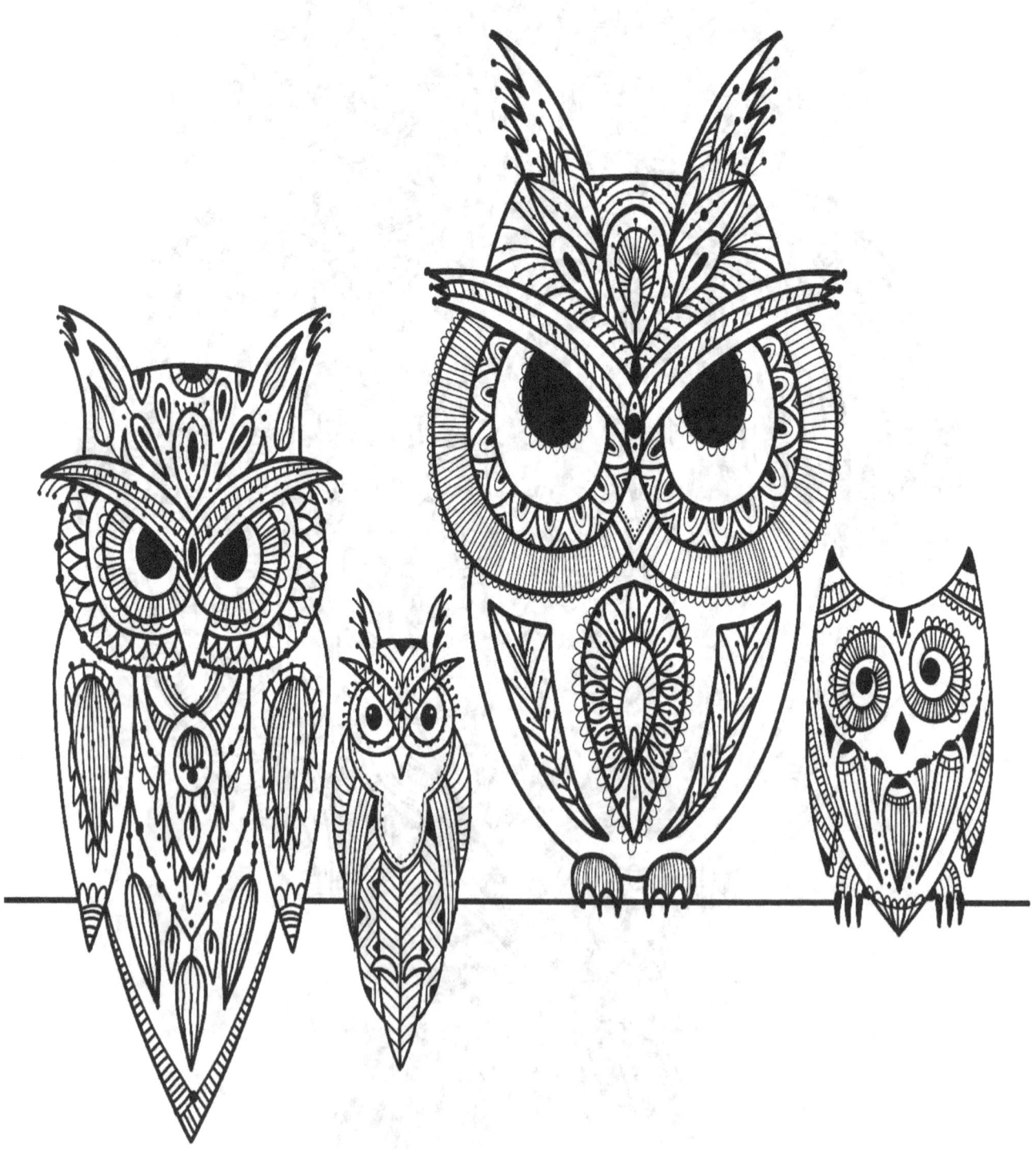

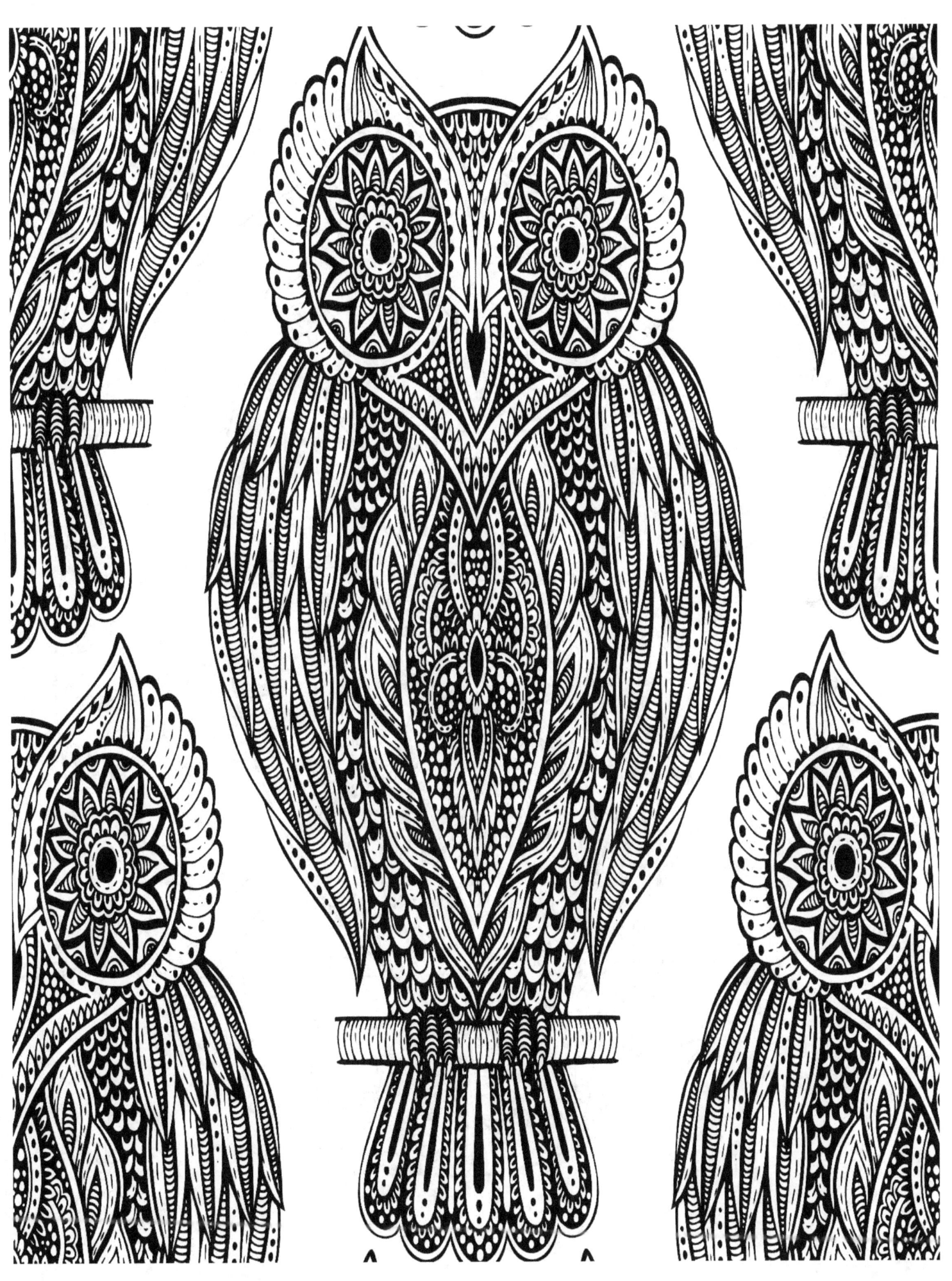

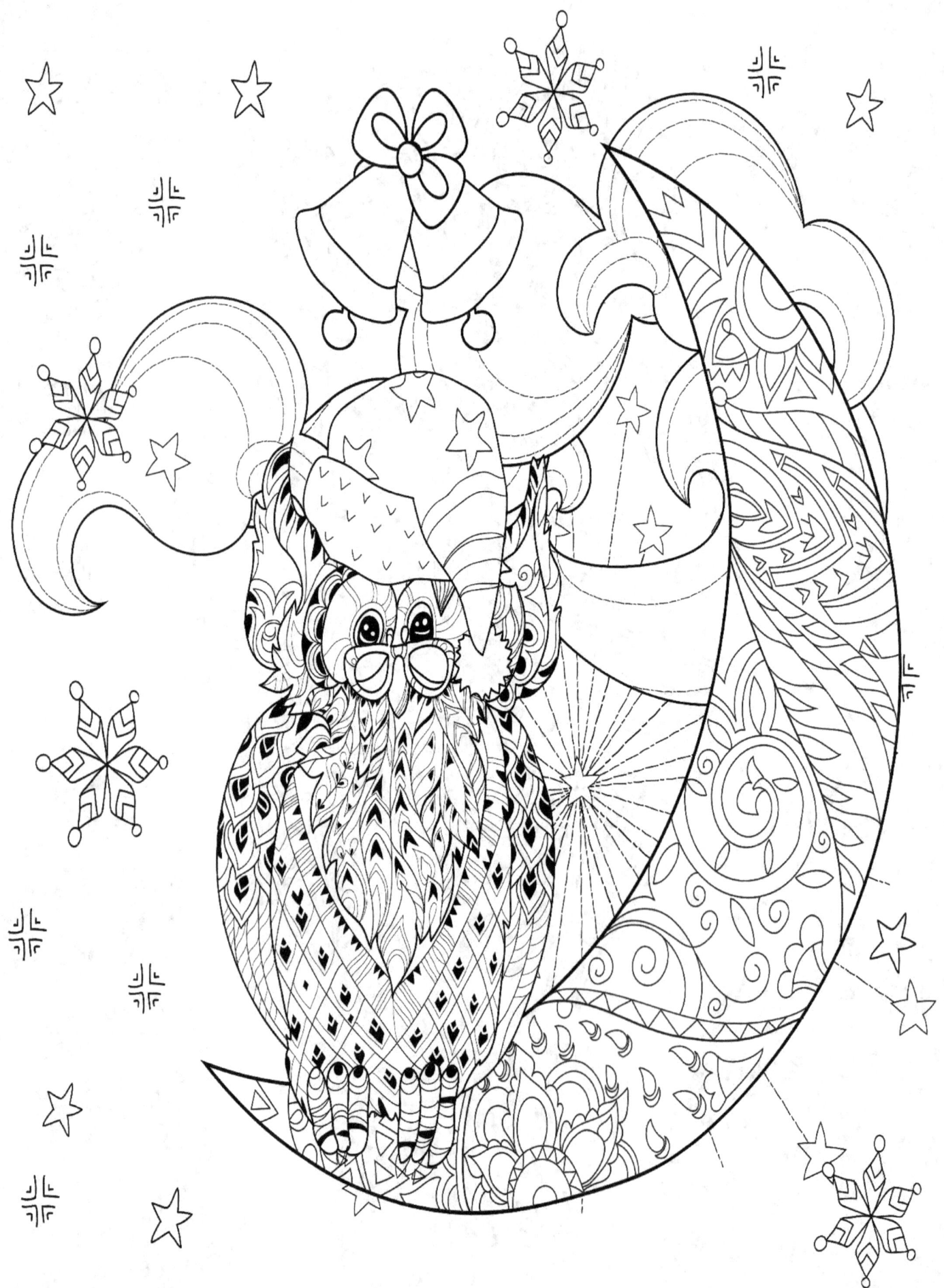

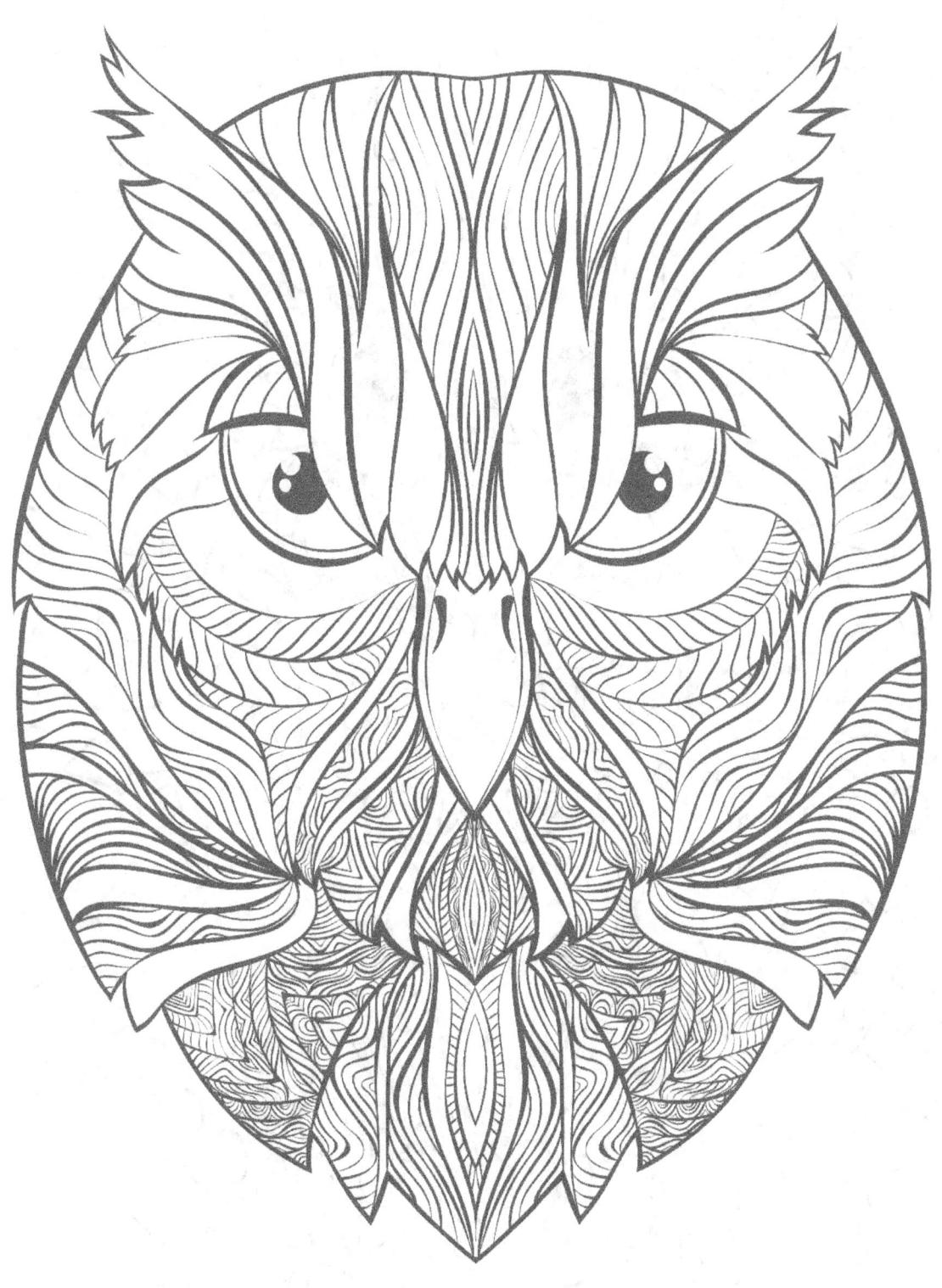

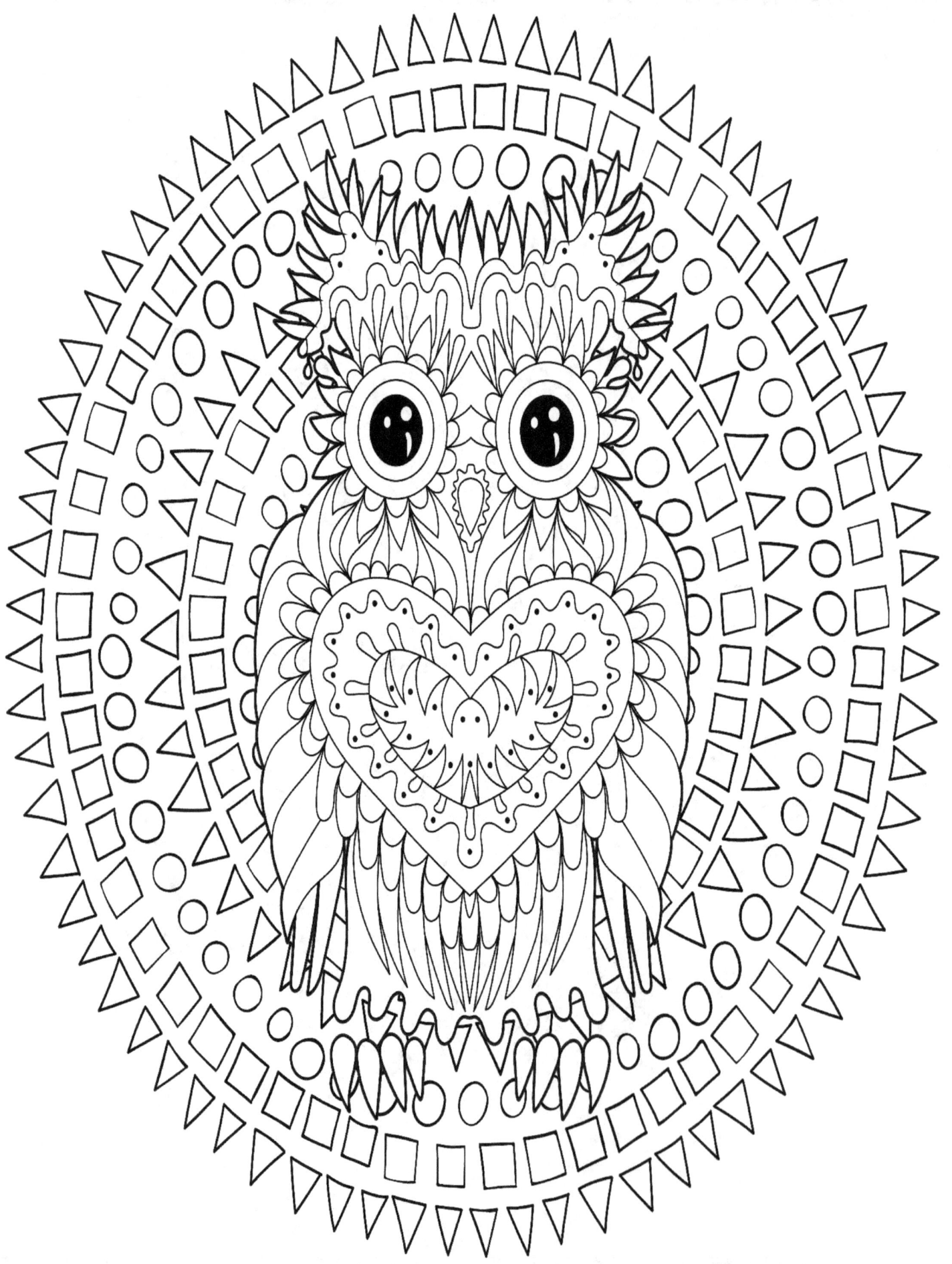

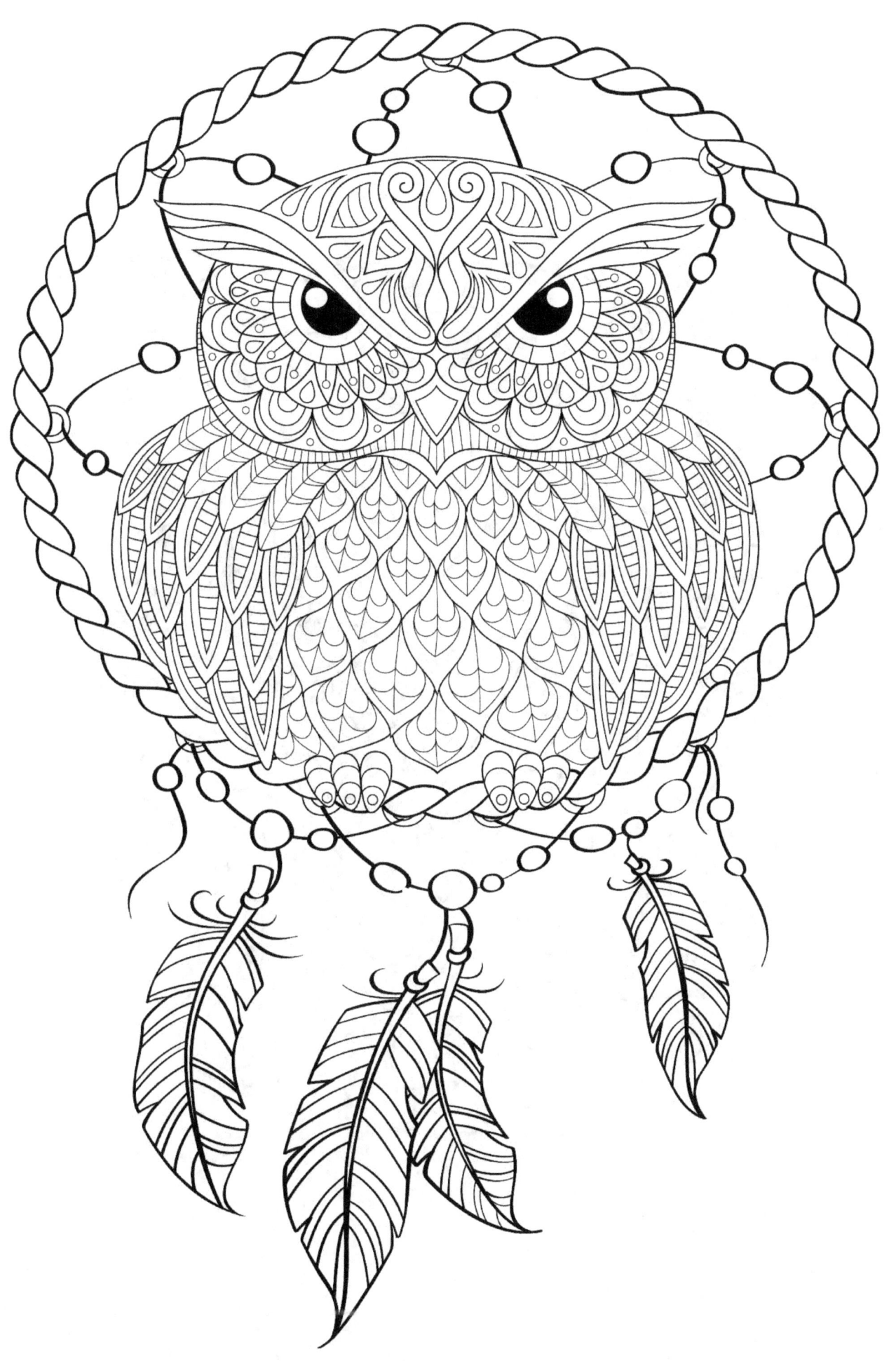

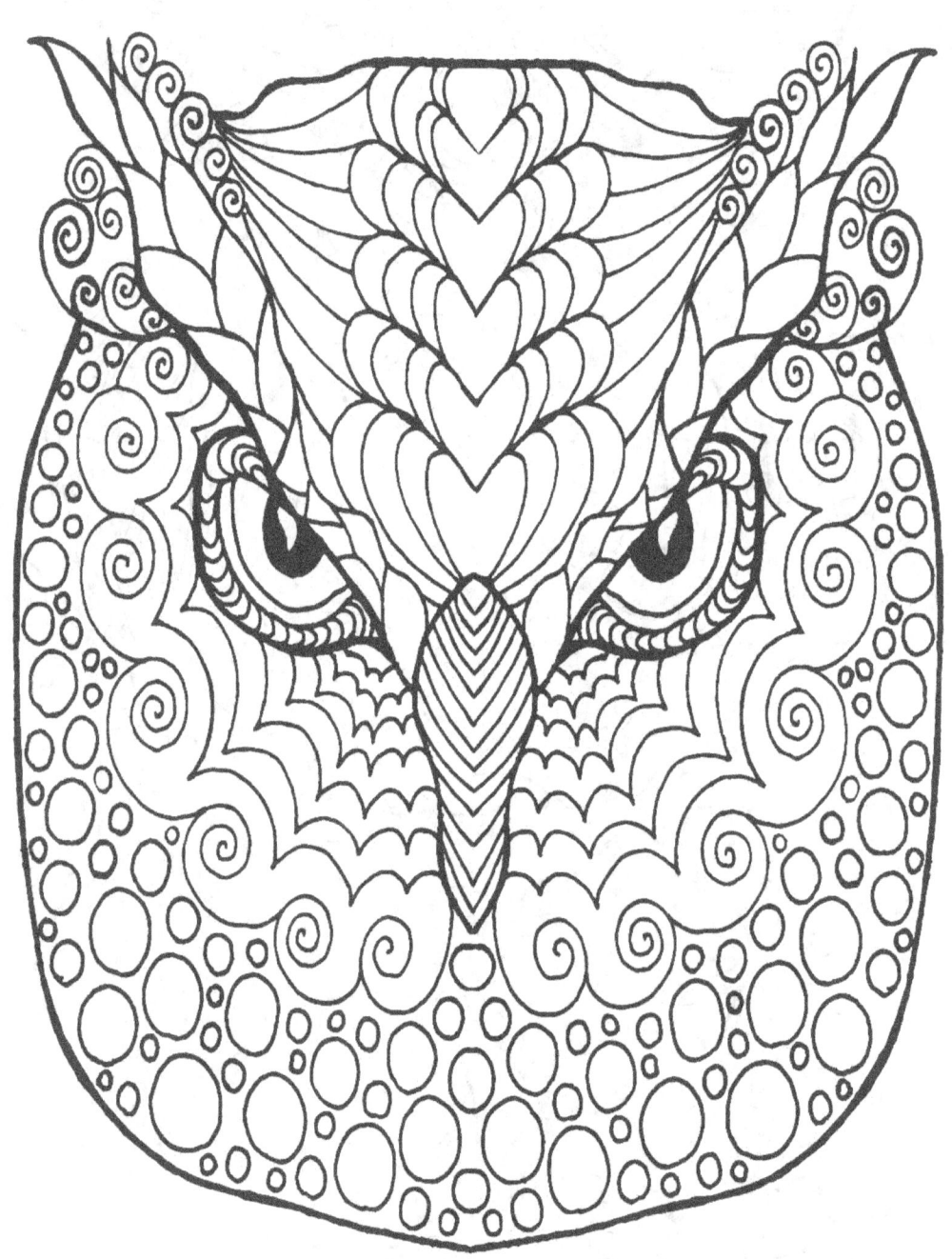

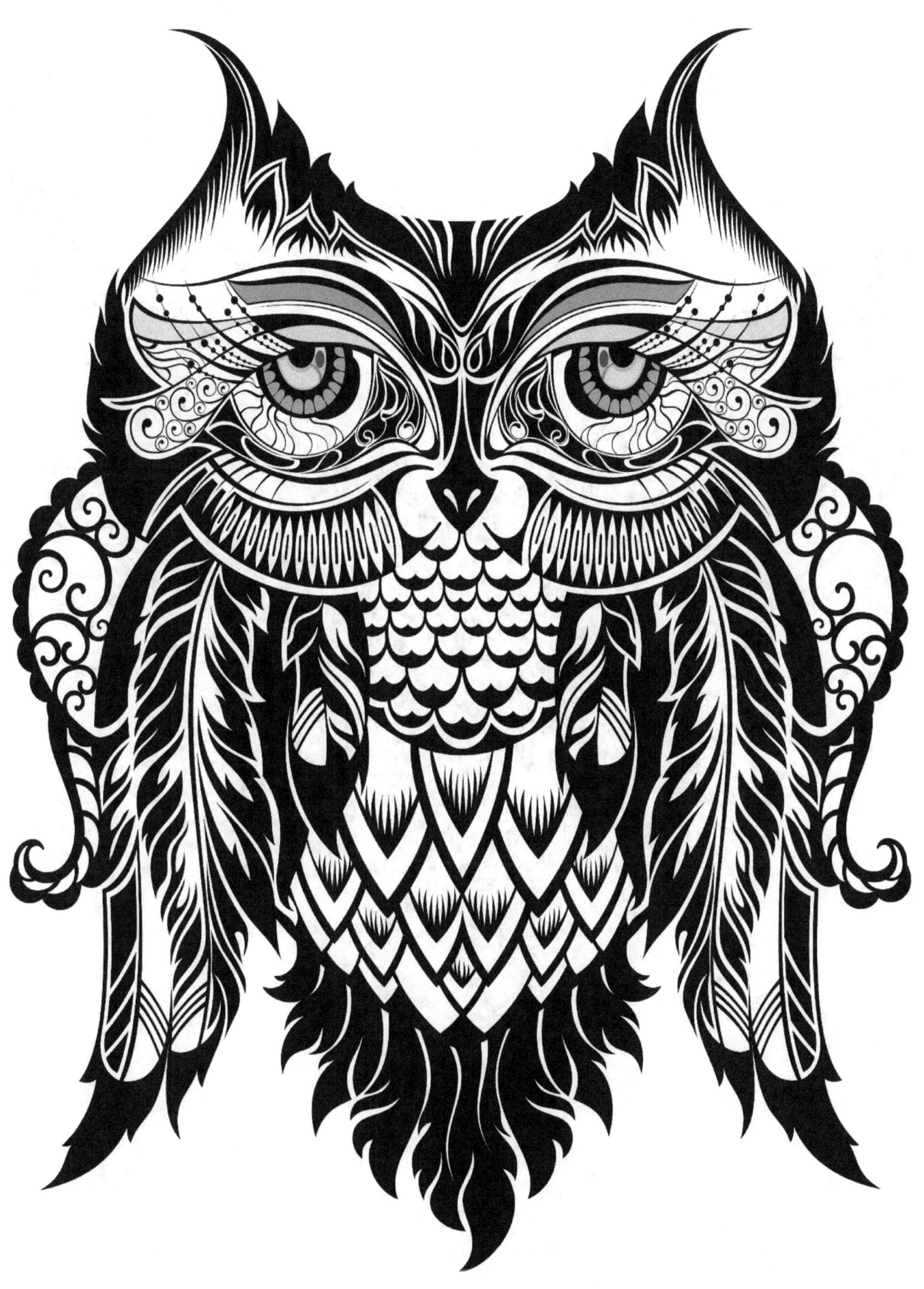

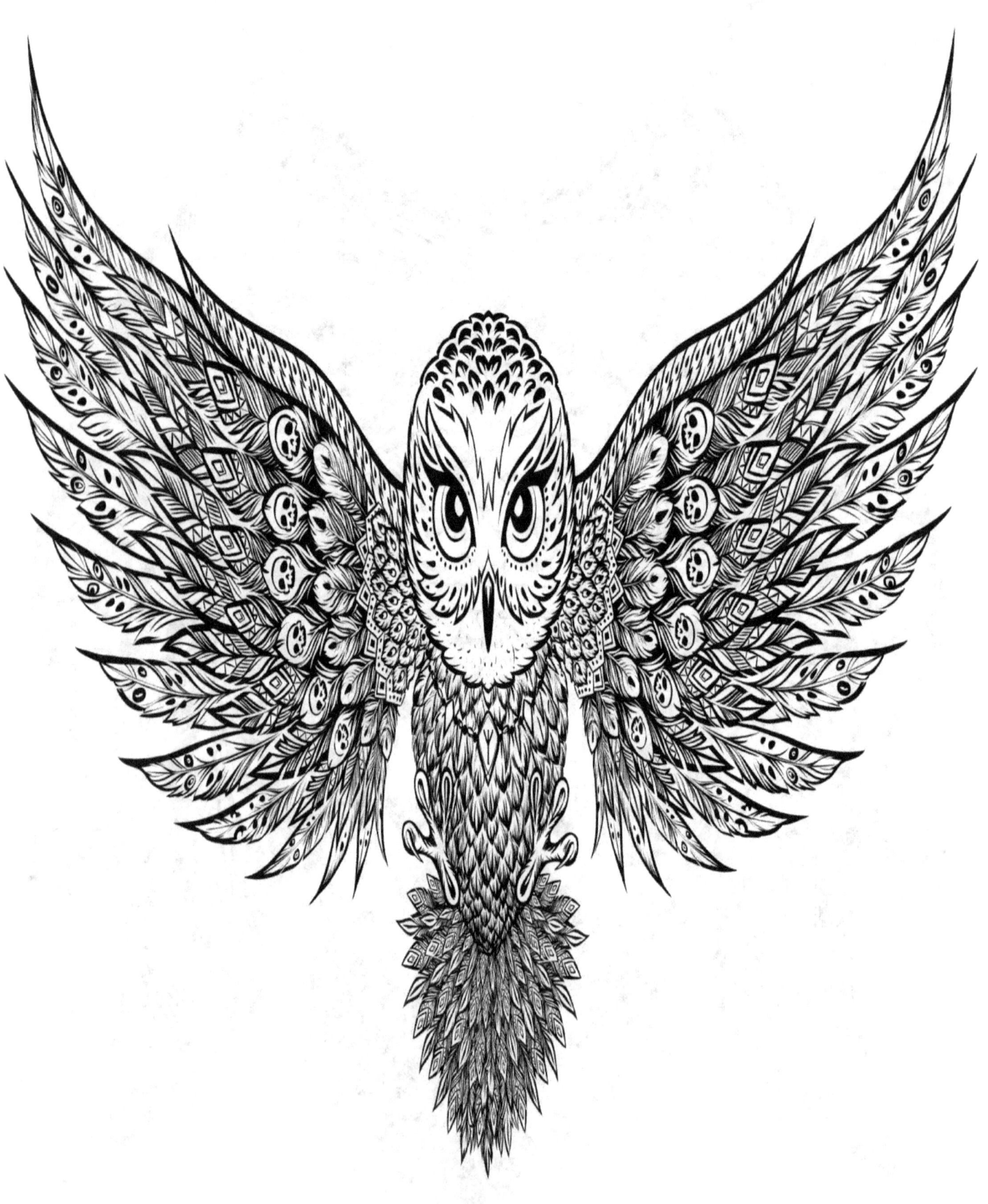

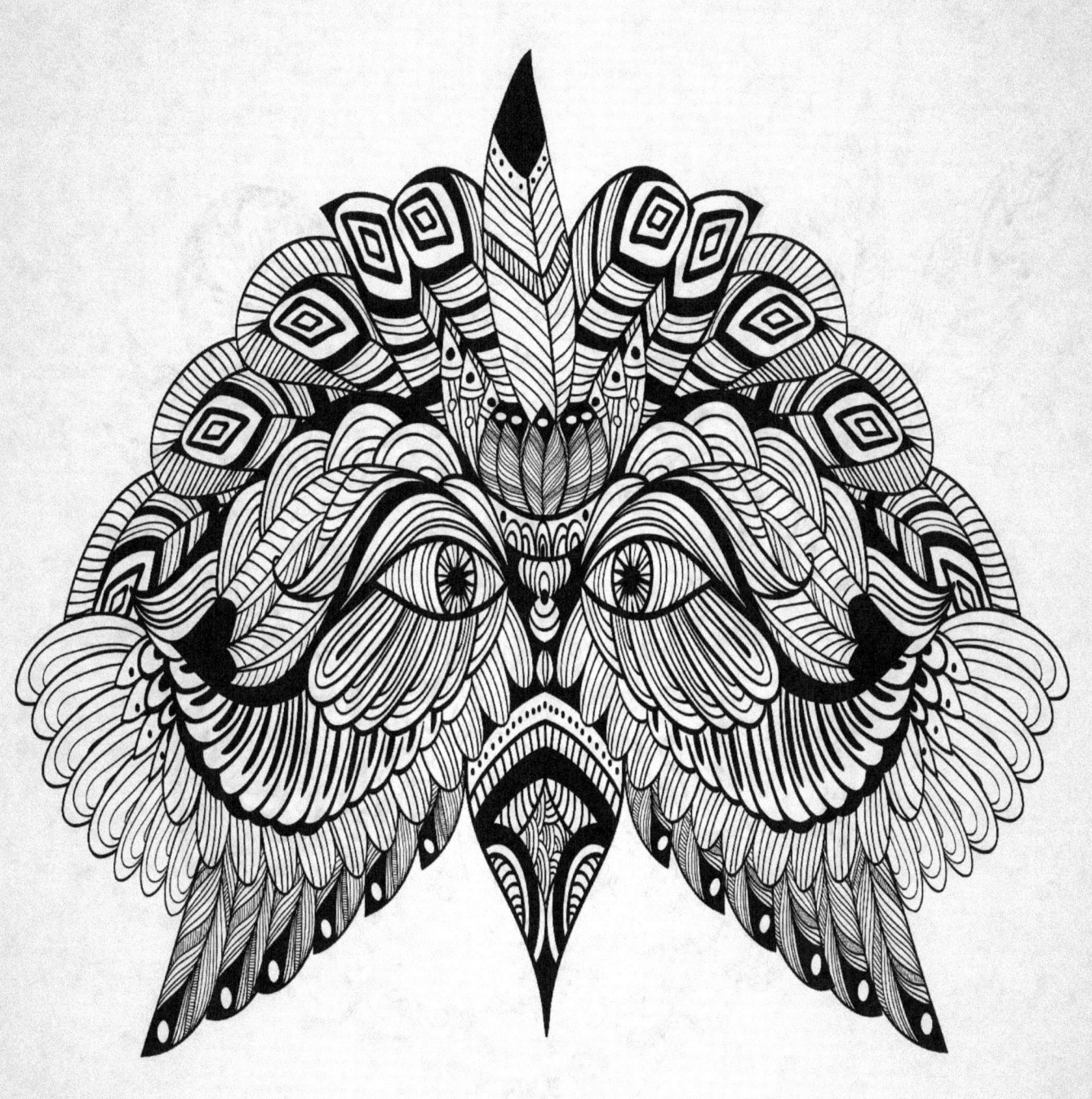

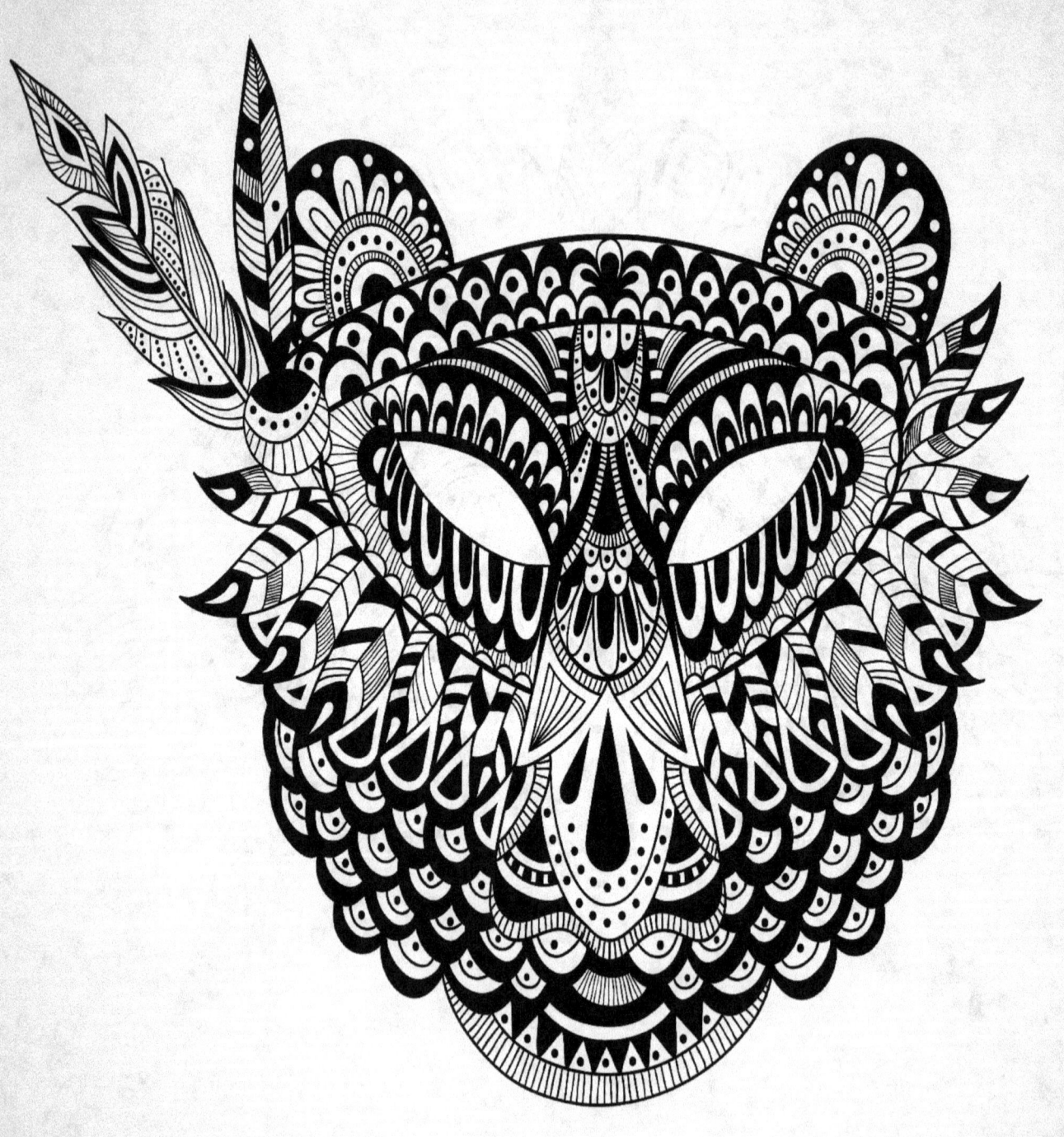

If you enjoyed this book, please leave me a review online.

ABOUT THE AUTHOR

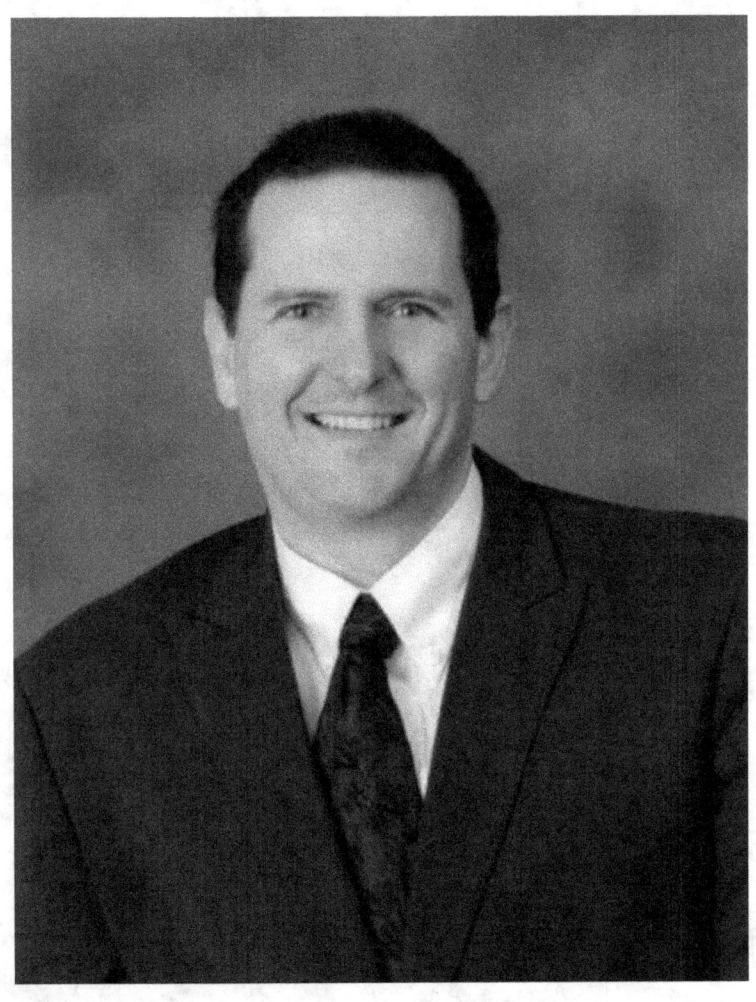

Dr. Wheeler is a physician by day and a writer by night. He enjoys beekeeping, travel, exercise, family time, and of course writing. He is a retired Tae kwon-do instructor. His two fantasy novels are published through Novel Star as well as self published. Collect his entire adult coloring book series: Fantastic Animals, Fantastic Designs, Fantastic Dogs, Fantastic Horses, Fantastic Cats, Fantastic Dinosaurs, Fantastic Birds, Fantastic Sea Life, Fantastic Flowers, Fantastic Skulls, Fantastic Christmas, Fantastic Foods, Fabulous Designs, and Mandalas and More. For younger children, look for The Adventures of Bumble the Bee, a 3 book series in both full color and coloring book formats as well as Fairy Tales, a 3 book series and The Boy Who Thought he was a Horse. For poetry lovers look for Mystical Musings: A Collection of Poetry. Dr. Wheeler's Fantasy books are The Witch of Endor: Vampires and Hammer of the Gods: The Nine Realms Book 1. He is currently working on the sequel to The Witch of Endodr, called Vampires Love and Blood.

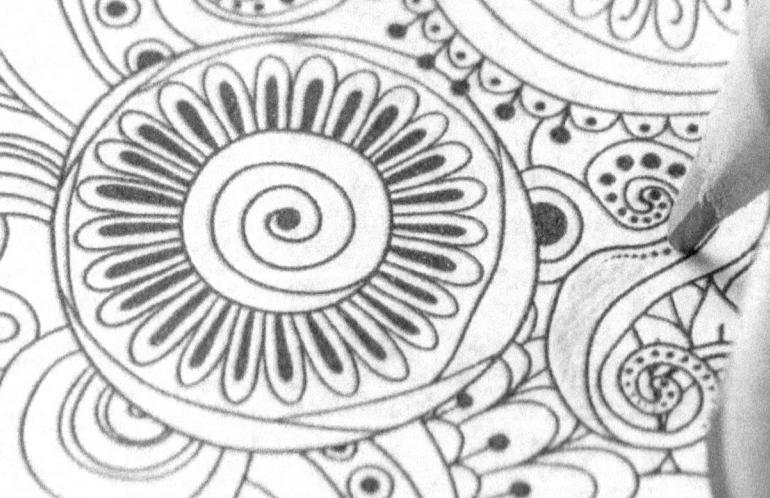

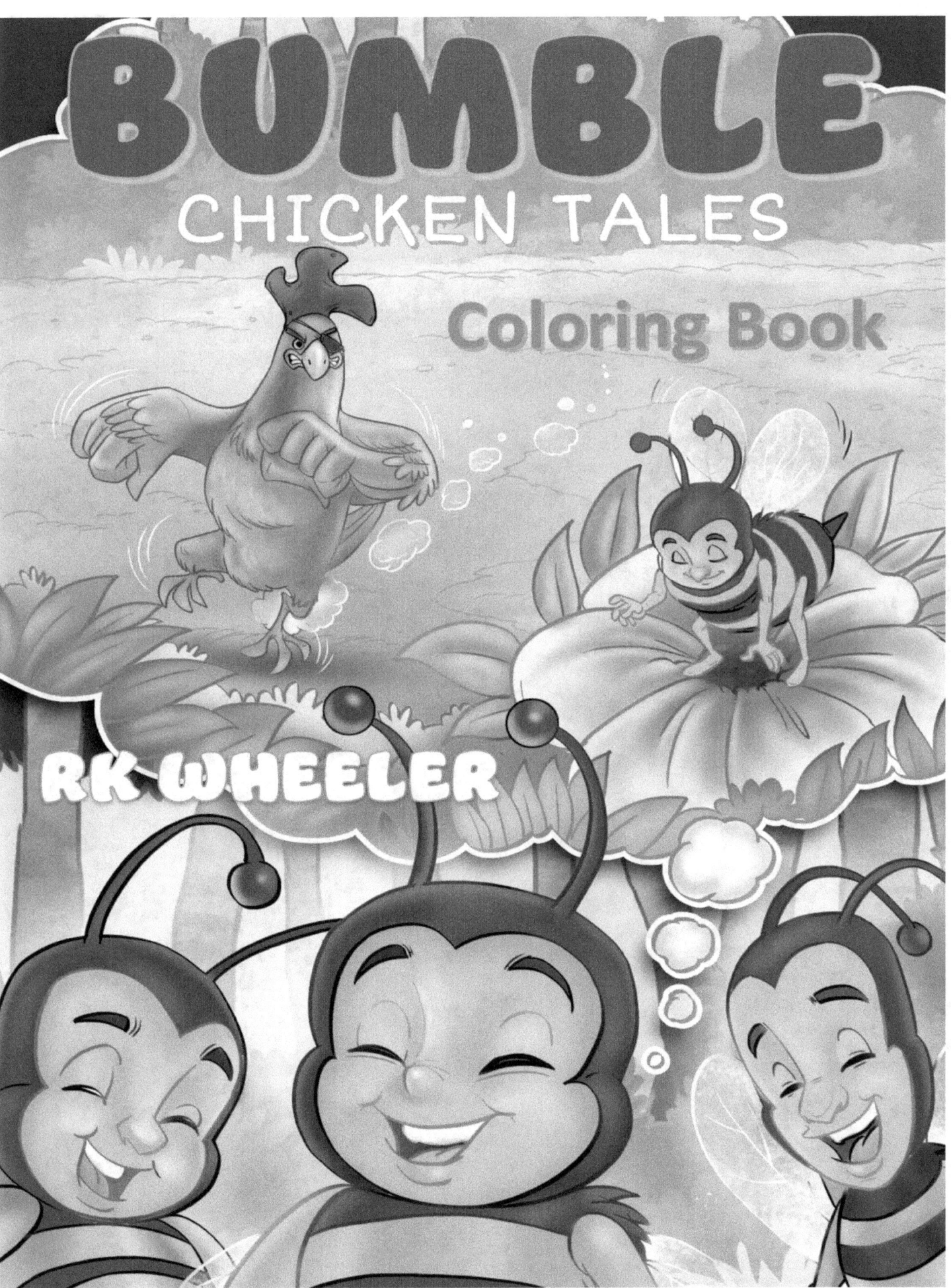

BUMBLE
The Bee Who Couldn't Fly

BY

RK WHEELER

The Adventures of Bumble
the Bee: Book 1

FANTASTIC ANIMALS

STRESS RELIEF

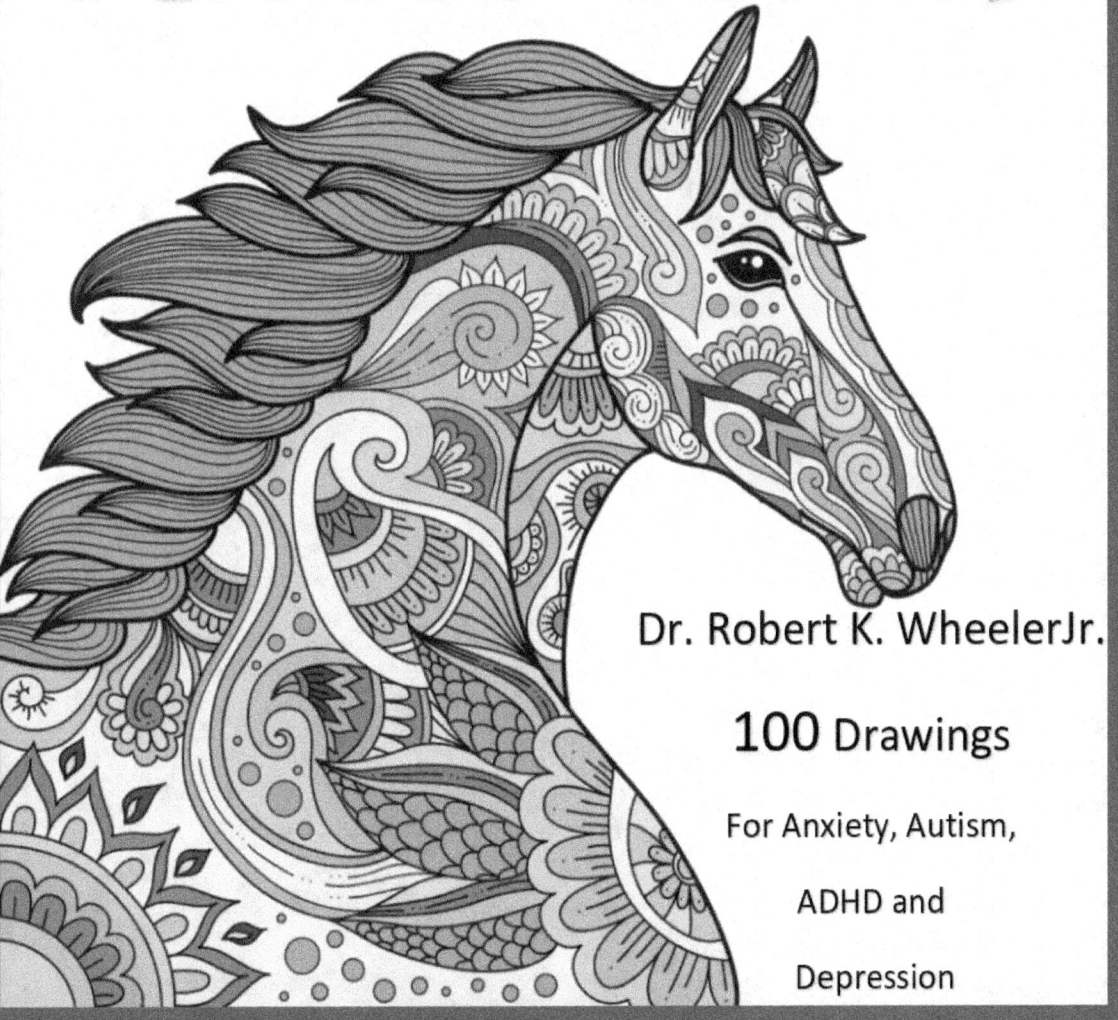

Dr. Robert K. Wheeler Jr.

100 Drawings

For Anxiety, Autism, ADHD and Depression

ADULT COLORING BOOK

www.ingramcontent.com/pod-product-compliance
Lightning Source LLC
Chambersburg PA
CBHW060423220526
45465CB00008B/2990